Praise for
You Don't Belong Here

"Becker, who also reported from Cambodia in the 1970s, fluidly sketches the history and politics of the Vietnam War and captures her subjects in all their complexity. Readers interested in women's history and foreign affairs won't be able to put this fascinating chronicle down."
—*Publishers Weekly*

"An incisive history of the Vietnam War via the groundbreaking accomplishments of three remarkable women journalists . . . A deft, richly illuminating perspective on the Vietnam War."
—*Kirkus*, Starred Review

"A riveting read with much to say about the nature of war and the different ways men and women correspondents cover it. Frank, fast-paced, often enraging, *You Don't Belong Here* speaks to the distance traveled and the journey still ahead."
—GERALDINE BROOKS, Pulitzer Prize–winning author of *MARCH*, former *Wall Street Journal* foreign correspondent

"Riveting, powerful, and transformative, Elizabeth Becker's *You Don't Belong Here* tells the stories of three astonishing women. This is a timely and brilliant work from one of our most extraordinary war correspondents."
—MADELEINE THIEN, author of *Do Not Say We Have Nothing*

"Elizabeth Becker's luminous book not only belongs, it demands at last that these daring, resourceful, and pathbreaking women take their rightful place in the history of the Indochina wars and journalists who covered them."
—DAVID MARANISS, author of *They Marched into Sunlight: War and Peace, Vietnam and America, October 1967*

"Every journalist should read this stunning book. Actually everyone should. Elizabeth Becker has that rare ability to weave the fascinating stories of three groundbreaking, very different women journalists with a riveting history of the Vietnam War. She challenges you to see who these women were in a place they allegedly didn't belong, while describing what and how they witnessed it."

—ANNE GARRELS, former NPR foreign
correspondent and author of *Naked in Baghdad*

"Ms. Becker has done us a great service by shining a light on three hidden women stars of the wars in Indochina: Francis FitzGerald, Kate Webb, and Catherine Leroy. They fought their way through opposition from the 'men's club' of war corresponding to focus on reporting the truth, proving that they actually *did* belong there. Put *You Don't Belong Here* on your reading list!"

—JOSEPH L. GALLOWAY, coauthor of *We Were Soldiers Once*

"Elizabeth Becker resurrects the long-forgotten stories and enormous sacrifices made by a generation of women who paved the way for the rest of us. Elegant, angry, and utterly engaging, it is a long overdue story about a small band of courageous and visionary women. *You Don't Belong Here* is a masterpiece of a book."

—RACHEL LOUISE SNYDER, author of *No Visible Bruises:
What We Don't Know About Domestic Violence Can Kill Us*

"When these three women were born, 'lady journalists' wore flowery dresses and white gloves and wrote about fashion and housekeeping. Today, because of the tenacity and bravery of women like Leroy, FitzGerald, and Webb, women report from the frontlines of the bloodiest conflicts . . . and they aren't wearing white gloves."

—TONY CLIFTON, veteran Australian journalist

"Here is a unique and valuable perspective on the Vietnam War. Elizabeth Becker has gracefully weaved admiring but clear-eyed portraits of three remarkable women who reported from its front lines. At a time when most female journalists were relegated to covering food, family, and fashion, these fought for a chance to take on the biggest story of their day, battling the military, their families, and male colleagues—hostile and amorous (sometimes both). Their work, in Becker's description of French photographer Catherine Leroy, 'eschewed classic heroics,' recording both the courage and the human toll of war, earning the amazed respect of soldiers, and making an indelible contribution to our understanding of the war, then and now."

—MARK BOWDEN, author of
Black Hawk Down and *Hue 1968*

"In this meticulously researched and drama-filled book, we can feel the sweat and heat of the jungle, hear the explosion of bombs, and witness the lies and political machinations justifying the doomed Vietnam War. Most importantly, Ms. Becker, a master international journalist herself, profiles the extraordinary courage, talent, and raw determination of three wartime female journalists, who succeeded in a man's world and helped pave the way for women everywhere to receive the recognition and respect they deserve."

—ALAN LIGHTMAN, author of
Einstein's Dreams and *The Diagnosis*

YOU DON'T
BELONG HERE

YOU DON'T BELONG HERE

How Three Women
Rewrote the Story of War

Elizabeth Becker

PublicAffairs
NEW YORK

PublicAffairs
Hachette Book Group
1290 Avenue of the Americas, New York, NY 10104
www.publicaffairsbooks.com
@Public_Affairs

Printed in the United States of America
First Edition: February 2021

Published by PublicAffairs, an imprint of Perseus Books, LLC, a subsidiary of Hachette
Book Group, Inc. The PublicAffairs name and logo is a trademark of the Hachette
Book Group.

The Hachette Speakers Bureau provides a wide range of authors for speaking events.
To find out more, go to www.hachettespeakersbureau.com or call (866) 376-6591.

The publisher is not responsible for websites (or their content) that are not owned
by the publisher.

Print book interior design by Linda Mark

Library of Congress Cataloging-in-Publication Data
Names: Becker, Elizabeth (Journalist), author.
Title: You don't belong here : how three women rewrote the story of war /
  Elizabeth Becker.
Description: First edition. | New York : PublicAffairs, 2021. | Includes bibliographical
  references and index.
Identifiers: LCCN 2020024549 | ISBN 9781541768208 (hardcover) |
  ISBN 9781541768215 (ebook)
Subjects: LCSH: Vietnam War, 196–1975—Journalists. | Women war correspondents—
  Australia—Biography. | Women war correspondents—France—Biography. | Women
  war correspondents—United States–Biography. | Photojournalists—United States—
  Biography. | Leroy, Catherine | FitzGerald, Frances, 1940– | Webb, Kate, 1943–2007 |
  Vietnam War, 1961–1975–Press coverage—United States.
Classification: LCC DS559.46 .B53 2021 | DDC 070.4/4995970430922—dc23
LC record available at https://lccn.loc.gov/2020024549

ISBNs: 978-1-5417-6820-8 (hardcover), 978-1-5417-6821-5 (ebook)

LSC-C

Printing 1, 2020

This is dedicated to the Becker-Nash clan

Will the Vietnam conflict be the first war recorded better by women than men? . . . The story of war is not the same as the story of men at war.

RICHARD EDER, *Los Angeles Times*, 1986[1]

The Vietnam press corps was a male bastion that women entered only at the risk of being humiliated and patronized; the prevailing view was that the war was being fought by men against men and women had no place there.

PETER ARNETT, Pulitzer Prize–winning war correspondent[2]

Contents

Illustration section appears after page 158

CHINA

Red R.

Black R.

Dien Bien Phu

MYANMAR

Hanoi

Haiphong

Gulf of
Tonkin

Louangphrabang

Hainan

NORTH
VIETNAM

LAOS

Vientiane

DMZ   17th Parallel

Khe Sanh   Con Thien
Hué

THAILAND   Danang

South
China
Sea

SOUTH
VIETNAM

Bangkok

CAMBODIA

Siem Reap/
Angkor Wat
Battambong

Kampong Thom

Dalat   Nha Trang

Mekong R.

Phnom Penh
Kompong Speu
Takeo

An Loc
Tay Ninh

Saigon
(Ho Chi Minh City)

Gulf of
Thailand

My Tho

Mekong Delta

0   100 miles

SCALE

Preface

W HEN I ENCOUNTERED HER AT THE HONG KONG AIRPORT, A
cigarette dangling from her free hand, I had never met anyone
like Kate Webb. It was January 1973, and I was on the penultimate leg
of my flight from Seattle to Cambodia to become a war correspondent.

She was immediately recognizable from the news photographs: the
thick-cropped brown hair, shy smile, and intense brown eyes. After I
waved to her, she steered me through arrival formalities and into a dim
sum restaurant with a view of the harbor. Our mutual friend, Sylvana
Foa, had arranged for Webb to host me overnight and make sure I
caught the morning flight to Phnom Penh.

Webb had been in the news for surviving capture by the North
Vietnamese and then writing a book about the experience. Soft spoken and to the point, she asked, Why had I crossed the ocean to
cover a war?

The short answer was a nightmare I was all too keen to leave behind. My master's adviser had rejected my thesis on the Bangladesh
War of Independence after I refused to sleep with him. He said the one
was not related to the other.

I had worked my way through college, petitioned to create a degree program in South Asian studies, and won a fellowship to graduate school. The professor essentially kneecapped my academic future. So, determined that he would not control the rest of my life, I found another dream: I would use my education to become a journalist. I filed a complaint against him with the campus Women's Commission, a meaningless but important act for me, cashed my fellowship check, and bought a one-way ticket to Cambodia.

That's where Foa came in. For a year she had been urging me to join her in Phnom Penh and become a reporter, as she had done. We'd met by chance in India when we were both traveling students in 1970. She left graduate school and went on to Vietnam and Cambodia. She sent me heart-stopping letters that were anything but tempting:

"War has broken out in the southeast with a ferocity I have never seen in Cambodia—tanks, B-52s, everything and despite the fact that the major battleground is 40 miles from here, the smell reaches Phnom Penh," she wrote in 1972. "Take care of yourself and think again about coming to live here. . . . It's more important than graduate school."[1]

As a member of the Committee of Concerned Asian Scholars that used historical and political research to oppose the war, I had never wanted to go within a hundred miles of a B-52 raid. But once I was pushed out of graduate school, Foa's invitation suddenly looked like a lifeline.

I justified the decision to Webb by pointing out that Cambodia was integral to my studies of India and the countries influenced by India.

Webb looked at me, a flicker of a smile in her eyes. She had been through so much more than my sad tale. Then she laughed out loud. She had done the self-same thing—bought a one-way ticket from Sydney to Saigon with no idea whether she would find a job in the war zone. "You'll do fine," she said. And that was that: I left the next day.

Foa was waiting for me at Phnom Penh's Pochentong Airport, from where she drove me into the city. I was dazzled by the city's beauty—the

golden spire of the Buddhist temples and the shaded sidewalk cafés—
but mostly by Foa's self-confidence. The friend who had shared dosa
and thick chai with me in Delhi was now a war correspondent with an
office, interpreters, a manager—and a desk for me.

That day I was under the wildly mistaken impression that it was
normal for young women to show up in Indochina and become battlefield reporters. In my backpack I carried a careful selection of paperback books on the war and one hardcover: *Fire in the Lake* by Frances
FitzGerald, the American woman who had made her name as a reporter in Vietnam. I thought I was ready. I was twenty-five years old
and had no idea what I had gotten myself into.

~ ~ ~

FOA WAS EXPELLED from Cambodia three months later at the beginning of April. In the middle of a massive American bombing campaign,
she published her investigation revealing that the United States embassy was illegally directing the pilots. Washington was furious. The
US ambassador Emory Swank told her boss that "Miss Foa distorted
the US role and activities in Cambodia" and it would be best if she
stays out of Cambodia.[2]

Sydney Schanberg wrote nearly the same article in the *New York Times*
one week later with no dire consequences to his reputation or career.[3]

With Foa gone, I was the only female foreign correspondent in the
country. The *Far Eastern Economic Review*, an Asia-wide news magazine published in Hong Kong, hired me after a two-week trial period
that I passed thanks to Foa's help. My base salary was $150 a month,
and I rented the least-expensive room in the best hotel for $50 a
month. (It came without hot water and was "cooled" by a colonial-era
ceiling fan.)

I had arrived in time to cover the escalation of the American bombing campaign in support of the Cambodian government army that was
fighting the guerilla Khmer Rouge with machine guns, rockets, and
mortars—the heavy artillery of war.

I was paralyzed the first time I saw the smoldering wreckage from a bombing campaign. Tropical palms were reduced to black stubs. The carcass of a water buffalo lay bloated in a cratered rice field. Displaced villagers told me they had no idea why fire had fallen from the sky. In the three months of March, April, and May 1973, 140,000 tons of American bombs were dropped.

The risks were beyond anything I had imagined but so were the rewards. In the US, I would have been lucky to write for the local women's page. In Cambodia, I was covering the central story of the war and learning the trade alongside reporters like James Markham of the *New York Times*, H. D. S. (David) Greenway of the *Washington Post*, Ed Bradley of CBS News, Tiziano Terzani of Der Spiegel, and Jacques Leslie of the *Los Angeles Times*—a cumulative masterclass in journalism.

But they didn't live in Cambodia. They arrived on assignment from their bases in Saigon, Hong Kong, and a few other cities. That meant news staffs were stretched thin and news organizations needed a resident reporter, or stringer, in Cambodia to fill in the gaps. They were sufficiently desperate that I became the contract stringer for the *Washington Post*, NBC radio, and *Newsweek* magazine in Cambodia just four months after I arrived.

When he hired me, Tom Lippman, the *Washington Post*'s Saigon bureau chief, said that I was the only person vaguely qualified for the job, and it did not matter that I was a woman. Not to him, perhaps, but mine became a rare female byline from the war, and I quickly became a target.

An anonymous parody written on Reuters stationary was circulated among the press corps casting me as a woman with "high school cheerleader looks" who had used her feminine wiles to win prize assignments. (I still have a copy.) I learned to barricade my door at night in case a colleague decided I was lonely. At a news conference, US ambassador John Gunther Dean asked a reporter to repeat a question, saying he had been "distracted by Miss Becker's legs."

I found friends: Ishiyama Koki, the correspondent for Kyodo News Service and translator of George Orwell into Japanese; Stephen Heder, an American freelancer who became a top scholar of the Khmer Rouge; and James Fenton, a British poet and unlikely war correspondent who wrote the best poetry of the war; and the diplomats Louis Bardollet, first secretary of the French embassy, and Renji Sathiah, head of the Malaysian mission.

Writing for the *Post* was more than a privilege. It felt like a higher calling, and I broke several important stories: I witnessed a US Army officer illegally advising the Cambodian army under attack, and I published an investigation of the Khmer Rouge identifying their leader for the first time as a man named Solath Sar (who would later be known as Pol Pot) and describing his revolution as brutal and ruthless as well as antagonistic toward their Vietnamese allies.

As the war neared its end, the great women correspondents returned. Kate Webb arrived in Cambodia on assignment, and we reported together; she showed me how to use my feet to measure a bomb crater and surreptitiously send rice to refugees, circumventing the journalist stricture against helping anyone you interviewed. One night we went to Café le Paradis for Chinese noodle soup. I complained about various indignities I had endured, but her frustrating advice was that I should keep a low profile. Perhaps my troubles seemed slight to her. She said her problem was nightmares. She would wake up trembling and not know which atrocity she had remembered in her sleep.

Frances FitzGerald was also back reporting on the war from Vietnam, crossing over to the Viet Cong area with Greenway, one of my bosses at the *Post*.

Then, out of the blue, two French women my age showed up in Cambodia to work as photographers. Françoise Demulder, a novice, arrived on a motorcycle with her boyfriend and a camera. Christine Spengler was something of a veteran after photographing the troubles in Northern Ireland. Suddenly I found myself alongside these French dynamos who were breaking into the rougher male world of war photography.

They were the unofficial protégées of Catherine Leroy, the diminutive French photographer whose images in *Paris Match* changed how the Vietnam War was imagined. During her first year, Leroy was the only woman photographer on the battlefield. She became the first woman to win important photography awards and became one of the photographers who helped make Paris the center of the photojournalism world. Demulder and Spengler were right behind her, inspired by her raw courage and winning their own share of prizes.

We were all so fixated on reporting the war that it took us decades to understand what we had accomplished as women on the front line of war.

Before Vietnam, the US military forbade women on the battlefield, and news organizations routinely sent men to chronicle war. Nearly every woman had to pay her own way to Vietnam and then find work and prove herself once she arrived. After Vietnam, that era was over. News organizations sent women as well as men to cover wars, and the US military dropped its prohibition against women covering the fighting.

The few dozen women who managed to cover the Vietnam War forever changed who wrote about and photographed war. The term *woman war correspondent* was no longer an oxymoron.

Leroy, FitzGerald, and Webb were the three pioneers who changed how the story of war was told. They were outsiders—excluded by nature from the confines of male journalism, with all its presumptions and easy jingoism—who saw war differently and wrote about it in wholly new ways.

Catherine Leroy spent most of her time on the battlefield taking striking photographs of war in the moment, stripped of patriotic poses. Frances FitzGerald, the American magazine writer, filled a huge void by showing the war from the Vietnamese point of view and winning more honors than any other author of a book about the war. Kate Webb, the Australian combat reporter, burrowed inside the Vietnamese and Cambodian armies and society with such determination that a top journalism prize for Asian journalists is named in her honor.

They kept a low profile, as Webb commanded me, and shied away from publicity, especially any that pigeonholed them as "girl reporters," as if that were a different and inferior category to male war correspondents. They didn't write their memoirs. Two of the women have already died.

They made their way to Vietnam at the beginning. I came at the tail end, following their paths, which I've retraced, scouring their diaries, notebooks, letters, photographs, classified military files, and writings and interviewing those close to them. Together, their lives offer a new way to see the war. And it is long overdue.

CHAPTER ONE

Petite Lady

THEY RECEIVED THE TWENTY-MINUTE WARNING. CATHERINE Leroy was waiting in her assigned seat on the left-hand side of the C-130 cargo plane, the air thick with the heat of Vietnam's dry season. She was quiet, trying to blend in. Leroy was the only journalist on the plane, the only photographer—she had two cameras draped around her neck—the only civilian and the only woman. Her US Army–issued parachute nearly swallowed her. At five feet tall and weighing eighty-seven pounds, she was less than half the size of the dozens of US Army parachutists sitting alongside her.[1]

In February 1967, Leroy was selected as the best person to capture on film the United States' first offensive airborne assault of the Vietnam War. The Pentagon hoped to repeat in the tropical jungles the success of World War II airborne operations that helped shift the course of that war. After more than a year of mixed results, the US military wanted a big win.

The day before Leroy had been called to the office of public information at the Military Assistance Command Vietnam, or MACV, the headquarters of the US Armed Forces in Saigon. Not sure if she was in trouble, Leroy was relieved when she was asked just one question: Did she still want to jump?

For the next twenty-four hours she was with the Second Battalion of the 173rd Airborne Brigade and sworn to secrecy until the operation began. She barely slept, rose with the troops before dawn, and climbed onto the truck convoy to Bien Hoa Airport. She boarded the seventh plane to shouts of "airborne all the way."

The target was a battleground near the border with Cambodia.

Leroy listened as the plane rose, excitement overwhelming her. Her stomach cramped.

She had lobbied to jump with the troops ever since she arrived in Vietnam from Paris. Few other press photographers were remotely qualified. Leroy had earned first- and second-degree parachute licenses in France while still in secondary school, egged on by a boyfriend who had dared her to try it, where she jumped eighty-four times over the vineyards and meadows of Burgundy.

The cavernous plane flew for more than an hour before the paratroopers heard the telltale drone of the engine slowing, signaling the pilot was near the target zone. Leroy photographed the game faces of the soldiers the moment the jumpmaster began the countdown.

"Ten minutes," he shouted, "ten minutes."

"Six minutes!"

"Get ready!"

"Stand up! Hook up! Check static lines!"

Soldier after soldier hooked onto the line of steel cable suspended above them, stamping their feet and shouting. The green light above the door lit up.

"Go!"

Leroy fell in with the others. The jumpmaster grabbed the static lines, guiding each soldier out with a "go, go, go, go."

Like a controlled explosion the men thundered down the long dark aisle toward the back of the airplane, Leroy keeping pace with them.

She jumped out the door with butterflies in her stomach, her dark blond pigtails lifting as she fell. Then: "Everything became light."

Leroy's parachute opened into cool air with no trace of wind. From above, the menacing jungle was an undistinguished blur of deepening shades of green. Almost beautiful. She grabbed the Leica, then the Nikon cameras around her neck, and photographed the hundreds of parachutes as they opened. She shot their images from above and below and sideways. Even in their helmets and heavy boots the soldiers reminded her of flowers opening their petals.

In no time the lush earth raced up to meet her. "I landed in a drained rice paddy, lovely and springy and soft, rolling over in my easiest landing."

Operation Junction City looked majestic in Leroy's photographs that first day. Parachutes filled the sky in artful patterns; soldiers hit the ground running, echoing the operations over France and Holland against the Nazis. But there the similarities ended. This tropical assault was a search-and-destroy mission in Tay Ninh Province in southwest Vietnam. It was not a set piece battle intended to capture a city or heavily armed positions. These soldiers were dispersed over rice paddies and villages looking, sometimes blindly, for the elusive headquarters of Vietnamese communists.[2]

In Washington, President Lyndon B. Johnson was waiting for news, anxious for a winning operation. His experience of World War II had been a series of battles that led inexorably toward victory. He had been a naval officer awarded a Silver Star for bravery as the observer member of bombing missions in the South Pacific.

Vietnam stumped him; the war was nothing like that. After nearly two years of disappointment as commander in chief, Johnson expected Operation Junction City to deliver a classic military turning point, an outright success that would impress the American public.[3]

With so much riding on the operation, other reporters had demanded to be on the ground with the paratroopers. Many were upset, some even disdainful, when they found out Leroy would be the only accredited journalist to jump. For over a year, Leroy had been the only woman combat photographer in Vietnam and had given up trying to change attitudes. Even the great photographer Don McCullin, who admired Leroy's work, was taken aback seeing her on the battlefield.

"She did not want to be a woman amongst men but a man amongst men. Why would a woman want to be amongst the blood and carnage? . . . I did have that kind of issue with Cathy."[4]

After the initial landing, the rest of the press arrived by land and filed their stories. The next morning Brig. Gen. John R. Deane showed up in the press tent with a surprise for Leroy. He pinned the master jump wings badge, its gold star signifying a combat jump, onto her shirt. "Wear this," he said. "That was your eighty-fifth jump."[5]

She wore the badge permanently on her crumpled fatigues, an eloquent rejoinder to anyone who had questioned whether she was qualified to cover the war.

~ ~ ~

Leroy's photographs from that day became historic. She had memorialized the first and, it would turn out, the only airborne US assault of the Vietnam War.

Only one other woman had preceded Leroy with a camera in the paddy fields and jungles of the Vietnam War—the celebrated photographer Dickey Chapelle. Chapelle became famous in World War II photographing battles of Guam and Okinawa. She had maneuvered around the official American ban on women covering combat by accepting an assignment aboard a navy hospital ship off the coast of Iwo Jima in 1945 and from there getting local permission to go on the island. On Okinawa she was caught photographing combat and placed under arrest in quarters. After the war, she photographed the struggles of postwar Europe, the uprising in Hungary, and wars in Algeria and Lebanon.[6]

Chapelle spent several months in Vietnam in 1961, before the American buildup, when President Kennedy sent 3,205 US troops as advisers to the South Vietnamese army. She burnished her reputation by winning a George Polk Award for her memoir. Her return to Vietnam in 1965 as the sole woman combat photographer was treated like a news event.

Chapelle was killed in November 1965, only months after she arrived. While on patrol with the Marines in Quang Ngai Province, she was hit by a piece of shrapnel from a booby trap. Her death made history: she was the first female war correspondent to be killed in combat. The news was published around the world, with accompanying photographs. When news organizations saw the picture of a Marine bending over her bloodied body crumpled on the ground, her pearl stud earring barely visible, they solidified their policies against allowing women to be combat photographers.

"There was a horror of assigning women to sports much less war," said Hal Buell, the New York photo editor of the Associated Press who worked with the Vietnam War photographs sent from Saigon. "Look at the history of photography. It was male oriented for so long: the equipment, the printmaking. We didn't think women could handle it. Women just weren't part of that pool."[7]

Leroy was the first woman photographer daring enough to follow Chapelle to cover combat in Vietnam and stick with it. For two years, Leroy remained the only one.

~ ~ ~

HER MOTHER SAID that Catherine Leroy was born angry, on an angry night of heavy Allied bombing toward the end of World War II. Their home in suburban Paris was not hit, and Catherine grew up in peace, in a prosperous bourgeois household where her father, Jean Leroy, an engineer, managed an iron foundry and her mother, Denise, doted on her only child.[8]

Young Catherine's anger and stubborn temperament may have been part of her DNA, but it was exacerbated by severe asthma. Tiny and in generally poor health, Catherine had to endure traditional treatments that failed to alleviate her condition. Despite the cost, her parents sent her to a boarding school in the French Alps for one month at a time to strengthen and clear her lungs. She despised the school, but the fresh air worked. Back at home, young Catherine was routinely forbidden to overexert herself. "You can't do that" was a familiar refrain of her childhood.

Her Catholic parents sent her to strict Catholic schools in their community of Enghien-les-Bains, best known for its casino. Monsieur and Madame Leroy were loving parents but repressed their feeling much of the time. Catherine saw her father break down only twice. In 1954, when she was ten years old, her father was listening to the radio, tears running down his face, as the announcer described the rout of the French army at the battle of Dien Bien Phu. Catherine had heard her father argue with his brother over the war to keep French colonies in Indochina. Until then, she hadn't grasped its profound importance to her father.

The second time was over the death of Michel Leroy, her father's twenty-one-year-old son from a previous marriage. Michel had died suddenly at a Catholic seminary where he was studying for the priesthood. To Catherine, he was a distant figure, more like a cousin.

As a young teenager, Catherine took up piano with a discipline she hadn't shown before. She was talented, and with practice she mastered the keyboard and found a style she loved. Catherine told her mother she preferred the blues, to which Denise answered simply: "Do you want to end up in a brothel?"

Catherine was determined to concentrate on popular music, and when she was fourteen years old was granted an audition with Bruno Coquatrix, the director of L'Olympia in Paris, Europe's biggest music hall. Top celebrity artists like Édith Piaf and Jacques Brel performed on the Olympia's stage. Acceptance by Coquatrix would bring Catherine close to her dreams of playing American jazz.

Her audition went well. Coquatrix complimented her, saying she was very good but also very young. Come back in a few years, he told her. Leroy would have none of that. Instead, she closed the lid of her piano and said: "I know all I need to know about piano."

She stopped playing forever.

She still loved music and stole away to Paris at night to hear jazz and meet boys. She was more than ready for the 1960s and a looser lifestyle and spent nights with her best girlfriend to avoid her mother's restrictions. To her parents' horror, Catherine dropped out of second-ary school. Frustrated, they sent her to England, to London, where she was supposed to learn English.

Rather than play cat-and-mouse games with her English teacher, Catherine explained early on that she had no interest in formal language lessons and offered a compromise: she would make herself useful washing windows in exchange for enough money to disappear into the London nightlife.

Her parents called her home.

Back in France, in need of an alternative source of excitement, she took up sky jumping. One of her instructors was a veteran French Foreign Legionnaire who had been scarred from stepping on a land mine. His stories brought to life the photographs of war and conflict in *Paris Match* magazine she admired, especially of the French paratroopers. She took photographs of the instructor with a small Instamatic camera.

"We talked a bit," she said. He introduced her to a professional skydiver who had been a freelance journalist in Saigon. She was intrigued. "I persuaded myself that if I could not be a blues singer like Billie Holiday, I would be a photographer," she wrote in a fragment of an unpublished memoir.

She was serious about photography and found a mind-numbing job at a temporary hiring agency in Paris, abandoning any idea of returning to school. In her free time, she roamed Paris, practicing with her camera. Working overtime, she saved enough francs to cover the costs of a Leica camera and a one-way ticket to Vietnam. After her twenty-first birthday, when a French child could legally leave home without parental consent, Catherine told Jean and Denise Leroy that she was going to Vietnam on her own for three months. In France, this was especially gutsy for a female, since the French were behind the times for gender equality. French women only gained the right to vote in 1944. But Leroy told her parents a white lie saying she would go only long enough to photograph a nice feature story on women in Vietnam. In fact, she was fully focused on being a war photographer, getting as close to the battle as she could.

"Photojournalists are my heroes. I want to be a photojournalist. The biggest story in the world right now is the Vietnam War," she wrote. Knowing next to nothing about Vietnam, Catherine Leroy arrived in Saigon in February 1966.[9]

~ ~ ~

JEAN LEROY HAD raised his daughter to believe in France's civilizing mission in Indochina—Cambodia and Laos as well as Vietnam. In her first vote in a French election, Leroy cast her ballot for Jean-Louis Tixier-Vignancour, an extreme right-wing politician who never forgave the French loss at Dien Bien Phu.

The history behind the end of the colonies wasn't discussed in her family, nor how and why the United States came to replace France as the reigning foreign power in Vietnam. Preferring to look at photographs rather than read long newspaper articles, Leroy had a negligible grasp of the history of the French and American occupations.

During World War II, Vietnam and every other colonized country was promised "the right of all peoples to choose the form of government under which they live" at war's end. The American president Franklin D. Roosevelt convinced Great Britain and then the other allies to make the pledge in the Atlantic Charter of 1941. The United States, at least, considered this a European promise to give up their colonies in Asia and Africa once the Axis powers of Germany, Japan, and Italy were defeated. President Roosevelt was determined to prevent France from resuming its colonial rule in Indochina.[10]

The British kept their word in India, Pakistan, and Burma by 1950, though the African colonies were not yet free of colonial interference. But France hesitated.

French leaders in Paris, trying to boost the local population's confidence after the war's devastation as well as the shame of occupation by the Nazis, were divided over whether to relinquish their colonies despite the Atlantic Charter.

After a series of failed negotiations, the French army returned to Vietnam and in 1947 began fighting to dislodge the provisional independent Vietnamese government of Ho Chi Minh in Hanoi. During World War II, Ho had worked with the United States Office of Strategic Services (OSS), the forerunner of the CIA. He was recruited in Kunming, China, at the Dragon's Gate Café. As Agent 19 of the OSS, Ho shared intelligence on the Japanese invaders with the OSS. Importantly, the Americans worked with Ho and his government in exile knowing they were communist.

But by 1948, the United States viewed communism as a global threat and was manipulated by France to change its priorities to line up with the French goal of retaining the Indochina colonies. Ho Chi Minh, once the intelligence asset, became the enemy.[11]

By the 1950s, Asia had changed dramatically. Communist Soviet Union developed and exploded an atomic bomb. China became a communist country after Mao Zedong's army won the civil war at the end of 1949. The anticommunist Red Scare in Washington, fueled by Senator Joseph R. McCarthy, led to accusations that some of the State Department's top China specialists had been disloyal and "lost China," the baseless accusations ruining their careers. The US Army faced off against the Chinese communist army in a war in Korea ignited by an invasion of the south by Soviet-backed Korean communists. The war ended in 1953 with a standoff that has endured into the twenty-first century.

Fear of a worldwide communist movement defined the politics of Washington. The United States considered itself in a cold war with the Soviet Union, which under the dictator Joseph Stalin had turned Eastern European nations into captive communist states. Every Soviet-allied communist country was considered an enemy to the US. The Atlantic Charter would take a back seat to this new and frightening threat.

With ease, the French convinced the United States government that Vietnam was a critical theater of the new Cold War, not a relic of colonial days. The American public went along and accepted the US decision to bankroll the French fight in Vietnam.

The French defeat at Diem Bien Phu was wrenching for Leroy's father and much of France because they believed that with American wealth supporting French forces they would win and France would revive its stature by keeping Vietnam and Indochina as overseas territories. Defeat was an unimaginable humiliation.

At the 1954 Geneva Conference, which followed the defeat at Dien Bien Phu, the French agreed to withdraw from Indochina. Vietnam was divided into two parts, North and South, until a national reunification election could be held. President Dwight D. Eisenhower decided that Ho Chi Minh was likely to win the election and predicted that would lead to disaster: "The collapse of Indochina would produce a chain reaction which would result in the fall of all Southeast Asia to the Communists."[12]

Eisenhower fully backed South Vietnam and rejected holding an election, citing a theory that each Southeast Asian country would fall once Ho Chi Minh won power. This became known as the domino theory. The Soviet Union had no such intentions in the region. It was fixated on controlling Eastern Europe. China barely had the resources to care for its own people after the Korean War and had a long history of antagonism with Vietnam.

President John F. Kennedy inherited Eisenhower's war in 1961. By then, South Vietnam was mired in the corruption and cronyism of President Ngo Dinh Diem, a Catholic. The Vietnamese, especially the Buddhists, were increasingly disenchanted with the political leadership and with war against the North. Kennedy increased American aid and military advisers to give South Vietnam's civilian and military leaders time to iron out their differences and unite against North Vietnam and the Viet Cong, the communist guerrillas in the South.[13] The South Vietnamese generals decided the solution was to overthrow and assassinate their own President Ngo Dinh Diem. Kennedy had tacitly agreed not to stop the coup d'état against Diem but had not imagined it would lead to Diem's murder.

Three weeks later, after Kennedy was assassinated in Dallas, Vietnam became Johnson's war. One year after his own election in 1964 as the candidate of peace, Johnson ordered American troops to Vietnam to fight as the main force against the communists. In March 1965, Maxwell Taylor, the US ambassador in Saigon, had given the South

Vietnamese premier one-week advance notice that an initial deployment of 3,500 Marines would land in Da Nang to kick off America's direct involvement in fighting the war. They were joining 23,000 American soldiers already in Vietnam as advisers. Later that summer, President Johnson announced he would raise the number of combat troops in Vietnam to 125,000.

~ ~ ~

DURING HER FIRST days in Saigon, Leroy was dutiful. She called on Vietnamese and French contacts—friends of friends whose names she had collected in Paris. She introduced herself to officials at the American military headquarters where she received press credentials based on a letter from *Paris Match* magazine promising to consider publishing her photographs. Leroy called the press pass her "open sesame card."

After bouncing around, she rented a room for a few nights at the elegant Continental Palace Hotel, a French oasis in the heart of old Saigon across from the ornate Opera House. She convinced Mr. Le, the hotel manager, to allow her to use the hotel as a mail drop once she found much cheaper lodgings.

Half of the trees had been cut down along the streets in central Saigon to make way for the wartime traffic of jeeps, black limousines, motorbikes, automobiles, and GMC trucks, which clogged streets made for rickshaws and bicycles. Yet Saigon still resembled a tropical provincial French city as the colonialists intended. Leroy wrote her mother reassuring letters that she had landed on her feet. Saigon, she said, "is a very pleasant town that you would like. People are insouciant and smiling. Many Americans in civilian dress. All this doesn't give the impression of being in a country at war."

Christian Simonpietri, a photographer who met Leroy in the early days, saw something else: a slight young woman distinctly out of place. "She was walking around the city center with only a few dollars in her pocket and a Leica camera strapped around her tiny neck. A tiny French person with a blond ponytail," he said. "She looked lost, so helpless. That is why we became friends."[14]

Simonpietri was part of a Corsican-French network that had kept Indochina running since colonial days. Born in Vietnam, he knew the country, the press corps, and the French expat community. For all those reasons, he was a valued guide for visiting foreign journalists.

With one look, Simonpietri knew Leroy needed help. They lunched together at the Continental, talking about war coverage over plates of spaghetti carbonara.

"I was giving her a few tips on how to cover the war in South Vietnam and how to behave with the troops," he said.[15]

Simonpietri was right. Leroy needed help. She was dangerously naïve about the hurdles she faced. But she was also a quick learner. Her letters home included descriptions of beggars, lepers, "thousands of dogs," and expats gone native. These old-timers, she wrote "are reliving the Indochina war all night long . . . 'When I was in Tonkin' . . . the key word, their faces light up. As far as I am concerned, I don't give a shit. What I'm interested in is today."

The far more sophisticated French and international society she met at diplomatic meals and social gatherings, like the French Cercle Sportif, a tennis and swim club, was more proper, and Leroy's wardrobe was barely adequate. She asked her mother to send her more stylish clothes: a new dress from Galeries Lafayette in Paris and, from her closet, the classic red silk dress, her navy-blue bikini—oh, and the top of her white bikini.

The better wardrobe would also help her in her work. After meeting several American officers, she realized that "being a woman, particularly a French woman, really brings a lot of advantages."

~ ~ ~

IN LATE FEBRUARY 1966, her confidence and wardrobe boosted, a petite woman with a long elfin face and piercing blue eyes walked into the Associated Press office in the Eden Building opposite the Continental Hotel. Unannounced, she introduced herself to Horst Faas, the editor of photography. Catherine Leroy had decided to jump-start her professional life.

Faas was a minor deity to photographers, especially freelancers. A talented photographer himself—he had won the Pulitzer the year before for his Vietnam War photographs—Faas was also an unusually gifted editor. His organizational skills, his grasp of history and photography's influence on events, and his deft handling of photographers helped put the Associated Press at the top. Above all, he had an eye for the most expressive photographs. Under his watch, the AP was the source of the best war photographs in Vietnam.

He was also a kingmaker. Faas took one look at Leroy and, new wardrobe notwithstanding, was not impressed. "She was a timid, skinny and very fragile young girl who certainly didn't look like a press photographer," he thought.[16]

He told her as much. "I'm not used to a young woman photographer," he said. "I don't know how you'll be perceived out there. Maybe you should concentrate on the Vietnamese and life in Saigon—pictures war photographers normally wouldn't like to take."

Leroy would have none of it. "No, no," she answered back. "I am a paratrooper."

Faas laughed: "You—a paratrooper—I can't believe it."

Luckily for her, beneath his daunting façade, Faas had a distinctly open-minded attitude within his profession. A German born in Berlin in 1933 who grew up with war's sorrows, he left his country as a young man, becoming cosmopolitan as he photographed conflicts in Algeria and Africa before arriving in Vietnam in 1962. He won the respect of the troops he photographed by living the war with them, famously wading through streams hoisting his camera above his head.

He worked easily with photographers from around the world: the US, Britain, Japan, and France, along with a few Italians and Vietnamese. They all respected him, not only for his evident talent but because he was fair, decisive, and exceedingly hardworking. And he gave them a chance to prove themselves.

But women? Faas's policy as photo editor, then a rarity, was to buy good photographs no matter who took them. Even, now, from a woman.

During that first meeting, they spoke in French. Leroy barely remembered English from her party days in London, although she had already started to Americanize her name, introducing herself as Cathy. Faas gave her several rolls of film, an essential gift since freelancers couldn't afford to buy their own. Then he delivered his routine conditions leavened with his dry humor. Once you've taken your photographs, he told her, bring back the film and AP will develop it in the bureau's darkroom. Photographers receive $15 for every photo purchased by AP, and AP retains the copyright on all these photos. No discussion.

With Faas's implicit encouragement, Leroy won a degree of legitimacy denied to other young women who had to spend months proving they were good enough to even be considered for freelance work.

Leroy's first assignment in Vietnam was an immersion in American culture, not war. She photographed the Swedish American actress Ann-Margret who was touring Vietnam to bolster troop morale. Leroy stood offstage as Ann-Margret performed at the US base in Da Nang in front of thousands of American men, all military, all in a frenzy at the sight of the actress in a skintight white costume. All Leroy could hear was raucous American noise—shouting, catcalling, and four thousand pairs of hands clapping, as every eye in the house converged on the dazzling woman singing and dancing onstage.

The coverage in the *Stars and Stripes* military newspaper was exuberant. How Ann-Margret, one of Hollywood's hottest stars, brought along a backup band of Johnny Rivers, Mickey Jones, and Chuck Day. How she danced the swim, the frug, the jerk, and the monkey to the deafening cheers of the troops, some of whom tried to dance along.[17] The mood in 1966 was optimistic. It was the first full year that American troops were actively engaged in combat in Vietnam. President Johnson had ended years of US vacillation between sending in American combat troops or searching for a peace settlement that would allow them to withdraw. Vietnam was now an American war, with the South Vietnamese in a secondary role. The Marines were gung-ho.

~ ~ ~

THE NEXT DAY, Leroy followed Ann-Margret to the Da Nang hospital where she greeted soldiers with smiles and close-ups. For a French woman who had never been to the United States, knew few Americans, and had never been close to the military, it was a heady initiation.

Leroy came away from the assignment impressed by the American military, especially by the traffic of warplanes steadily taking off from the base on bombing missions over North Vietnam, raids begun by President Johnson in 1964 that signaled his decision to jump into the war.

The heat on the bases was overwhelming. It felt like a sauna. Sweat coated her scalp and collected around her neck. She took the next day off to swim in the waters of the South China Sea before hopping on a military flight back to Saigon. A Swiss magazine bought two of her color photos of Ann-Margret. Her career had begun.

Buddhist demonstrations broke out one month later in April. They appeared to be a resumption of the huge 1963 Buddhist crisis symbolized by a Buddhist monk who burned himself to death on a busy Saigon street in protest of the corrosive policies of President Diem, protests that helped lead to the president's downfall.

Now in 1966, the Buddhists were agitating against the escalating American military role, which they saw as a foreign power taking over their country. President Nguyen Van Thieu feared the Buddhists were becoming effective rivals and struck back. He fired a popular Buddhist general and claimed the Buddhist clergy was under the influence of communists.

Most of the recent South Vietnamese history was lost on Leroy. When she went back to Da Nang to photograph the growing protests, she wrote in a letter home that they had been "skillfully led by the Buddhists, who in turn are manipulated by the communists."[18] She was parroting the South Vietnamese government's baseless charges.

Da Nang itself was off-limits when she arrived. A military jeep dropped her off at the press center outside the city. From there, she walked toward the fighting in Da Nang on "a deserted avenue lined with wooden shacks, in the crossfire of automatic weapons."

Her first time under fire, she instinctively ran for cover and joined a group of Vietnamese who had been chased from their homes. They gave her a bowl of soup and chopsticks. "This is delicious," she said in French, and then ran further to avoid the fighting as it closed in.

"I ended up near a shop making headstones, I was not the only one. I took a photograph of a man. Woman? Terrified and taking cover behind a headstone."[19]

She took more pictures of Vietnamese civilians—children as well as adults "huddled under sniper fire behind gravestones in the stone mason's yard." It was a chaotic insurrection with no sign of communist propagandists or communist provocation.

Faas bought two of her photographs, haunting images of Vietnamese civilians hiding behind headstones as they were fired on by their own government. When he sent Leroy's first photos over the wire to New York for sale around the world, her excitement matched only her determination to continue photographing for Faas.

From that moment, the AP Saigon bureau became a second home to Leroy. Returning from the field, she walked up four flights of stairs because the elevator rarely worked. The familiar walls of the office were crowded with framed articles and photographs of reporters who had died covering the war; the floors were strewn with flak jackets, boots, and the gadgets photographers required, and the hallway permanently smelled of *nuoc mam*, the ubiquitous Vietnamese fish sauce, and urine. She slumped into an armchair, wrote her captions, and handed the negatives to Faas.

Just as familiar was her routine after leaving the AP office. She would return to her small rented room, shower off the dirt from working days in the field, and then crawl into bed, sleeping eighteen hours at a stretch, sometimes a whole day: "I slept as if I had no desire to ever wake up."[20]

CHAPTER TWO

As Dirty and Tired as They Are

N O ONE HAD TOLD LEROY THAT THE US MILITARY HAD A
long-standing but now dormant rule that prohibited women
from reporting on the battlefield. The ban was rigidly enforced during
World War II and specified that women journalists stay behind with
military nurses. Among the thousands of male reporters covering the
American military, very few women managed to make it anywhere near
actual battlefields; most were caught and told to leave.

Vietnam was wildly different. Military rules for media were not applied there. President Johnson had refused to declare the US at war
in Vietnam and instead relied on open-ended powers granted him by
Congress under the 1964 Gulf of Tonkin Resolution. And without a
declaration of war, there was no censorship. Vietnam was the first and
last uncensored American war. American journalists were not required
to submit their reports or film for review. Nor were they embedded
as they are today, where access to the front is under tight control and
allowed at the discretion of the unit commander "whenever possible."[1]

Amazingly, the military even provided transport for the press. Reporters were free to come and go wherever troops were deployed,
albeit always with permission from the unit commander. All that was

required to board the transport—often a helicopter—was official press credentials.[2]

Jonathan Schell, journalist and author of *The Village of Ben Suc*, arrived the same year as Leroy and, as an American, understood how rare the freedom was that journalists had in Vietnam. "That press pass turned out to be magical—sort of like an all Europe rail pass except you could go on the planes, you could go on the tanks, live on the bases. You could hitchhike with helicopters from one place to the next," he said. "It was wide open. You could go out and see that war."[3]

For women, this uncensored, unrestricted entry to the battlefield was an incomparable gift: a door to a profession that was closed to them at home. Without a declaration of war, the military also left dormant the ban on women journalists on the battlefield.

For Leroy, the press pass was also a temporary answer to her abysmal finances. She was running out of money. After paying for meals, professional expenses, and rent on a tiny room in a Vietnamese boarding house, she was broke. Her press pass allowed her to live in the field with the soldiers where she ate rations, slept rough, and spent no money. It was a godsend. A newcomer with no training in photojournalism or familiarity with the military, she didn't know the rules so she made up her own. She would go from base camp to base camp, take in-depth photographs, fly back on a military chopper to Saigon to sell the photos, and then return to the field.

She set a record for the number of military operations covered by a journalist in 1966. She had followed US troops from the demilitarized zone (DMZ) on the northern border to the Mekong Delta in the south and back again several times.

One of her first operations was on the Chu Pong Massif near the Cambodian border and the DMZ at the base camp of the Second Battalion of the Twelfth Cavalry of the army's First Cavalry Division.

"A helicopter has just put me down in the middle of the jungle at the same time as boxes of C-rations, munitions and mail," she wrote. "I stayed there for a few seconds, lost among all these men staring at me."

She was wearing combat fatigues she had tailored to her size in Saigon and size 5 combat boots she bought on the black market, after an extensive search for the smallest pair available. The overall effect was of an adolescent boy going to a costume party.

The commander had approved her visit and welcomed her, not knowing how long she would stay or how she would adapt. Leroy wasn't sure herself. Hesitantly, she established what became her distinctive modus operandi. She accepted no help whatsoever. She carried her own pack, and she crossed streams and climbed hills unassisted. She was determined: "The terrain is extremely difficult. I have to learn to hold on tight, to not sink, looking where to place my foot."

"I walk around dressed like them (not a pretty sight), eat like them, twice a day I tell them I'm fed up of seeing your faces, I go behind a tree when it's time to pee."[4]

She slept under her poncho or in a tent with several soldiers. There was no sex with the troops. That was a given, or Leroy would have been shipped out immediately for causing disruption among the ranks.

At the same time, she was French and understood the magic of presentation. Using dreary military C-rations, she made the troops hot chocolate, calling it "French cocoa," convincing them it was delicious because of a special French ingredient. At night, she proudly offered cans of *vin ordinaire* that tasted like champagne in the field.

After a few weeks, she became used to the military, from the throbbing whirl of the helicopter blades to the rattle of machine guns or the slicing sound of machetes cutting pathways through the head-high elephant grass as the troops reconnoitered. She got used to the body bags too. And the army got used to her and her camera. They started talking to her, teaching her English with their questions: Where do you come from? What are you doing here? Her answers were delivered in a Parisian accent they adored and tried to mimic. Soon, they barely noticed as she photographed their arduous and tedious marching, their anxious moments running to the mail drop to see if someone had written them a letter, their exhaustion at the end of the day as night fell in the jungle. In her photographs, she caught the offhand nobility, the anxiety and loneliness in their faces, the fear as they marched past villages where smoke billowed from burned-out houses.

When Captain Bobby C. Allen, a Protestant chaplain, arrived and the soldiers gathered in the inhospitable jungle, backs to a tree, legs bent, helmet-less heads bowed with eyes on the ground, Leroy captured the moment in a tableau as composed as a Vatican painting, the soldiers caught in a moment of reflection, listening as the chaplain addressed them, lifting them out of the moment where the sound of battle couldn't reach them.[5]

In a letter to her father she described the rite of passage when she went out with a new unit. "I've got one day to prove myself. They expect me to break my neck every 100 meters. There would be 10 guys to help me up, but all would be lost.

"In the morning I'm just as dirty and tired as they are, so our relations are very friendly. They forget I'm a gal, I've been adopted."[6]

One soldier, knocked over by the novelty of her at the camp, told her: "When I write to my pals that I slept in a tent with a French woman in the Vietnamese jungle, no one will believe me."

All the time spent with troops bred a ruggedness in her that was considered anything but feminine. She learned the English lexicon of war: how many wounded or dead, incoming and outgoing, mortars and machine guns—what she called her "language of violence."

She learned to swear with the soldiers and Marines. She matched their "fuck you" and "fuck this," always pronounced with her strong French accent as "fuck zees." She called this language colorful, but others called it foul. Dickey Chapelle had taken on the same habits. After she died, she was remembered by Vietnamese troops as a foul-mouthed woman.[7] In the 1960s women were not expected to curse aloud.

And Leroy smoked as much as any soldier. She was rarely without a cigarette dangling in her hand. The woman whose parents spent most of her childhood worried she would succumb to asthma without special care always carried a pack, which she shared casually with the soldiers as they did with her.

Spending inordinate amounts of time in the field allowed her to experiment. She was so short, she could move among the tall Americans without being noticed and aim her camera at unusual angles. She started to lie on the ground to be close enough to zero in on a soldier's face. She focused on the eyes.

As the war escalated in the summer of 1966, and the rhythm of the deployments intensified, Leroy sold enough photographs to earn real money. The Associated Press was still her best client. She would go directly from the field to the office of Horst Faas "ill at ease in my filthy battle dress" but determined not to miss a news cycle. With a professional eye as discerning as a diamond cutter, Faas would review her film, choosing the few he would buy and paying the $15 a photograph he had promised her from the beginning. *Paris Match* gave her assignments and paid much more handsomely. She worked for CBS. United Press International bought a few photographs left over by AP.

After forty-eight hours in Saigon, Leroy would be back in the field, disciplining her nervous, wild energy on photographing war, the most intense subject any journalist ever faces. Every photograph she took that caught a moment of agony or triumph had the potential of generating a public reaction that might move global politics and make history. Every photograph could be her last if she was hit. Leroy was beginning to understand what every male journalist has known since the Crimean War: there is no assignment more rewarding and exciting or more dangerous. There's nothing like a war.

The first months were exhausting, especially for a woman who had trouble bringing her weight up to ninety pounds. Her arms and legs were skinny skeins of muscles and nerves. And she had to learn to manage on her own: she was a freelancer with no health insurance, no company regularly depositing a check in her bank account or funding her for expenses, and no spouse waiting to help her recover in a well-kept home in Saigon.

Without real friends, the daughter who had rebelled so forcefully against her parents was discovering how much she needed them. Her letters home were a release valve, an antidote to loneliness, and a rich diary.

She told her mother things she would have never expressed back home in France. "As a woman, it's tough to be respected in Saigon. You're either a whore or a bitch: 20,000 guys in town, but virtually no European women. It's nowhere near as much fun as you'd think," she wrote.[8]

That description proved comically prophetic.

One evening after returning from the field "dog tired," Leroy was woken by loud shouting and screaming in Vietnamese. Then a knock on her door.

"I found myself face to face with three military police—American, Vietnamese and Korean. They look into my room . . . a desk, a bed, a chair, a few photos on the wall, on the floor a dirty battle jacket, boots and an operations bag."

She asked them: "What do you want?"

After surveying the room and realizing that this French woman was a professional journalist, the American policeman looked down at his boots and said: "We're sorry, but we're looking through all the prostitute houses."

The other young boarders with angelic smiles she had taken for Vietnamese students were actually sex workers in a brothel. In some ways, life in Saigon often seemed more difficult than in the field.[9]

Leroy took a different tack when writing to her father: "You would be proud of your daughter if you saw her shaking hands with [US general] Westmoreland and curse in English just like certain colonels in the Marines with more decorations than General de Gaulle himself. I could write pages and pages about 'my Marines,'" she wrote him. "The young Marines in particular are very impressive: calm, very relaxed, the tough youths do a real professional job. In these units there are some absolutely crazy heroic acts."[10]

The photojournalist Christian Simonpietri saw her transformation and was concerned that she was too coarse. She was becoming a confident journalist, yes, and gaining in professional stature. United Press International had already written a short story about the French woman war photographer. Among her colleagues, though, she was an oddball. There was, simply, no one like her. Weeks would go by and Simonpietri didn't see her in Saigon. When she did show up, she had changed, and he told her so. "Her personality, her bad language was really not appreciated among colleagues," he said. "She was too loud."[11]

Leroy could feel the tension and knew she needed a break. She had earned it in every sense: by July she was bringing in $500 for a single month's work, a tangible acknowledgment that she had built the beginnings of a career in Vietnam. With plans for guilt-free relaxation, Leroy flew to Hong Kong. There she indulged herself, swimming in a hotel pool and window-shopping for clothes she couldn't afford. She did buy a Nikon camera with a telephoto lens and a few additions to her wardrobe. But three days away felt too long. "There's so much going on in Vietnam, I don't want to start getting involved with events elsewhere."

By the time she returned, she discovered some of her "colleagues" were trying to get rid of her.

~ ~ ~

WHEN LEROY FIRST arrived in February 1966, there were 184,314 US troops in Vietnam, a vast increase on the initial deployment a year earlier of just 3,500. By the end of 1966, the US military said it needed a total of 429,000 American troops.

The war was escalating. The word *escalation* became shorthand for the explosive expansion of the American military role and presence in Vietnam that transformed South Vietnam into the biggest battlefield on the planet. Tens of thousands of American troops arrived with their sophisticated warplanes, weapons, and equipment to be used to attack and bomb at an intensity never seen before. Construction crews built massive bases with airstrips and fuel depots. They carved out roads through remote jungles and rice paddies and threw up military bridges over rivers in a traditional Asian countryside of water buffalo and ox carts. South Vietnam was in the immensely powerful hands of the American military. The social and political costs were enormous but hidden.

The original war plan of Gen. William Westmoreland, the commander of US forces in Vietnam, was conventional, relying on America's modern, high-tech firepower as well as US troops. In the first stage, his forces would seal off South Vietnam's borders from North

Vietnam. Then American troops would be deployed along the DMZ, along Vietnam's long coastline, and at new US bases around Saigon's defense perimeter to defend against enemy infiltration. Once the National Liberation Front of South Vietnam or Viet Cong were cut off from North Vietnam, Westmoreland would launch massive search-and-destroy operations to find and eliminate the enemy in the South.

His plan's biggest vulnerability was Vietnam's western border. During the war against the French, North Vietnam had created a web of paths and roads along that border, used by its soldiers to travel through southern Laos into northeastern Cambodia and then cross over to South Vietnam. During the American war, the paths became highways and waterways that transported millions of troops and supplies to the communists in the South. Named the Ho Chi Minh Trail by the Americans, this route bedeviled Westmoreland, and destroying it became an obsession.

The other problem with the plan was the American inability to find the enemy. It was close to impossible for Americans to discern the loyalty of rural South Vietnamese. Militarily, Westmoreland's conventional strategy underestimated the guerilla nature of much of the war. The Viet Cong had mastered the hit-and-run tactics of the insurgent, hiding in tunnels or blending into villages, waiting for night to mount operations before disappearing again.

"There is no front line," Leroy wrote to her father, trying to explain how the Vietnam War wasn't like World War II. In Vietnam, you couldn't plot a march toward victory on a map. Westmoreland's strategy did not include front lines in part because US troops were not charged with capturing and then holding territory. They were trying to capture and kill the illusive enemy. Leroy hopped from helicopter to helicopter to keep up with these moveable battlefields.

In Vietnam, the war eventually became known as the American war.

Leroy's photographs told this story better than words. Stunned villagers huddled near their empty huts, ordered out by the towering American soldiers in a search-and-destroy mission. Their faces resigned, the villagers were rounded up and banished from their homes, leaving behind their ancestor altars and pig stys. They cradled bedrolls and cooking pots; they were displaced to refugee camps.

Elsewhere, B-52 bombers dropped 500-pound bombs on rice paddies where water buffalo pulled plows. Warplanes dropped deadly chemical defoliants and herbicidal agents that overnight destroyed jungles and any animal or person in its path. Vietnam became the battlefield where the United States used the most sophisticated and lethal arsenal in modern history.

In the village of Co Luu in Quang Ngai Province, Leroy photographed Marines moving several hundred villagers into tents surrounded by barbed wire. Leroy took images of an interrogation, which she later described in a diary. A South Vietnamese officer is asking standard questions to an old man who is wrinkled and trembling: "'How old are you?' 'Where are your sons?' . . . The soldiers are professional, their faces serious, the background of destruction is menacing."[12]

The buildup of journalists paralleled the military buildup. In one year, the number of accredited correspondents in Vietnam ballooned from less than one hundred to over six hundred.[13] Leroy scrambled, wanting to take advantage of her newfound success. She was making a name for herself and believed her colleagues should treat her as a legitimate member of the press corps. She wanted respect. Instead, she was ostracized.

The reasons given were couched in personal terms. Leroy was pushy, ambitious, shoving to get on a helicopter to the battlefield or back to Saigon with her film. She had no manners. In the field, she could be a hothead. When she didn't get her way, she would flare up, sometimes using profanity. She swore.

It made no difference that male reporters and photographers also had tempers, also swore, also threw their weight around to get what they wanted, and also were ambitious. Leroy was expected to be ladylike. She was an interloper who had become an affront to the profession. It came down to her gender: she didn't belong because she wasn't a guy.

Alain Taieb, a French photographer, had briefly befriended her, seeing her as a lost soul until he realized she was serious and was actually becoming a real war photographer. For him, this was impossible. She was strange and small; she tied her Leica camera around her neck with a shoelace. He told her that being a photographer in Vietnam was a boy's job, not a girl's job. In no time, he and other French journalists refused to work with her. "We would tell her—you can't come with us—you are bothering us—this is for boys."

And they insisted that she wasn't qualified: "She had no money, no job, no manners, no nothing." This was also absurd. Taieb had arrived in Vietnam with no experience, no money, and no job—exactly like Leroy.

Leroy was astounded that her colleagues had betrayed her. She wrote her mother that Taieb and another French photographer were acting like "real bastards."[14]

Decades later, Taieb apologized to her and said he was "not very proud of the way we treated her."[15]

The worst was yet to come. Some reporters decided to lobby the US military for Leroy's official exclusion. On October 1, 1966, François Pelou, bureau chief of Agence France-Presse—the equivalent of the dean of the French press corps—went behind Leroy's back and denounced her in a complaint to the US military press office. He said her behavior "cast reflections upon the whole press corps to the extent that others are having difficulty winning the cooperation of troops after she leaves an area."[16]

Once Pelou broke the ice, others followed.

Leroy became a target. Peter Arnett, who won a Pulitzer Prize for his Vietnam coverage for the Associated Press, wrote in his memoir that he saw Leroy swear at an aircraft commander at Dang Ha when she was told there was no room for her in his helicopter. Another reporter wrote an anonymous complaint about that incident in Dang Ha to MACV, and it became a second strike against her. A male reporter engaging in such behavior would have generated no protest whatsoever.

Filed alongside that complaint was a handwritten note from a local American commander at Dang Ha, warning an official in Da Nang that "the unwashed one" was heading his way.[17]

That "unwashed" slur is a classic and grotesque insult against women as old as the Bible. Unclean and unwashed referred to women who were impure because they were menstruating or were women of loose morals. Unwashed women were isolated and denigrated. Taken literally, the accusation against Leroy didn't make sense. All journalists covering the battlefield stunk until they got home to Saigon and a hot shower. But it made for an easy insult against her that resonated. It stayed in her file permanently.

Other military spokesmen piled on. One wrote an unsigned note: "Why can't we remove one ugly Caucasian from the Far Eastern scene? Isn't the evidence sufficient to lift accreditation?"[18]

That became the goal: create a thick secret file, nicknamed "the black book," that would justify taking away Leroy's press credentials so she couldn't work.

Another poison dart read: "An [unnamed] American correspondent reported . . . that Miss Leroy seems to be doing all she can to discredit the efforts that American troops are making to win the war. She criticizes their work, food, efforts to help her get her material and twists facts to suit her purpose of discrediting their actions."

That accusation against Leroy was outrageous. Her politics were more conservative than most of her colleagues, and she was one of the biggest boosters of the military. She told anyone who would listen: "I love the Marines." And she did.

One of the most serious charges in the secret file came from the Marine media liaison officer who wrote on October 20, 1966, that Leroy was "not welcome" aboard the USS *Repose* hospital ship because she used "coarse and profane language" and acted in an "arrogant and obnoxious" manner when making demands. T. M. Fields, deputy of information in the Information Office of MACV, wrote: "This continues to damage the otherwise excellent relations in the I Corps area between the military units and members of the press . . . and is unfair to the many sincere and responsible reporters who deport themselves in a proper manner."

Her colleagues did not stand up for her. As Arnett wrote: "The Vietnam press corps was a male bastion that women entered only at the risk of being humiliated and patronized; the prevailing view was that the war was being fought by men against men and women had no place there."[19]

Instead, Arnett said, the men actively worked against the women. "We reporters tended to disparage the abilities of women and gossip about them and their relationships and were uninterested in helping them out with the authorities."

But when the military moved to take away her press credentials, they had a problem. Leroy had obeyed the basic rules. She had not violated security considerations, endangered troops, written bad checks, assaulted military spokesmen, or fabricated journalistic credentials. They had to make up an offense, and in a wicked twist, the military said she was being suspended because her obnoxious behavior hurt her fellow journalists. "Her actions were such as to alienate working relationships with military personnel to such an extent as to make it difficult for newsmen to function effectively."

On October 24, 1966, Col. Rodger R. Bankson, chief of information at MACV, officially suspended her press credentials:

"Miss Le Roy," he wrote, "Since my last letter to you, we have received additional reports concerning your conduct while associated with military units in the capacity of a correspondent. These incidents are of such a serious nature that a decision has been made not to renew your MACV accreditation. You are requested to turn in your present accreditation card to the Special Projects Division on 30 October. Sincerely yours."[20]

Without her press credentials, her photojournalism career in Vietnam would be over. The military even sent letters to Leroy's outlets in Paris to tell them that her behavior had led them to suspend her credentials. No stone was unturned to ruin her career just weeks after it had finally blossomed.

Leroy panicked. She "felt like jumping in the Mekong." She had been shoved out the door by the military with the assistance of some of her colleagues. She was furious. If the ban was not lifted, she would be forced to return to Paris and work in a dreary "insurance office." She was so humiliated that for weeks she couldn't write her parents or anyone else. For the first time in her young life, Leroy couldn't resolve her difficulties by simply running away.

Instead, she had to learn to stand her ground and fight back, quickly. She was told the most serious charge of bad behavior was made by officials from the hospital ship *Repose*. She got in touch with her host on the ship, and three days after MACV revoked Leroy's press credentials, Lt. Paul E. Pedisich of the navy's Seventh Fleet's information office sent a short, unequivocal message to MACV that rebutted the charge against Leroy. It read in full:

"Miss Leroy conducted herself in a complete, charming and lady-like manner while on board the REPOSE. Left with warm invitation to return whenever she could."[21]

With this courtly description of Leroy, the top officials of the USS *Repose* hospital ship denied that she had been a nasty, foul-mouthed woman or that she was no longer welcome on his ship.[22]

While some friends in the press were less sympathetic, her strongest supporter was the man whose opinion counted the most: Horst Faas, at AP. He wrote a letter attesting to her professional standing and dispelling any hint that she was an unwelcome colleague or a fraud. Writing on the Associated Press letterhead, Faas used the clear, commercial language of success: Leroy's photographs were good enough to be published in the highly competitive world market. She had sold spot photographs and photograph series she took of combat operations in all of the US military corps areas in Vietnam, earning at least $1,000 (which was the equivalent of $7,900 in 2019) after only seven months in Vietnam.[23]

In other words, Leroy was not the uncouth amateur undermining her colleagues as portrayed in that black book of complaints nor was she a vagabond who should be dismissed as a frivolous woman seeking adventure, as her male colleagues called women freelancers.

Bryce Miller, bureau manager of United Press International, followed Faas with a more perfunctory note "to certify" that UPI had purchased photographs from Leroy and "will consider any pictures in the future she may have to submit."

Leroy's reputation, though, would never recover. From then on, she was branded a spitfire and a troublemaker, an uncouth, foul-mouthed woman.

The story spread through Saigon. When she went to the Continental Hotel to collect her mail Mr. Le, the manager, said he had received a letter from her father who was worried when she hadn't written home in weeks. He handed her a second letter from her mother. She read it over a drink at the hotel's terrace bar and wrote her family back. "My problems were serious, and I wasn't in the mood to not take it seriously," she wrote. "Things are going better today."

Leroy backed away from much of the press corps. She didn't know whom to trust and was slightly punch-drunk from the battle to keep her press card. She sought other people to mix with, including men. In the free atmosphere of Saigon, Leroy was beginning to enjoy casual sex as much as her male colleagues did. As she wrote her mother in her usual frank fashion, she would have fun when she wasn't working and lead a life "without problems of guys and romance. I take [romance] where I can get it. I'm keeping my heart for other things. It's not egoism. I call it experience."

She found ways to mix pleasure with work. Whenever possible, she took an extra day from the field to swim at one of the magnificent but largely empty beaches. She turned an assignment for AP into a short vacation at Vung Tau, the old French beach resort known as Cap St. Jacques, sunbathing on the rocks and swimming in the ocean. In Saigon, she swam in hotel pools. At night, she photographed GIs in bars like the San Francisco, Blue Moon, Number One, and Chez Mimi, ending up across the river on a strip called Soul Alley, where the bars played soul music with a heavy emphasis on Aretha Franklin and James Brown.

She occasionally sought out the younger English-speaking crowd closer to her age and temperament—like the photographer Tim Page and CBS television journalist John Laurence. She could relax around them because they required no apologies from her and made no judgments about her behavior. When she needed a place to crash, their door was open.

Page, who became one of the most famous photographers of the war, had a special respect for Leroy. He was amazed at how hard she had to work to prove her talent as the first woman on the scene with a camera, made all the more difficult as a French woman in an American war. "She became a loner in the purest sense, broke the mold, defied odds few others could have faced."[24]

Since Leroy spent so much time in the field, a lot of her socializing with Laurence was at the Marine Corps press center in Da Nang, where the food was reasonably good and the drinks were cheap. He considered the gossip about her being unclean and unkempt as mean-spirited nonsense. "Of course, you look dirty and smell foul after you've spent a few days in the field with the troops . . . to single her out for criticism on that count was wrong."[25]

A few months after Leroy redeemed her accreditation, she was selected as the only accredited journalist to parachute with the troops in Operation Junction City. Finally, she was back, triumphantly wearing her master jump wings.

Leroy's photographs of the assault were impressive, dramatically framing the parachutes in the broad sky, illustrating the size and strength of one of the largest US Army offensives of the war. But Operation Junction City itself was a wash, at best.[26] Over six weeks, US aircraft bombed villages, and 25,000 American and South Vietnamese troops were sent to find even a trace of the COSVN (Central Office for South Vietnam), the communist headquarters. There was heavy fighting with the Liberation Army of South Vietnam, the official army of the communists of the South known as the Viet Cong. The Americans reported heavy damage to the enemy, bombing communist positions and destroying acres of jungles and fields. During the offensive, nearly 7,000 Vietnamese civilians fled the fighting, becoming part of the refugee exodus filling the slums and suburbs of the cities of the south. Officially, 2,728 enemy soldiers were killed while 282 American soldiers died.

The US military declared the mission "inconclusive." The Vietnamese communists had controlled the tempo, choosing when and where to engage with the Americans. After a few months, the American troops withdrew, recalled to other battles, and the Vietnamese communists quietly returned. The US military concluded from Operation Junction City that airborne assaults were not suitable in the guerilla wars of Vietnam. On the ground, they found systems of tunnels under the villages, signaling that the communists had local control if not support and could evade conventional tactics, even from a force with such superior firepower. By year's end, the military was even questioning the value of big operations.

Instead, Vietnam became the first helicopter war. Army air cavalry units used helicopter formations in combat for the first time to find and attack enemy forces and transport US forces to battle. Helicopters also carried out the wounded and supplied troops in the field, as they had in the Korean War.

The disappointing military results of Operation Junction City did not dampen Leroy's pride. She wrote to her father: "I've always thought I should succeed because I never gave in." She signed it with "warm kisses, and to Mommy, too, C. Leroy."

After that near career-ending episode, she was even more driven to prove her worth. She won awards never before given to women and changed the look of war photography.

~ ~ ~

LEROY'S PRESS CREDENTIALS were soon jeopardized again. In 1967, all female journalists were put on notice that the US military was planning to reimpose a lighter version of the World War II regulations prohibiting them from reporting on the front lines—the military still didn't believe women belonged in a war zone.

This ban was triggered by a fluke encounter in April 1967 between Denby Fawcett, a former women's page reporter for the *Honolulu Star-Bulletin* newspaper, and Gen. William Westmoreland. Fawcett, who had a degree from Columbia University, had left the society pages, paid her own way to Saigon, and become the *Honolulu Advertiser* newspaper's stringer in Vietnam.[27] A careful journalist with the looks of the actress Sally Field, Fawcett had had to convince unit commanders that she was sturdy enough to report from combat areas. At the beginning, many refused her, some saying she reminded them of their daughters and they didn't want to see her in harm's way. Finally, the Marines gave her permission, and she accompanied a unit in I Corps (pronounced "eye core"), proving her mettle. Then she ran into Westmoreland.

Fawcett was in the Central Highlands reporting with a unit from Hawaii—the First Battalion, Eighth Infantry of the Fourth Infantry Division—when General Westmoreland made an unannounced visit. After pep talks to improve troop morale after heavy fighting, Westmoreland continued with inspections and was surprised to see Fawcett with the troops.

He knew her as the daughter of friends in Honolulu, where the two families were neighbors. His wife played tennis with her mother. After pleasantries, the general asked Fawcett how long she had been at the forward base. "Several days," she answered, believing it was part of a friendly exchange.

It was nothing of the sort. Back in Saigon, Westmoreland was furious that any woman would stay days and nights on a forward base. His concern wasn't cloaked in a denunciation of her character, as it had been with Leroy. He framed it simply as a question of gender. The commander of US forces in Vietnam did not believe women belonged near the fighting.

As explained to Fawcett, Westmoreland feared women "might inconvenience or endanger soldiers who would rush to protect us." He also worried that women correspondents would collapse emotionally when "faced with the horrors of war." Westmoreland proposed a compromise edict that would prohibit women journalists from spending nights with troops in the field. It wasn't a complete imposition of the World War II ban, but it might as well have been.[28]

By requiring a commander to guarantee that any woman journalist would travel to and from a battle in a single day, Westmoreland was asking the impossible.

The handful of women journalists in Saigon recognized that their "livelihoods are being destroyed." Five American women, largely strangers to one another, set up an ad hoc committee to fight the ban.

With her gritty reputation and recent run-in with MACV, Leroy was asked to be one of the ten women who signed a letter asking that the edict be nullified.

The American women then petitioned the Pentagon to drop the proposed Westmoreland ban since the MACV accreditation was under its auspices. Ann Bryan, editor of *Overseas Weekly*, an alternative newspaper for GIs, wrote a history of women war correspondents to buttress their position that women were as qualified as men to cover battles and were no more likely to cause problems than their male counterparts. They sent their request to Defense Secretary McNamara and invited him to meet them on his next trip to Saigon.

McNamara said he would listen to their argument. On a visit to Saigon, he sent Phil G. Goulding, the deputy assistant secretary of defense for public affairs, to meet with the women. They included Jurate Kazickas, a freelance reporter who went on a quiz game program to win her airfare to Saigon, and Anne Morrissy, a young but seasoned field producer who had convinced ABC News to send her on a three-month assignment to Vietnam. (She extended her tour to nine months.)

As the group's unofficial leader, Morrissy spent an afternoon and an evening of martinis with Goulding, keeping him on topic. Before long, it became clear to her that the ban was unsustainable and that Goulding knew it.

Goulding told Morrissy that Westmoreland's proposed ban "would be lifted and we could go back out in the field."[29]

MACV officials added one stipulation to demonstrate to Westmoreland that they took his concerns seriously. The ten women journalists in Saigon—either resident or visiting—had to sign a letter addressed to any new female journalist working in Vietnam "asking them not to place the burden on the field commanders on whether it is safe for the girls to stay overnight in battle areas." In other words, the women had to promise not to ask for special treatment or protection not given to male journalists. In fact, the women had made no such requests in the first place.[30]

All ten women, including Leroy, signed the letter. Women were still on a leash, even though the ban was effectively shelved.

No one publicized the near expulsion. The women never wrote stories about it or told their male colleagues. Fawcett found it embarrassing. She had been blocked from the field so many times in her early days she knew better than to bring up the subject. The other women agreed. Too many in the military still felt women didn't belong there.[31]

They waited thirty-five years to tell that story.

Nonetheless, the impact of their pushback was profound. They had removed the American military's biggest impediment to women war correspondents. The United States military never again attempted to prohibit women reporters en masse from the battlefield.

This was the only time the women journalists banded together, let alone as sisters or even friends. Afterward, they went their separate ways, cut off by their work, by the stress of proving their professionalism, and by the pace of war. Kazickas called it a "very, very lonely time" without the company of other women.[32]

For Cathy Leroy, her career saved from a second near collapse, the next step was simple: she informed her parents that despite her promises to come home she was staying on.

CHAPTER THREE

Fortunate Female

T HE NEWS QUIETLY CIRCULATED THROUGH THE US EMBASSY
in Saigon: Frances "Frankie" FitzGerald, daughter of Desmond
FitzGerald, the powerful CIA deputy director of plans, was coming
to Vietnam. She arrived in February 1966, the same time as Leroy.
FitzGerald was also a freelance reporter, part of the surge of hundreds
of new journalists coming to the war in 1966, although her VIP status
was stronger than her journalism credentials. Wanting a break from
writing New York personality profiles, FitzGerald had packed a single
suitcase and headed for Southeast Asia.

Her first stop had been Vientiane, Laos, where she was a guest of
US ambassador William H. Sullivan. Laos, a poor landlocked nation
of largely subsistence farmers, had become an extension of the war in
Vietnam. The US officially considered Laos an important domino and
supported the government in Vientiane against the communist Pathet
Lao, aligned with the far more powerful North Vietnamese.

Unofficially, the CIA had launched a "secret war," underwriting the
Hmong, an ethnic minority in Laos, to fight as a counterinsurgency
force against the North Vietnamese communists in their northern
and central Laos sanctuaries near the Vietnamese border. Desmond

FitzGerald inaugurated this secret war, the first war in US history led by the CIA, not the US military. The secret war also included American bombing of communist-held enclaves near the Vietnamese border. At the time of Frankie's visit, her father had successfully lobbied to expand the Hmong forces and dramatically increase American bombing.[1]

Ambassador Sullivan, FitzGerald's host, had taken a proprietary role in approving the secret US bombing, setting the pace for a campaign that eventually set the record for the most bombs per capita ever dropped on a country—more than all the bombs dropped in World War II.

FitzGerald knew nothing of this or of her father's pivotal role.[2] She enjoyed her short stay at the ambassador's residence in the sleepy Laotian capital as well as a visit to the hinterlands, writing an article in the *Village Voice* that was both awkward and tongue-in-cheek. "Of course," she wrote, "there is a sort of war going on in Laos. In fact the Enemy occupy one-half to two-thirds of the country—take your pick of estimates. But it's not something one talks about a lot. Involved as it is with the neighboring war in Vietnam, vast distances separate the action from its effect. Families of refugees drift down from the sparsely populated highlands, a few of the wounded come to Vientiane for treatment."[3]

It was banal, but the embassy so liked her writing, officials posted it on the common bulletin board.

Once in Saigon, FitzGerald came down to earth.

She landed at Tan Son Nhut airport, as militarized as a civilian airport could be. During the ride into town, she inhaled dust and fumes from decrepit buses and military jeeps and was jarred by the sight of the once beautiful city—the Paris of the East—defiled by the demands of war.

Frank Wisner, an ambitious young diplomat at the embassy, was her informal liaison. They were old friends whose families were part of the same world of privilege and influence that extended from Wall Street to high-level Washington policy makers, many from the Ivy League upper crust, often supported by old money.

From her first day in Saigon, FitzGerald moved in different directions and more rarified circles than Leroy. While Frankie FitzGerald may have arrived in Vietnam with only a cursory knowledge of the country and an outsized reputation as an overprivileged dilettante, she brought with her a sophisticated understanding of how Washington worked at the highest levels, an understanding few other reporters could match. She had also embraced the early critiques of the war, matching wits with her father, among others.

Her father was uneasy about Frankie's trip to Vietnam, even though she insisted it would just be a short visit. In a lengthy letter to her about his recent tour of Africa for the CIA, Desmond consciously played down his concern for her safety in a war zone. He simply asked her for more news after reading her first letter from "chez Sullivan."

"Am up to date with you to Laos only," Desmond wrote on Pan Am stationery while flying across the Atlantic. "Am dying to hear how Saigon goes for thee and hope to find word waiting at home. Please be careful. Love, Daddy."[4]

When Frankie had graduated from Radcliffe in 1962, Desmond deposited $100,000 in her bank account, the equivalent of $830,000 in 2019.[5] Without his extraordinary generosity, she could not have become a reporter headed toward Saigon. Magazines would not hire her. When she applied for a reporter's job at *Newsweek* magazine, she was told women could only be researchers there, never writers. She walked away thinking "if *Newsweek* won't hire me to hell with them. I'll write for someone."

In January 1966, she bought a $1,314 round-trip ticket on Qantas Airways, using money from her father's gift. After a stop in Vientiane, she planned to write a few articles from Vietnam and then complete her monthlong trip in Singapore.

She was counting on young Wisner to smooth her way. In letters, he had described the boredom of the war. Promoted to staff aide to William Porter, the deputy ambassador, Wisner was locked in an office all day, where he had to "read cables, listen to phone conversations, dial [the telephone] constantly."

He told her that as a woman "this is not your world—the guns, tanks and brutality all seem so pointless save in the very obvious point of it all, and the obvious is alive here."

He was so busy he was late answering her practical concerns about how she would manage once in Saigon. With effusive, apologetic language, he promised he would take care of everything: "Your letter was of great beauty—read and reread," he wrote. "You ask how it is in Saigon. Hot, dusty, hurried, impossible, overcrowded, rumor filled, exuberant and morose, choking, ugly and . . . charming. I can't wait for you to see it—and more—to see something of Viet Nam."[6]

He said he would arrange her press credentials and find her a place to stay. "Done—have no worries about lodging. We'll work out something."

He ended with: "I yearn to reach out and touch you. You save me from forgetting. Much love, Frank."

However, when FitzGerald arrived in Saigon in early 1966, Wisner had done next to nothing for her. He apologized and said his work had been overwhelming. Besides, in his rare spare time, he was engaged with "beguiling Vietnamese females."

Wisner was being honest. FitzGerald arrived in a moment of crisis in South Vietnam and disappointment in Washington, creating insurmountable problems for the US embassy in Saigon. American combat troops had been in Vietnam for nearly one year without making significant progress. President Johnson wasn't pleased.

The Johnson administration had lost faith in the South Vietnamese government's ability to lead the military fight to defeat communism by early 1966 and instead went all in with US troops. The president told Gen. William Westmoreland to "assume no limitation on funds, equipment, or personnel."[7]

This was the moment when the North Vietnamese understood that they had to prepare to fight a different kind of war and began the mammoth project of transforming the Ho Chi Minh Trail into a modern highway with sturdy bridges to send tens of thousands of North Vietnamese Army (NVA) troops, along with their weapons, ammunition, and food, to the South on the trail that became Westmoreland's Moby Dick.

Wisner and the embassy were charged with making sense of the political and military realities on the ground, translating them for Washington while absorbing missives from the government, answering constant queries, including from the newly concerned members of Congress. William Fulbright, chairman of the Senate Foreign Relations Committee, was unsettled by Johnson's rapid buildup in Vietnam and told the president he feared that a "massive ground and air war in Southeast Asia would be a disaster."[8]

FitzGerald knew the outlines of the proposed escalation, and as a friend of Robert Silvers, editor of the literary *New York Review of Books*, she had absorbed some of the toughest critiques of war. "People used to sit and talk to Bob about the war, and if they were not antiwar, they were highly skeptical." During a charged Manhattan evening, drink and cigarette in hand, she met Jean Lacouture, the influential French journalist of *Le Monde* who had covered the wars for independence from colonial France in Africa and Asia. Hearing Lacouture explain why he believed the United States was repeating the failed French policy, citing historical fact rather than ideological imperatives, impressed FitzGerald. She thought: "Anyone who knew about the French war would feel this wasn't a good idea."[9]

When Wisner saw FitzGerald in Saigon, he realized she had changed. A tall blond, she was now willowy, her blue eyes brighter, even piercing. Her serious side was showing.

He found her lodging in the empty apartment of embassy officials away on temporary assignments. Then he planned to introduce her to the Saigon press corps, where she could find colleagues to show her around and help her write those two or three articles before she moved on to Singapore.

Wisner's solution was a party: he would escort FitzGerald to a birthday celebration on the rooftop of the Caravelle Hotel, the modern luxury hotel on the Saigon River that had become the foreign journalists' watering hole. Talented, experienced, and entertaining American journalists were crowded into this splashy party hosted by Dean Brelis, the new NBC television correspondent. He was celebrating the birthday of his sweetheart, Jill Krementz, a young New York photographer. Brelis had exchanged his first-class airplane ticket for two round-trip coach tickets so she could come with him when he was given the coveted assignment in Saigon.

Scruffy reporters and photographers like Leroy were not part of the mix.

Vietnamese waiters passed trays of champagne and Asian hors d'oeuvres. Thanks to river breezes the evening was cool. Guests watched rockets and mortar fire exchanges across the river. When Wisner arrived with a beautiful young woman, the crowd took notice. Wisner made introductions, first to Brelis and Krementz. Neither she nor FitzGerald recognized each other even though they had been debutantes together in the 1958 New York season.[10]

Wisner then steered FitzGerald toward Ward Just, the elegant *Washington Post* reporter who happened to be Wisner's best buddy. He had a similar background to Wisner—a graduate of the elite Cranbrook School near Detroit, also a favored escort at debutante balls and an heir to a modest newspaper fortune. Newly arrived in Vietnam, Just had become as comfortable on the battlefields as he was at cocktail parties. He was considered one of the defter writers in the press corps.

Newly divorced, Just took an immediate liking to FitzGerald. She's a looker, he thought, a head-turner. Wisner left them alone. He could tell his work was done.

Normally the master of political banter, Just found himself in the presence of a quiet young woman with a surprising understanding of American politics. After a few rounds of drinks, Just had an idea. Why shouldn't the two of them bicycle over to the Cercle Sportif, the private French country club, and swim in the moonlight?[11]

Just paid the Vietnamese guard ten dollars to look the other way and let them in. They had the pool to themselves. When they climbed out and dressed, Just discovered the guard had stolen his battered but beloved Timex watch. Somehow the mindless theft added to the romance of an evening that could only have happened in a war zone.

FitzGerald was surprised how much she was attracted to Just. She had left New York deeply hurt by the end of an affair with a married man. But after her night in Saigon with Just, she felt restored.

The romance was a prelude to the hold Vietnam and the war would have on her. Vietnam hit FitzGerald like a thunderbolt. She found the war unbelievable. It challenged her understanding of how the world worked and how she could convey that vision in writing. She threw out her old plan and decided to stay on. Turning her life upside down to become a war correspondent was a monumental decision, one she made far from the restraints and privileges of her New York life. She was twenty-five years old with little understanding of what she was getting into.

Ward Just captured this moment of Frankie's innocent introduction to wartime sophistication in a book he wrote after they had both left Vietnam. He describes a scene in a Saigon restaurant, a dinner with a few friends: plates of entrecôte grille, washed down with glasses of Bordeaux.

"The girl was blonde and Radcliffe and in Vietnam on assignment for magazines. In time she would grasp the Vietnamese condition as well as anyone in the country but then she was a very shy girl, uncertain why she was there. She talks about the Buddhists in I Corps, and said she was going to Quang Nam Province.

"She wants to talk about Vietnam, but her dinner partners want to hear about New York and Washington and the mood in the United States. There is a long dialogue about what Vietnam is doing to America, as ice cream and coffee makes its way around the table."[12]

After dinner, the group headed toward a bar, filing past the Air France office, stumbling over homeless beggars, and getting splashed by an American army jeep speeding through a monsoon-drenched street. At the Sporting Bar, they drank their nightcaps while GIs played cards with young Vietnamese bar hostesses, many of whom were prostitutes.

In this way Frankie FitzGerald was inducted into Saigon society and the life of a war correspondent.

~ ~ ~

AT EIGHT YEARS of age, young Frankie was tested and discovered to have an extraordinarily high IQ. She was born into a family of enormous wealth and social advantages that were unimaginable to most Americans, much less Vietnamese. She was raised in mansions by maids and nannies and chauffeured to school in limousines. She rode horses to hunt, summered on a thousand-acre estate on Long Island. Her behavior was impeccable, a girl with a pleasant, almost patrician demeanor.

Her mother, Marietta Peabody FitzGerald Tree, was a famous blond beauty with a near perfect New England pedigree: her lineage included the Peabody and Parkman families, two of the oldest clans of New England, a grandfather who founded Groton, a grandmother who helped found Radcliffe College, and a father who was the Episcopal bishop of central New York state—the very definition of high WASP. With Marietta's marriage to the handsome Desmond Fitz-Gerald, her mother became a New Yorker as well, with a New Yorker's appetite for glamour and the spotlight.

Frankie had almost no memory of her parents together. Her father enlisted in the army in 1942, when she was two years old, and spent the rest of the war in Asia. Her mother worked at *Life* magazine as a fact checker and socialized at night. She had a high-minded view of her responsibilities and helped establish a nursery school in Harlem. (Marietta's first choice of a career was as a diplomat until she was told women were ineligible.) Desmond returned home in peacetime to find his wife had had an affair with the movie director John Huston.

The precocious Frankie chronicled their divorce in a school essay. "Mummy and I went to Lake Tahoe, which is near Reno," she wrote. John Huston was also in Reno, as was Ronald Tree, the multimillionaire heir to the Marshall Field fortune. Frankie knew that both men were vying for her mother's hand.

"I wanted Ronnie because he had a pony that I could ride in England. I got my wish. You may think that this sudden divorce and marriage was rather trying for me but if you do you are wrong, for although I was sad about leaving Daddy it didn't bother me a bit." She did admit that she may have been "too young to really realize the full meaning of it."[13]

Underneath the bravado, FitzGerald was very upset about her parents' separation. "Of course, I lied—to protect my mother, the only parent I had. I hadn't had a father, period. I desperately wanted my father—a theme of my life."[14]

Frankie and her new family sailed across the Atlantic to their new home at Ditchley Park, one of England's finest country estates. She now owned a miniature racehorse named Beauty and a springer spaniel puppy named Whiskey. She was the only child in the one-hundred-room mansion with servants and nannies waiting on her. Chauffeurs drove her to the Crescent School in Oxford.

That English country idyll didn't last long. In two years, her mother was bored and a change in British tax law had diminished Tree's wealth. The family returned to New York with Tree's butler and Frankie's dog, moving into a home on East 72nd Street off Central Park. Frankie went to the exclusive Dalton School, and her mother gave birth to Penelope Tree, Frankie's half sister. During winter breaks, the family vacationed in their Barbados mansion. In the summer, Frankie traveled to Maine, splitting her time between her father and his new family and her Peabody grandparents—a gilded childhood, with a deep undertow of loneliness.

As a teenager, Frankie went away to Foxcroft, a girls' boarding school in the Virginia hunt country. She was not impressed. "The teachers were just terrible. They hadn't been teaching me math and when we went to get our S.A.T. scores the headmaster told me: you did well for a girl."

She escaped boredom by boarding her horse at school and riding on weekends with other young women. Her high school albums are filled with friends and their horse shows. No dances, no boyfriends, no slumber parties, no football games, and no weekends in the city.

At Radcliffe College, she finally began dating: "After having not seen a boy until I was 18, I suddenly saw a lot of them." She attended class with the young men at Harvard, discovered dancing, brilliant professors, and freedom. She developed into something of a nerd. Meg Douglas-Hamilton, who roomed with FitzGerald off campus at Henry House, admired Frankie's discipline, how she researched and wrote papers like a professor instead of slopping them together in two nights like the others.[15]

FitzGerald tackled the hardest questions in her papers on Middle Eastern history and politics, exploring the creation of a Jewish state in Palestine and the Abbasid succession as a revolution in Islam. In a paper entitled "The Caliphate and the Kingdom," FitzGerald wrote: "It is very difficult—if not impossible—for an observer of one culture to analyze the impact of his world upon another culture," the kernel of the questions she raised in Vietnam five years later.[16]

Her classmates were struck by her good humor. She seemed immune to the petty difficulties and arguments that undid other young women.

Her father rarely if ever visited. She only saw him during summers and occasional holidays, and those visits were often canceled. As if making up for his absence, he wrote his daughter letters filled with affection.

Her mother, Marietta Tree, was, however, all too noticeable. When she visited Harvard, she captured everyone's attention like a celebrity. She dressed like a Vogue model and charmed like a politician, especially around the young Harvard men. Some of her classmates thought it wasn't easy for Frankie to be Marietta's less glamorous daughter.

FitzGerald graduated magna cum laude and decided she wanted to write. After she was rejected at *Newsweek*, she realized how hard it would be to find rewarding work as a woman. Opportunities at the *New York Times*, her hometown newspaper, were no better since it sequestered its few women reporters in the women's section, cut off from the main newsroom and dedicated to what was considered women's news. Her dilemma was characteristic of the uncertainty facing the other women in her graduating class.

She turned to her mother for help. Marietta Tree had become a grand dame of Democratic politics and New York society, hosting soirées, dinners, and cocktails for the city's most powerful and cultured men.[17]

Adlai Stevenson, twice the Democratic nominee for president, had become her mother's discreet lover sometime after he lost the 1952 presidential campaign to Gen. Dwight D. Eisenhower. When Stevenson lost a second time to Eisenhower in 1956, he recovered with the whole Tree family at their Barbados home. He invited the Tree family—Ronald, Marietta, and Frankie—to accompany him and his sons on a semiofficial eight-week tour of Africa with Alicia Patterson, founder and editor of *Newsday* newspaper. Ever conscientious, Frankie wrote a forty-eight-page report of the trip for her father and sent him copies of Patterson's seven-part newspaper series.

In 1961, the newly elected President John F. Kennedy named Stevenson as ambassador to the United Nations and Marietta Tree as US representative to the UN Commission on Human Rights. After Kennedy's assassination in 1963, President Johnson asked Stevenson to stay on as the UN ambassador, with Marietta Tree as a special adviser.

This was the moment her mother came through with a job for Frankie. There was an opening for her at the Congress for Cultural Freedom in Paris, which, unbeknownst to Frankie, was a front for the CIA. When she arrived in Paris, she realized the job had been created to please her mother.

Undeterred, Frankie spent two years on the Left Bank trying and failing to write a novel. In some ways, it didn't matter. She needed distance from New York and her mother to find herself by herself. When it was time to return to New York, she extended her stay out of fear that back home she would fall once again under the maternal shadow, which would curtail or somehow smother her.

She shared her anxiety in a letter to her mother: she felt she had yet to live up to the great expectations of her family and her overachieving mother.

Marietta Tree replied immediately.

"Thank you so very much for your sweet and thoughtful letter. It moved me to tears. I am honored and grateful that you can write me what is in your mind and heart—a most difficult feat between mother and daughter and especially vice versa. . . .

"From the day you were born I have always been extremely proud of you and surprised that I could have such a superior child. You have been born with far higher intellectual talents than I, and you have developed them through hard work. . . .

"You are beautiful and will become more so. You are healthy and strong. You have a nice and loving family who are responsible people in the community, and you are financially independent. With all of this

I suddenly realize that you are probably the most fortunate female of your age in the world.

"You know you could have your own apartment on your return and will chose your own job and of course know that I am not offended by your decision. The question is—are you having some kind of interior battle of an important nature and have substituted me for your conscience or better judgment? I love you with all my heart."[18]

Frankie took her question to heart and returned to New York in 1965, still trying to keep the right distance from her mother. It wasn't easy: "I was so identified with her in my mind. She was the one constant in my life. She was so beautiful, so admirable, and so brilliant in so many ways—every man fell in love with her. I felt like the ugly duckling in the story. I didn't want to go back to her orbit."[19] Marietta Tree was too supportive to be easily dismissed as a vampire mother and too self-absorbed to be relied on.

～ ～ ～

THE NATIONAL CONVERSATION had changed while FitzGerald was writing her novel in Paris. Passions that had focused on civil rights were shifting toward the buildup of the Vietnam War. While the two were twinned around the issue of social justice, Vietnam was hitting white American families in a way the racial issue did not. The military draft skyrocketed that year to the largest since the end of the Korean War. The draft exempted most young men in college, which meant that men of the lower classes and men of color were disproportionately sent to the new war. Julian Bond, the cofounder of the civil rights group Students Nonviolent Coordinating Committee, was blocked from taking his seat in the Georgia state legislature because of his early opposition to the war. He appealed all the way to the Supreme Court and won.

At first Martin Luther King Jr., the leader of the civil rights movement, avoided open opposition to the war out of respect for President Johnson, who had championed the landmark 1964 Civil Rights Act. When the troops landed in Da Nang, King would only say the war in

Vietnam was "accomplishing nothing." By late summer of 1965, King was more forceful, unsettled by the violent escalation of the conflict and calling for a halt to the bombing of North Vietnam as well as a negotiated settlement. At year's end, he was preaching against the immorality of the war: "As a minister of the gospel, I consider war an evil. I must cry out when I see war escalated at any point."[20]

On campuses across the country, students who came out of the civil rights movement were allying with pacifists and the nascent new left to protest the US involvement in the war. They organized teach-ins where they questioned the government's rationale behind sending Americans to a small country across the globe, and they invited the press to their events, just as they had done in the South while registering black Americans to vote.

In this atmosphere, Frankie decided to try breaking into journalism again. Her mother obliged. She hosted a small dinner party and introduced her to Clay Felker, the charismatic editor of the magazine of the *New York Herald Tribune*. Felker was a champion of new journalism and was publishing writers like Tom Wolfe. He was game and gave Frankie freelance assignments that played to her strengths: writing magazine profiles of men who were changing New York, men like John Torres, a young leader in the barrios of the city, and David Merrick, the impresario of the New York World Fair. She was becoming a published journalist, her name in print. Still, she saw no clear path toward a full-time career with the *Tribune*, where women on staff were stuck in the "flamingo-pink ghetto" of the women's department.[21]

Now as a journalist on her own, FitzGerald began mixing in rarified intellectual circles at Felker's magazine and, accompanied by various boyfriends, at Bob Silvers's *New York Review of Books*.

Unlike these intellectuals, FitzGerald thanks to her father actually knew officials carrying out the war even if she was largely in the dark about what they were up to. Her father had doubts about the war's effectiveness—he had told Robert S. McNamara that he relied on statistics too much—but he always defended the mission. Adlai Stevenson, her mother's lover, dutifully supported Johnson's Vietnam policies at the United Nations while privately arguing for a negotiated settlement.

He was ignored. Her mother fell on the dove side of the debate. She knew no one actually fighting in the war.

Missing Europe, FitzGerald went on a vacation during the summer of 1965 and was in Greece when she received a cable from her mother telling her Stevenson had died of a heart attack walking down the streets of London with Marietta.

FitzGerald was stunned with grief. "Mummy was with him. He fell down on the pavement outside the American Embassy. She tried to give him artificial respiration," she wrote in her diary. "What am I doing here alone in Athens. . . . We are all alone when people die away from us."

Then FitzGerald added to her diary a disturbing and deeply private moment when Stevenson visited her in Paris: "that night in the park on the Ile de Cite when the Gov. [Stevenson] asked me whether he should propose to Mummy. We sat under the weeping willows and dangled our feet close to the water and listened to guitars. He kissed me on my mouth and wanted to hold my breasts. Then was horrified. How are things so necessary and so impossible?"[22]

Since her childhood, FitzGerald had had to absorb the deep disappointments and pain from the behavior of powerful adults in her life. For days she tried and failed to write a consoling letter to her mother.

That autumn FitzGerald attended a boozy dinner with her father in Washington at the home of Joseph Alsop, an influential conservative newspaper columnist.[23] Alsop always dominated his dinners, peering over his round eyeglasses and challenging any and all to disagree with him. That night he praised the "nobility of the Vietnam War" and mentioned Frank Wisner as an example of a young lord of the Delta.

Frankie FitzGerald and the other young guests couldn't disagree more, saying the war was a disaster.

Desmond FitzGerald sided with Alsop. He told his daughter and the other younger guests that they didn't know what they were talking about, that they were "all wet." American combat troops had been fighting a mere seven months and already Vietnam had provoked a rare but amiable disagreement between FitzGerald and her father. Desmond continued writing long, deeply affectionate letters to Frankie, but always from a distance, as he traveled the world for the CIA.

It was a few months later that Frankie, adrift after an affair with a married man had ended in heartache and with her mother still consumed by grief over the death of Stevenson, designed a trip to Southeast Asia that would include reporting stops in Laos and Vietnam. She expected her father to be pleased with her travel to a region he loved. But while he approved, he was clearly worried. He feared "dark forces" would discover she was his daughter and kidnap her. He told the embassy to avoid any mention of her relationship to him.

She collected letters of accreditation from the *Village Voice* and *Vogue* magazine. At a farewell dinner, he tried to seduce her. "Clay 'got personal' and I fended him off with beastly abstractions," she wrote in her diary. "A pass was made. I shriveled—hating myself for shriveling and said: there are many ways to tell a lie."[24]

In this way a woman of extreme privilege and attributes—wealth, status, intelligence, beauty, and sophistication—ended up competing in the grubby, dangerous, and wholly masculine world of the war correspondent. Before Vietnam, Frankie FitzGerald had never lived among the middle class, much less the poor. Her only experience of misery was that VIP tour of Africa with Adlai Stevenson, where she visited the apartheid ghettos of Johannesburg, South Africa. Yet she gave up her Manhattan apartment and Parisian jaunts to live amid Vietnam's heat and disease, its refugee camps of mud, shit, and despair, and its corpses—corpses everywhere.

Without her advantages, it is hard to imagine how Frances FitzGerald could have beaten the odds against a woman becoming a war correspondent in Vietnam, enduring the snubs, the refusal to take her seriously or acknowledge her accomplishments. With the security of her family money, she didn't have to scrounge for assignments to pay her expenses. With her upbringing among the elite, she was neither easily intimidated nor fooled.

It never crossed her mind that, if she had been a man, *Time* or *Newsweek* would have hired her, trained her, and sent her to Vietnam as a war correspondent. She didn't dwell on the barriers she faced. They were so ingrained they seemed natural, inevitable. She knew Vietnam offered her an opportunity of a lifetime—graduating from writing occasional profiles for a small if promising New York newspaper to covering the most important story in the world.

~ ~ ~

FRANCES FITZGERALD'S POLITICAL awakening in Vietnam came in March 1966 during the Buddhist insurrection, just as it had for Catherine Leroy.

The monks were agitating against the South Vietnamese junta, and the year-old American takeover of the war. Their protests shook Hue, Da Nang, and eventually Saigon. Vietnamese dockworkers in Da Nang refused to unload American ships, resulting in a shortage of bombs. Demonstrations led by Buddhist monks stopped traffic and daily life in Saigon to protest the military junta ruling South Vietnam under the thumb of the Americans rather than a democratically elected Vietnamese government.

For foreigners, the sight of monks wrapped in scarlet robes leading thousands of protestors, some wielding truncheons, belied the one-dimensional view of pacifist Buddhism. The protests were centered in Hue, the cultural and political hub of Vietnam for centuries. At that time, it was also the country's haven for intellectuals, nationalists, and political organizations.

For the Vietnamese, there was nothing exotic about monks, or even nuns, leading a political rebellion. Under the banner of *mission civilisatrice*, the French colonial government had tried to break the Buddhist hold on Vietnam's culture. French priests converted a sizeable minority of Vietnamese to the Roman Catholic faith, and the French government rewarded Vietnamese Catholics with privileges and elite status in colonial society. When the French lost control of the country in 1954, the Buddhists expected to recover their primacy in South Vietnam. Instead, they watched as Diem, a conservative Catholic, led the new government. The Buddhists became the strongest critics of the Saigon government, not only for its close ties to Catholicism but for its corruption and for handing over power to the Americans. They were also anticommunists. Thich Tri Quang, an influential monk who led some of the protests, said he feared the communists would win "because this government is unpopular and always seems to do the wrong thing."[25] Buddhist protests had helped fuel the coup d'état against Diem in 1963. The Buddhist protests in 1966 seemed just as ominous.

Like Leroy, FitzGerald realized that the Buddhist uprising was a window into an unsettling truth about Vietnam, but neither woman was sure what it meant. Washington couldn't understand the insurrection either. The military was saying the war was going well, so why were the South Vietnamese starting riots? President Johnson's military commanders had assured him that the US would win the war, though they warned it might take longer than predicted. And American troop strength had increased ten times in the year after the US took over combat operations. Lt. Gen. Victor Krulak, commander of the US Marines in the Pacific, had said: "We are not only going to win, we are winning."[26]

But the American takeover of the war effort and the endemic corruption it helped nurture in the South Vietnamese society exacerbated the clash between the Catholic regime and the Buddhist believers.

The month that FitzGerald and Leroy arrived in Vietnam, Prime Minister Nguyen Cao Ky, the head of the South Vietnamese junta, had flown to Honolulu to meet with President Johnson for a hastily assembled conference. Johnson projected an air of confidence to distract from growing dissent among influential senators back in Washington who were holding hearings questioning Johnson's dramatic escalation of the American war.

Ky was hoping for Johnson's blessings to continue what had become unlimited spending on the war. A dapper flatterer, Ky said he would replicate Johnson's Great Society in Vietnam with a new "social revolution," giving Johnson the democratic talking points he needed. Johnson beamed and told Ky he spoke "just like an American." Johnson gave Ky his approval.[27]

Given the assurance of American support, Ky returned to Saigon and mounted a brazen power play. He removed his rival Gen. Nguyen Chanh Thi, the popular military leader in Central Vietnam. The move blew up in Ky's face. General Thi, a native of the region, was a hero of the region from the Central Highlands to the plains, the coast, and the city of Hue. He had the support of villagers, students, and Buddhists who called for a popular insurrection against Ky.

At the very moment that the Americans were ready to declare victory against North Vietnam and with the backing of a solid South Vietnamese government, Ky had ignited a battle within his own political base.

On the battlefields of Central Vietnam, Army of the Republic of Vietnam (ARVN) troops loyal to General Thi blocked the ARVN troops sent by Ky from entering their region. The US military had to break up what threatened to become a civil war between ARVN soldiers.

The junta convinced the Americans that the Buddhists were pawns of the communists who were really behind the revolt, propaganda that Cathy Leroy had initially believed. In fact, the communists were caught by surprise and criticized themselves later for failing to take advantage of such popular anger.

FitzGerald traveled with Ward Just to report on the Buddhists. While Leroy captured the visual horror of the political breakdown, FitzGerald went in search of answers or at least an outline of the implications of this confrontation.

She and Just grabbed seats on a military helicopter traveling from Saigon to the imperial city of Hue. A small detachment of Marines met them and was surprised to see her. They surrounded her, trying to talk to this blond American woman, and blocked her way to the jeep waiting to take them to the protests. FitzGerald kept her cool and smiled a wicked smile that Just rarely saw cross her patrician face.[28]

The two reporters interviewed the American and Vietnamese military directly involved in the standoff. FitzGerald filled her notebook with quotes about the underlying political rivalry that nearly became a full-scale battle between pro junta troops against rebellious pro General Thi troops.

They roamed the dynastic city, the elegant seat of Vietnam's Nguyen dynasty, which evoked a culture and era that stirred Fitz-Gerald's curiosity. Surrounded by a moat, Hue's citadel had the imposing air of an Asian fortified palace-city, with six major gates, several pavilions, and impressive gardens. Nothing in Saigon had prepared FitzGerald for this clearly Chinese-influenced citadel with elaborate carvings and halls expressing both serenity and power. She broke away from Just and lingered over the tombs and pagodas in the centuries-old former capital, wondering whether this Purple Forbidden City, as it was called, still held strong national political and spiritual meaning for the Vietnamese and how this filtered into the politics of the war.[29]

She left the citadel and roamed the city perched on the banks of the Perfume River. FitzGerald interviewed students protesting against Ky and then talked to the polished rector of a Catholic school. Further downstream, she found young men at the Hue yacht club about to sail boats on the river with no interest in the Buddhist uprising. This was her introduction to the layers of Vietnamese society foreign to Americans and unreported in newspaper stories of war. She didn't need an interpreter; her nearly fluent French worked almost everywhere.[30]

Ward Just arranged for them to sleep that night on a sampan moored on the river, a gesture that confirmed their romance. Hue was far enough from the war and the cacophony of Saigon's traffic and war machine that FitzGerald was surprised by the silence. They slept soundly and headed back to Saigon the next day. FitzGerald had the beginning of an article that analyzed the clash between the junta in Saigon and the Buddhists in Hue, considered the heart of Vietnamese culture, and what it meant for the American war. Her goal was to explain the social and political dimensions masked by the daily military reports.

~ ~ ~

IN SAIGON, FITZGERALD became a witness to the deep anger and frightening chaos of a massive Buddhist protest. The monks had been leading protests in Saigon streets, where police clubbed the protestors and knocked down monks. In a direct attack against the Americans keeping Ky in power, Buddhists strung banners across major boulevards in Saigon calling for an end to foreign domination of the country. Street gangs roamed and threatened violence.

She had been invited to the thirty-fifth birthday party of Daniel Ellsberg, a former Marine with a PhD in economics who was a Pentagon aide stationed in Vietnam as an intelligence officer. He had helped draw up the initial bombing targets against North Vietnam.

When FitzGerald arrived at Ellsberg's party, only a handful of guests had shown up, and they hadn't touched the bottles of cognac or plates of food. Everyone was worried about an unexpected protest that had broken out in Cholon, the Chinese quarter of Saigon and the center of the country's black market. Cholon was a world apart, a dense neighborhood of Chinese shops and villas shrouded in a reputation of mystery and greed, where merchants' main interest was profiting from the war. The most common sounds were the clicks of a merchant counting on an abacus or playing the tiles of mahjong. Political trouble in Cholon was newsworthy.

Most of the guests had stayed home out of caution. Ellsberg told FitzGerald he was calling off the party. She should go home; the city was too dangerous.

She said, "Well, let's go and see the protests then."[31] Without a thought, the few guests piled into Ellsberg's jeep, and he drove toward the Xa Loi Pagoda, a major center of Buddhist dissidents. As they progressed, the crowds grew larger, shouting loudly against the Saigon government and the Americans. Ellsberg came across an American civilian contractor whose car had been overturned and torched. When he stopped to offer help, the crowds pressed close to the sides of the jeep. Ellsberg realized they would never reach the pagoda and headed back home, quickly, driving down a major boulevard. A white-gloved Vietnamese policeman directed them away from the masses down a narrow side street. But the crowd followed, raining pebbles on the jeep. Ellsberg thought, "We've had it."

He looked at Frankie and was relieved that she seemed calm.[32]

In fact, she was very frightened; a white-knuckle fear burned underneath a stoic exterior. At that moment, a young Vietnamese man jumped in front of the crowd and onto the hood of their car. He shouted to everyone to move away, and they did. In this way, he skillfully cleared the way for Ellsberg to back out of the street, turn around, and drive off to the center of Saigon and to safety.

From that point on, FitzGerald sought out Ellsberg. He was the rare American official—civilian or military—who took her seriously, mulling over the war and her questions and answering as best he could. The longer she stayed in Vietnam, the more she appreciated the thoughtful conversations she shared with him. For his part, Ellsberg was surprised by FitzGerald. He knew her father—he had once briefed him on a top-secret study—and knew Desmond FitzGerald's fingerprints were all over Vietnam. Yet Desmond's daughter was the rare reporter who refused to define herself as a cold warrior dedicated to the US cause.

FitzGerald was not a reflexive fan of the US mission—unlike Ellsberg. She assumed her role was to report the facts and the truth with an eye toward what mattered and not automatically support the policies undergirding the American war. Her reporting led her to think about the nature of the war, neither justifying it nor opposing it.

She wrote her first article on the blue Olivetti Lettera 22 portable typewriter she had carried from New York. She read and re-read her notes from Hue and Saigon. She worked alone, without any guidance from an editor since her pieces were "on spec" with no promise to be published. The result was a highly original piece written in the style of an outsider, someone who asked different questions and admitted when she didn't have answers.

She slipped the article in an envelope addressed to the *Village Voice* in New York and walked to Saigon's post office to mail it. The ornate post office was across the square from the Cathedral of Notre Dame, in the heart of the French quarter. With its domed ceiling and bustling central hall, the post office resembled the Gare d'Orsay railroad station in Paris. FitzGerald walked past the carved wooden telephone booths, bought a stamp at one of the windows lining the far walls, and mailed her article. No one was paying her expenses, so she resisted paying the exorbitant cable prices to get her article to the US faster. She trusted the transpacific postal system and waited to see if the *Voice* would print her article.

She need not have worried. "The Hopeful Americans & the Weightless Mr. Ky" by Frances FitzGerald was published in the *Village Voice* on April 21, 1966.

It began: "For American officials in Saigon the five-week political crisis has been a long and harrowing ordeal. No normal, healthy little coup, it has emerged slowly from beneath the surface like some fearful miasma to invade the dry safe world of diplomacy and war casualty statistics."

She was unblinking in her description of the breadth of the crisis, telling readers of the *Voice* that it included "the resignation of General Nguyen Chanh Thi, the secession of Central Vietnam, the demands for elections and a civil government, the rising tide of violence and the new hostility to Americans.

"For the Embassy here the problem has not been how to deal with the crisis—there is no way to deal with it under U.S. Standard Operating Procedures—but rather how to explain what is happening in any coherent terms."

FitzGerald portrayed Ky as a man of little substance or independent power, whose government embraced "speculators, grafters, bribe-takers, black marketers or outright crooks. It suffered them in the silence of a government which needs a few powerful friends."

Her voice was quite unlike most of the other articles on the same subject. *Life* magazine published "Irony of Riots on the Heels of Hard-Fought Victories" by Don Moser and Sam Angeloff, both staff correspondents.[33] It covered much of the same ground and was written with precision and knowledge. But when the authors put the Buddhist riots into historical and political context, they identified themselves with the American war effort. "The U.S., under these circumstances, is peculiarly at a loss. Nothing we say can significantly influence the political direction South Vietnam is taking now," they wrote to justify Washington's refusal to alter its course of action or undermine Ky.

They even warned against the United States changing course and withdrawing: "Supposing we, in fact, were asked to leave. What then?" Implicitly, in the *Life* version, the US was a victim of a flaky Vietnamese government, not a cobelligerent.

FitzGerald measured the responsibility of the US government and President Johnson with the same precision as she employed for Saigon and Ky. "The Honolulu conference was the beginning of disaster," she wrote. "Having so publicly embraced, the two partners to the agreement were irrevocably locked together. They balanced each other curiously—the illusion of power for the illusion of leverage."

Once her article was published, FitzGerald could no longer be dismissed as a dilettante. Ward Just certainly knew it. "I had an intimation that Frankie was going to stick around. Right from the beginning she had a seriousness about her that wasn't usual."

Frankie wrote an illuminating note to herself: "You must not forget. You simply must not forget. That this war is a tragedy. That the greatest sin is to speak of politics in the abstract. . . . you must stick to the concrete because that way you will be able to see from more points of view than the abstract."[34]

That became the guiding principle of her Vietnam reporting.

CHAPTER FOUR

A Whole New Meaning to the Phrase Foreign Correspondent

T HE LIMP BEDSHEET WAS SPOTTED WITH THE DEEP SEPIA brown of old blood. Half hidden underneath was a figure bandaged like a mummy with the face of an old Chinese god. Except the flesh was pink instead of ivory. "Gas burns," explained Dr. Goodhope, an American physician from a private charity.[1]

Frances FitzGerald was shadowing the doctor, sidestepping the grime and excrement in the hallway as he made his early morning rounds. The stench was nearly intolerable. At his next stop, two women were lying end to end on a narrow bed. One woman's stomach was swathed in bandages. The baby she clutched had an arm in a sling. "Mortar wounds," said the doctor. "The mortars are the nastiest wounds of all—except for the M16 rifles and the white phosphorous."

The Qui Nhon Hospital, built by the French as a colonial medical center in the 1930s, was now a filthy relic. The US embassy had paid a Vietnamese contractor to clean the facility, provide new beds and furnishings, and install toilets, showers, and tubs. Instead, the contractor pocketed the money and disappeared. Nothing was done. No government authority seemed in charge of this hospital that was treating hundreds of civilians injured during Operation Masher, a joint US, South Vietnamese, and South Korean operation, in the central province of Binh Dinh. (The mission was later renamed White Wing by President Johnson, who found the original name gruesome.)

In Operation Masher, the American troops had used their overwhelming firepower to dislodge the North Vietnamese and Viet Cong forces from the Bong Song plain in central Vietnam. But the communist troops had withdrawn before a full battle ensued; there were more civilian than military casualties.[2]

In the aftermath, the American and Vietnamese military said they had no responsibility for civilian casualties. Their injured troops were treated in well-equipped and clean mobile army surgical hospitals, MASH units, and transported as needed to hospitals in Saigon or outside the country. For the local civilians, it was a different story.

Some of the lightly wounded villagers were treated by American military medics in the field, but most had to find their way to the hellhole of Qui Nhon. FitzGerald had opted to follow them as Operation Masher wound down.

Seven hundred patients crammed into the three-hundred-bed hospital. Besides Dr. Goodhope, three doctors and three nurses from New Zealand were the only other full-time staff, sent by their country on an aid mission. After hours and on weekends, several Vietnamese doctors from the nearby ARVN military hospital volunteered to help, working for free.

Dirt was everywhere. There were not enough latrines, so people not only defecated in the hallways but in unexpected hideaways. "They used to bury amputated limbs in the dirt outside until the dogs would come and find them," said the American doctor. Now they were disposed of farther away toward the jungle. "You don't want to see the kitchen."

She watched as one of the New Zealand nurses sawed off a cast from the leg of a slight Vietnamese woman. "Sorry, old girl," said the nurse. After the cast split off, it released a smell "for which there are no similes" and revealed an ankle covered in yellow pus several sizes larger than the leg. The nurse lifted her patient onto her back and carried her piggyback to a ward so the grotesquely infected wound might be cleaned. Nothing in her pampered existence had prepared FitzGerald for the sights, smells, or sounds in Qui Nhon. "I'd never seen such horror in my life. If I'm going to be in this war I have to be tough and not fall apart to see as much as I could," she wrote in her notebook.

She stuck with it, and for the rest of the day FitzGerald prowled the hospital's wards and hallways, forcing herself to view the casualties of battle that were never included in military briefings or official statistics.

She was witnessing the aftermath of Operation Masher, which was launched just before the Buddhist crisis unfolded in Hue and Saigon and lasted from January through early March of 1966. It was the largest search-and-destroy mission to date and revealed the immense human costs of the new American tactic.

The target was the Viet Cong and the North Vietnamese armies entrenched in the hamlets of the Bong Song plain in the An Lao Valley. The American and Vietnamese troops planned a pincher movement to assault their enemy from both the north and the south, forcing the communists out of their bunkers and foxholes.

It was never going to be easy. The communists had been in control of this rice-growing region for years, essentially since the French had left. Unbeknownst to the Americans, the Viet Cong had been tipped off by spies in the community and ARVN that an operation was being planned to destroy them. By the time the major fighting was underway, the North Vietnamese and Viet Cong had slipped away from the An Lao Valley and disappeared into the Annamite Mountains. They refused to fight a lopsided battle against American firepower.

As a result, the blunt force of American bombing and mortar fire savaged the homes of the villagers, not the enemy. Rice paddies were gouged by 500-pound bombs. The military had "called on every bit of firepower at their disposal"—tactical airstrikes, napalm, B-52 strikes, artillery, mortars—to protect the lives of American soldiers. One estimate said six civilians died for every military death. More than 120,000 Vietnamese were made homeless.

FitzGerald saw what that meant for the villagers: "In the process [the Americans] left hundreds of civilians dead and wounded and 'generated' so many refugees as almost to depopulate the fertile An Lao Valley."

The American and South Vietnamese troops withdrew and declared the battle a victory. The casualties included 288 US soldiers and an estimated 2,150 communists. Maj. Gen. Stanley Larson, the army commander overseeing the Central Vietnam coast area, said the troops had achieved their aim in the war of attrition of bringing the battle to the communists, "keeping them off balance," and wearing them down.

No American or ARVN units were ordered to stay behind and consolidate political or military control. Within a few months, the communists were back in place, building new fortifications, and the villagers of Binh Dinh Province once again lived in Viet Cong territory.

~ ~ ~

HER EXPERIENCE AT Qui Nhon planted questions that would shape FitzGerald's investigation of Vietnam, the Vietnamese, and the Americans in Vietnam. When she returned to Saigon, she made plans to visit the sordid camps around the capital where the refugees from Operation Masher ended up, but only after the Buddhist crisis abated.

The Buddhists were stubborn. Through April and May, they refused to give in to the Saigon government, organizing peaceful demonstrations and parades, which government troops broke up with bayonets and tear gas. Monks went on well-publicized hunger strikes. A Buddhist nun committed suicide by setting herself on fire. They were the last independent dissident group challenging the political power of the junta, and they were desperate.

Ky won approval from US ambassador Henry Cabot Lodge and Gen. William Westmoreland to do what was necessary to end the rebellion. The US would not tolerate infighting among the South Vietnamese while American soldiers were dying to defeat their common communist enemies.[3]

Ky sent his troops once again to Hue, where this time they fought and subdued rebel troops. They went further and arrested Tri Quang, the most influential monk, effectively blocking the movement's headquarters in the imperial city. Ky's officers jailed political opponents, finally ending the Buddhist movement and silencing further well-organized protests for the rest of the war. That left the communists as the sole alternative to the Saigon junta.

In return for American support for quashing dissent, Ky agreed to American demands to hold elections in South Vietnam, which he did the following year. The junta selected Thieu, the ARVN general and head of the junta, as its candidate. Thieu won the election, which was neither free, fair, nor democratic. The political life of South Vietnam was set for the rest of the war: Thieu would remain president until the regime's final days.

The political significance of the ruthless crackdown of the Buddhists and the Americans' benign acceptance of the junta was buried in mainstream reporting of the American military expansion of the war into every corner of the country.

In the face of the turmoil, Desmond FitzGerald wrote Frankie in his old-school manner and again said he was frightened for his daughter: "I shall not trouble you with my concerns about your safety during the current mess—except to say again 'be careful.'"

"Unfortunately," he continued. "I have no plans to visit Vietnam this spring much as I would like to see you in your new habitat."

He signed it: "Much love and do be wise and careful, Daddy."[4]

Frankie was disappointed she wouldn't see her father in Saigon: it would have been their first time together where they were both professionals in Asia, one of the pulls that had attracted her to Vietnam in the first place. By the time she received his letter, she had decided to extend her stay even further; safety wasn't her top concern. She had become committed to understanding and writing about the war, her new universe.

The momentum was shifting with the magnitude of the American presence. Her second article for the *Village Voice* was written like a fable.[5]

"This is the war in Vietnam. . . . This is the colonel with the well-pressed suit who directs the army to make war. This is the woman who chews betel nuts and who presses the suit of the well-dressed colonel who directs the army to make the war in Vietnam.

"It is a true story of the colonel who directs an attack against a Viet Cong unit that includes the son of his Vietnamese housekeeper. The bomb misses the V.C. unit and kills a baby. The mother continues to iron the colonel's uniforms."

The tone of mythical disbelief grew out of Frankie's initial impression of Vietnam as that of walking "through the Looking Glass of print into a land beyond the vanishing point."

She continued the piece with an American official in the provinces who told her it was impossible to count refugees from all the military operations, so he made up numbers to keep his superiors happy. "I just invent a likely figure—numbers seem to give [visiting dignitaries] a certain sense of security."

Then she quoted a French priest who sat in his yellowing office that smelled of rats and mildewed religious pamphlets and told her that it didn't matter whether the Buddhists failed to force the ouster of Ky as they had done in 1963, helping foment the overthrow of Diem.

"'Nothing will change,' he said, reflecting his years waiting for the war to end. 'I have been here for 35 years. Let us talk of something important.'"

This cross between a fractured fairy tale and a Samuel Beckett play was not the standard journalism of the day. A few weeks later, the *Voice* published a lengthy letter from a reader praising FitzGerald's unusual articles as "the best on-the-scene writing on Vietnam to be had in [New York]." He especially appreciated her refusal to accept "news" or "facts" that would be disowned as lies the next day.[6]

~ ~ ~

FILMMAKERS AND NOVELISTS build war stories around passionate love affairs to provide an intimate narrative to the chaos of the battlefield and as a relief from the body count. Buddy movies do the same thing.

At no other time are the senses so alive, the chance of survival so low, and a night of companionship so electrifying. A few intense months are as full as a lifetime. A night of tenderness can offer deeper relief from the sights and sounds of death than a night of drinking.

Ernest Hemingway was a master of the genre: *For Whom the Bell Tolls* has a doomed romance during the Spanish Civil War; *A Farewell to Arms*, set in World War I, ends with the death of the beloved in childbirth. Ward Just was a devotee of Hemingway, and in his mind his affair with FitzGerald had begun with the intensity of a Hemingway novel. They were each other's match in wit and intelligence, two sophisticated writers in a war zone, clearly a couple but never clinging to each other. One minute they were the handsome couple descending the staircase of the Continental, her arm in his, then the next week they were apart, as she disappeared to report from the provinces, and he followed an American unit to the DMZ.

For FitzGerald, the affair was a godsend for reasons she appreciated much later. Just was among the most admired and well-liked correspondents in Saigon. Ben Bradlee, the *Washington Post*'s new executive editor, had assigned Just to cover the war in 1965 to redeem the newspaper's reputation. While the *New York Times* reporters David Halberstam and then Neil Sheehan were digging deeply into the flaws and lies of the war, the *Post* reporters in Saigon had largely parroted the official American view of the war. Just changed all of that and not only wrote serious, thoughtful, and hard-hitting articles about the war, but also wrote them beautifully.

As his romantic partner, FitzGerald was protected by his status. None of his colleagues would make unwanted advances or oafish attempts to seduce her. That also meant FitzGerald was off-limits as a source of puerile sexual gossip and slander.

There would be no guessing games about how she might be "sleeping around," none of the crude gossip that had begun to circulate about Leroy and her casual sex. Nor was FitzGerald accused of using her sex appeal to win assignments or special favors from diplomats to boost her career—routine gossip that often had a poisonous effect on the rare young woman in Vietnam intent on becoming a journalist.

Different standards applied to the men. Male correspondents considered their own sexual behavior beside the point. They might frequent brothels and sleep with whomever was willing, whether they were single or married. Nothing critical was said. This was part of the male prerogative.

The glamorous mystique of being a war correspondent was seductive—especially for younger women.

When it came time for men to tell their Vietnam War stories and write their memoirs, they dismissed the women trying to become reporters without credentials as vagabonds looking for adventure. Men who arrived with the same lack of credentials were heroic. The few women reporters acknowledged were often those of considerable physical beauty like Pamela Sanders. In William Prochnau's *Once upon a Distant War*, an encyclopedic history of the first group of Vietnam war correspondents, Sanders is described largely as the romantic foil for famous journalists like David Halberstam and Charles Mohr.[7] Sanders's novel *Miranda*, about a woman journalist's view of the war, is quoted only to show how well she understood Halberstam. Marguerite Higgins, who began reporting in World War II, is the only female journalist treated seriously by Prochnau. But not flatteringly. In his telling, Higgins had once been a respected and talented reporter who during her reporting trip to Vietnam acts like an aging battle-ax, too willing to support the American war.

In *Dispatches*, deservedly the most admired of the Vietnam War memoirs, Michael Herr mentions there were "all kinds of girl reporters around" but says nothing more, later implying they were either girlfriends or wives of his male colleagues. They were the backdrop to men's heroics. He mentions only two by name and in one sentence: "Cathy Leroy, the French photographer" and Jurate Kazickas, "a correspondent of great, fashion-model beauty."[8] Nowhere did he think it fit to mention that Kazickas was badly wounded covering the battle of Khe Sanh or that her reporting was so impressive she was hired by the Associated Press back in New York. Or that Leroy became one of the most honored photographers of the war.

FitzGerald was saved from these slights and insults by keeping a low profile. As the lone resident magazine writer, not reporting for news magazines like *Time* or *Newsweek*, she had no male competitors; none of them were interested in what she was doing.

In the early days, she often decamped for days in Just's comfortable apartment with its well-stocked drinks table, working kitchen, and regular housekeeper who kept it in order. She reported by day and joined Ward on the Caravelle Hotel's rooftop for drinks—gin and tonics, beer, or coarse Algerian red wine—with other reporters by night. Ward called them "the guys." They were all men: Jonathan Randall, William Tuohy, and Neil Sheehan, among others. The talk began after their stories were filed at the PTT (post, telegraph, and telephone office), and the tropical sun had dropped below the horizon.

At first, FitzGerald was quiet, almost shy, listening to the men's back-and-forth. There was little conversation about what was going on in the United States or a new book someone had read. Instead, it was all about war, what the men saw that day in the field and how it compared to yesterday's fighting, or where the politics were headed. Just had warned her: "War is all we talk about. Anyone mentioning news from Washington, the conversation lasts six seconds."[9]

FitzGerald listened carefully to their chatter and braggadocio. Ashtrays filled with stubs of Marlboros, Camels, or British 555s.

Being accepted into this informal men's club of war correspondents marked FitzGerald as a privileged female outlier. Just was impressed with how quickly she sized up the gatherings and "became increasingly talkative, getting the atmosphere right, and understanding who were the real players."

She displayed her new savvy in the most pedestrian setting: the daily military briefings. Christened the five o'clock follies by the skeptical press corps, the briefings were held on the rooftop garden of the Rex Hotel, a few blocks from the Caravelle.

The MACV briefer rarely made news, preferring to recite dry statistics or the latest body count from military operations. The body counts mattered to MACV. Since Vietnam wasn't a war to capture and hold on to territory—it was to evict the communists from territory—one tangible measure of success was the body counts of the enemy versus friendly troops killed in action.

After attending several briefings, FitzGerald noticed that the official kill ratio of friendlies to enemies never ended in five or zero. She investigated further and found this was always the case. It was a statistical impossibility. She pointed out this flaw to the briefer in front of the press corps, in the process confirming what reporters knew from the field—military and civilians made up body counts for their superiors. Her observation infuriated MACV officials.

~ ~ ~

SLOWLY FITZGERALD UNDERSTOOD that underneath the camaraderie, her acceptance by the press and news sources was tentative at best. Even Frank Wisner did not treat her as the peer she had imagined he would.

When she tried to discuss an earlier halt to the American bombing over North Vietnam with him, Wisner cut her short. Instead of debating the merits of whether it fostered peace, as she had heard him do with Just and other journalists, Wisner grew angry with her. He said the halt allowed North Vietnamese to infiltrate South Vietnam and kill American soldiers. It devolved into a tremendous argument. FitzGerald retreated, regretting that she lacked the confidence to take him on. For his part, Wisner did not take her seriously. Later he admitted: "This was a man's world—this was a war—in a generation that did not foresee that genders were equal. . . . We operated in different worlds."

Wisner brushed her off again when she visited him at the embassy. She wanted to give him her new address, but he just smiled and walked away without even a perfunctory good-bye. As she wrote in her diary: "Frank was odd today. Wouldn't even ask me the address of my new apartment. Went off ahead of me out of [Edward] Lansdale's office after kindly telephoning another bureaucrat without saying a word. What is it?"[10]

She figured out what "it" was. Wisner and Just went out together without her, eating meals and talking about the war. It wasn't the first time she had been left out of the men's serious conversations about Vietnam or their occasional jaunts around Saigon, but she felt especially slighted: "I say I am furious at [Just] for not including me—but actually I am jealous of him, of his relations with Frank. I want Frank too and anything else that comes my way."

Meanwhile, the rest of the Saigon press corps falsely believed Fitz-Gerald had special access to US officials. Instead Wisner treated her like a social peer and family friend but not a serious reporter. The one time he actively sought her was to help him entertain Joseph Alsop, the conservative columnist, when he arrived in Saigon. Alsop was the fiercely pro-war family friend with whom FitzGerald had disagreed in front of her father at a Georgetown dinner. Wisner felt it was natural to expect FitzGerald to act as his hostess. She refused.

Just stepped into the breach: "Miss Fitz," Just wrote in a conciliatory note, "Mr. Wisner stopped by. Your Uncle [Alsop] arrives tomorrow at 12:30 and he asked that you and I meet him. I told Frank that I was going off with the first division. Frank then said for me to tell you to meet him, in a government car that would be provided. I said I'll tell her, but she won't do it.

"Well, she must do it.

"I'll tell her, I said, but I bet she won't.

"She must, he said.

"I'll deliver the message, I said.

"He is a visiting dignitary, he said.

"And must be met with all protocol, I said.

"Right, he said.

"I said we would have him to dinner tomorrow night. We'll defrost the lamb chops. W"

The two of them hosted Alsop at Ward's apartment. Nonetheless, Frankie refused to greet Alsop at the airport.[11]

FitzGerald learned through painful trial and error that Wisner would be useless for her, so she turned to Ellsberg, the Defense Department intellectual and aide to Lansdale. He sat with her for the five-hour discussions she craved to explain the war. Ellsberg was a hawk, like every other government official, and he tried to convince her of the underlying value of the war but with the honesty and openness of the brilliant systems analyst he was. He admitted when the "situation was unpromising." He didn't pretend that South Vietnam was a struggling democracy the United States was trying to preserve. He knew full well the flaws in US and South Vietnamese military tactics and even strategy. But he argued that American interests and America's commitments were at stake.[12]

When she was trying to sort out a story, he listened. He weighed her evidence behind every thesis, paying attention to the details. He enjoyed their conversations as much as she did. (She wasn't surprised five years later when he was the official who leaked the Pentagon Papers.)

His was the only apartment she visited that contained books, even poetry; it made her comfortable.

She sought other experts, including Gerald Hickey, an anthropologist who gave her memorably unhelpful advice. "He told me I must wear dresses when traveling to villages. So, I wore a sleeveless dress, and it was dreadful. Vietnamese women dressed modestly."[13]

FitzGerald rarely ventured outside the small social circle of senior reporters who were Just's friends. But once she accepted an invitation to the crash pad of journalists her own age that was ironically known as Frankie's house.[14]

Frankie was the nickname of Tran Ky, the owner of the nondescript villa in a sketchy part of Saigon where they met. Tim Page, John Laurence, and Michael Herr were part of an elastic band of English-speaking photographers and reporters who enjoyed the 1960s life of rock and roll and dope while making names for themselves in Vietnam. Precisely because Page and Laurence were easygoing nonconformists, Cathy Leroy often sought refuge at Frankie's house after she was ostracized.

The night FitzGerald visited, Page had mounted his latest photographs on the wall, and assorted friends were appraising his work to the accompaniment of rock music on tape—the Rolling Stones, Aretha Franklin, Smokey Robinson, the Supremes, Stevie Wonder—and smoking marijuana. Someone got the munchies, and food was delivered. The conversation grew livelier and weirder. FitzGerald was mesmerized by her peers who were anything but—but she never returned. She was definitely more of the white wine type.

~ ~ ~

FitzGerald began spending much of her time away from Saigon but not on the battlefield with US soldiers. She traveled south to My Tho in the Mekong Delta to track the American campaign to win over the hearts and minds of rural Vietnamese. It would result in her last article for the *Village Voice*.

Most of Vietnam is a long, narrow littoral bordering the South China Sea. At either end, the country fans out with wide river deltas. In the north, the Red River Delta creates a lush agricultural plain. In the south, the Mekong River empties into the sea, creating an even more spectacular delta that is so fertile it is known as the rice basket of the country.

My Tho is roughly in the center of the utterly flat southern plain. The United States wanted to secure it for the Saigon government. Besides pushing out the Viet Cong through military campaigns, the US brought aid to the hamlets to try to win back the loyalty of the region.

FitzGerald went on one of the USAID missions, traveling in two jeeps with American and South Vietnamese officials down Highway 1 from Saigon.

"We hurtle along," she wrote. "It's safer to drive fast as the mines tend to blow up behind you and cause the snipers to miss."[15]

They sped past endless rice fields and hamlets with Buddhist pagodas, arriving at an outlier village of "seedy looking shacks dominated by a capacious concrete Catholic church." The Vietnamese priest welcomed them, walking along a dusty lane where men were digging an irrigation ditch. Children in rags swarmed to their side to grab free provisions the officials had brought as gifts for the village: bags of wheat, cans of oil, and boxes of old clothes donated by the American Catholic Relief Service.

Across the field was a Cao Dai village that was so orderly it seemed to belong to another country. In fact, Cao Dai is a homegrown

Vietnamese religion: the syncretic faith blends aspects of Catholicism, Buddhism, and mysticism and matches them to secular saints as disparate as the writer Victor Hugo and the US president Thomas Jefferson.

Together, the group crossed a wooden bridge over "a stream thick with water lilies and the delicate outlines of fishing nets" and moved through the village that was a stark contrast to the Catholics. "Row upon row of palm-thatched houses interspersed with disciplined onion beds. It is clean and orderly enough to be the work of a single landscape gardener."

Two Cao Dai priests in white robes welcomed the aid mission and ushered it toward their temple, distinguished by a silk flag with a huge eye in the center of a red heart. The priests had bad news for the group. The day before, the Viet Cong had killed the hamlet chief. Members of the Popular Forces, the Saigon government's guard organization, who were supposed to protect the hamlet, had, instead, run away, disappearing with the deputy hamlet chief. The hearts and minds campaign was at a standstill.

With FitzGerald taking notes, the Americans reassured the Cao Dai that the guards would return and protect the hamlet. Before the Cao Dai could ask any more questions, the group climbed into their jeeps and returned to Saigon.

FitzGerald was intrigued. Who were these Vietnamese of all faiths and who were the Viet Cong and how did they fit into a story of the whole country including North Vietnam? More than a few American officials viewed the mass of Vietnamese as bit players in the war: the anonymous farmer, the anonymous communist, the anonymous widow, the anonymous monk, and the anonymous corpse. Journalists often weren't much better. Since the US had taken the lead fighting the war, reporters writing about the war focused on the American troops—the private from Omaha, the staff sergeant from Georgia—and American officials.

FitzGerald followed a different perspective. As a critical intellectual, she finally had a complicated and compelling subject in the Vietnam war that would require all of her talents and commitment. She approached the war by trying to understand the Vietnamese on their own terms and from there examining what the Americans were doing with their ideology of the Cold War, the domino theory, and the strategy of overwhelming firepower against a poor agricultural nation—pretty much the exact opposite of her boosterish male colleagues.

Ward Just remembers when FitzGerald took a turn down a road no one else saw. "She was looking at things in a completely different optic, like she was from a different country—a whole new meaning to the phrase *foreign correspondent*."[16]

When she went to war zones, she stuck with the military adviser and the survivors, far from the frontline reporters and photographers who covered the artillery, the mortars, or the airstrikes. She wrote about the difficulty in the Delta of getting food from one place to another and aid missions that didn't work. Just and his colleagues had little interest in those subjects, especially not the Viet Cong and their blatant propaganda. He saw how "the job she undertook for herself was difficult, very, very difficult. Much more difficult than battle coverage."

To do so, FitzGerald needed a magazine's larger canvas. She felt the same urgency as other reporters as the war escalated with half a million US soldiers slated to arrive in 1967. She had no trouble selling her stories. Every article she sent was published: in the *Daily Telegraph Magazine*, *Vogue*, the *New York Times Magazine*, and the *Atlantic Monthly*.

~ ~ ~

As IN ALL war zones, difficulties, small and large, dogged her. On a reporting trip to Da Nang, FitzGerald and photographer Philip Jones Griffith decided to swim off China Beach. It was the end of a hot working day, and she needed to relax. But as she entered the water, at least six Marines further down the strand plunged in the ocean after her. They were laughing—chasing her as a prank to amuse themselves. But she was frightened instinctively, as any woman would be, and managed to outswim them. She never forgot that episode.

FitzGerald suffered from emotional and physical stress, inadequate sleep, and skipped meals. Finally, the lurking germs and diseases accumulated, and her body reached a breaking point. In late April 1966, she awoke feeling weak, almost dizzy. Her menstrual period seemed interminable, lasting for weeks. By May, she had high fevers. She went to a Vietnamese doctor, a man who knew little gynecology. He gave her generic medicine and sent her home. She grew weaker, and her mind started wandering. Was this bleeding a reaction to all of the misery she'd witnessed, to the gore and blood she saw at hospitals, to the injured carried off the battlefield, the body bags? At one point, she hallucinated. "Three bonzes [monks] appeared to me in the room. They were so real. They didn't do anything. They seemed to be looking around in my desk."[17]

For the first time, she turned to the US embassy for help. The CIA found her a top-flight Catholic Vietnamese doctor from the old Diem regime who diagnosed her problem and recommended a dilation and curettage. The operation was performed at a modern private clinic. Even so, FitzGerald was terrified when she was put under general anesthetic. What if something went wrong so far from home?

The CIA anticipated FitzGerald's concerns and sent a nurse to care for her in the clinic and during recovery. Her mother was beside herself when she received the news. "My Darling Frankie, You must have had a horrible last few weeks," Marietta wrote in a June 4, 1966, letter. "Thank God everything went as easily as predicted and that it's all over. What a huge relief! When I got your cable, I felt dizzy and nauseated until I heard from your doctor."[18]

Her mother was already scheduled to visit Saigon on June 15 as the head of a United Nations delegation. She asked Frankie to rest and "spend a great deal of the intervening time taking it easy."

That proved impossible when, in the late afternoon of June 8, Ward Just was seriously wounded covering a battle in the remote jungle of Kon Tum in the Central Highlands, near the border with Laos. He was with a forty-two-man patrol, Tiger Force of the army's 101st Airborne Division, following a trail north through thick jungle searching for the North Vietnamese. On the second day, the patrol was attacked from three sides. A dozen American soldiers were killed, and the command post filled up with wounded. The North Vietnamese were lobbing grenades at them, and all they could do was hunker down and wait for reinforcements. Finally, a grenade exploded one yard from Just, tearing into his back and hurling him to the ground. At that moment, reinforcements arrived and held back the NVA who then retreated. Medics gave Just morphine and bandaged his wounds. At nightfall, a helicopter hovered over the encampment to pick up the wounded. Only then did Just allow himself to believe he would make it.[19]

FitzGerald and Wisner received news that Just had been seriously injured but no information on where he was being treated. The two scrambled until FitzGerald found him upcountry in a mobile field hospital. Wisner pulled strings to have him transported by helicopter to Saigon, where he was admitted to Grall Hospital. He recuperated under the shade trees in the private gardens of the venerable French hospital, grumbling that he would have preferred to stay with the wounded soldiers.

A few weeks later, Marietta Tree arrived in Saigon in a blaze of white: beautiful white dresses and stunning white hats. She took her daughter in hand, trying to cheer her up with an invitation to a formal dinner dance in Tree's honor hosted by the United States Agency for International Development. FitzGerald demurred but allowed her mother to pack her bags and guide her onto an airplane at Tan Son Nhut to flee the war and recuperate in nearby Singapore.

For once, Tree pampered her daughter to the exclusion of nearly everything else. She booked them into a luxury hotel and took Frankie to checkups with a gynecologist. FitzGerald was found to be anemic and gave herself up to her mother's care, resting and eating and falling asleep in crisp linens. Then, over her mother's protestations, she flew back to Saigon. She missed being immersed in the war.[20]

Just had already left for the United States when FitzGerald returned to Saigon. He had flown to Hawaii for a reunion with his parents and his two daughters, and then on to Washington for full rehabilitation.[21]

~ ~ ~

THAT SUMMER AMBASSADOR Lodge needed to convince Congress and the American public that it was the wrong time to negotiate for peace with North Vietnam. The stirrings of youthful protest were growing into an antiwar movement, especially as the number of Americans killed in action in 1966 rose threefold, from 1,863 to 6,143. Death was touching families and communities across the country; Americans were beginning to understand the sacrifice required to fight in Vietnam.

As chair of the Senate Foreign Relations Committee, Senator William Fulbright held nationally televised hearings on the war. He publicly worried that the United States was showing an "arrogance of power" and was "in danger of losing its perspective on what exactly is within the realm of its power and what is beyond it."[22]

At the hearings, George Kennan, the former ambassador to the Soviet Union and a respected foreign policy analyst, advised that the United States "withdraw as soon as this could be done without inordinate damage to our prestige or stability in the area" and to avoid risking war with China.[23] Angry at Kennan's testimony, President Johnson ordered FBI director J. Edgar Hoover to investigate whether his old friend Fulbright was "either a communist agent or a dupe of the communists."

Powerful voices were joining Middle Americans, asking: Why not end this war with a negotiated settlement? Ambassador Lodge found a surprise ally in Henry A. Kissinger, the Harvard professor who had been no fan of the war. But in 1966, Kissinger publicly came out against negotiations with North Vietnam, arguing that South Vietnam wasn't ready; it wasn't strong enough. Lodge invited Kissinger to visit Saigon in July.

It was the professor's second visit to what he called a "weirdly fascinating city" of dirty streets, hopeless traffic, and graceful people.[24] Lodge assured him that the war was practically won and insisted that a peace settlement shouldn't be on offer. Ellsberg, in a separate conversation with Kissinger, demurred, saying things weren't so good in the countryside: the local military cadre system wasn't working, and the provincial administration was so poor, "we are simply shuffling dirt in the wind."[25]

After a quick survey of rural Vietnam, Kissinger realized that Ellsberg's assessment was the more accurate one. But he stuck with Lodge, advising against negotiations, an opinion that became more important over time.

Before he left, Henry Kissinger met Frankie FitzGerald at a party. She remembered him from her Radcliffe College years when she took classes at Harvard. He paid close attention to her, flirting and recounting a meandering story from his rural tours.

A few weeks later FitzGerald received a letter, hand-delivered by John Negroponte, another rising young diplomat at the embassy:

> *Dear Frankie:*
>
> *This is just a note upon my return to the United States to tell you how much I enjoyed seeing you in Vietnam. I thought your article on Hau Nghia was extremely sensitive. Do let me know when you are back to the States and we can then form a society for picaresque talks of Vietnam. Kind regards,*
>
> > *Sincerely yours,*
> > *Henry A. Kissinger*[26]

FitzGerald dismissed his attention: "To him I was just a pretty girl." But that would not be the last of their exchanges.

～ ～ ～

DURING HER RECOVERY, FitzGerald read a book strongly recommended by Tran Ngoc Chau, a Vietnamese intellectual working with Ellsberg on pacification programs. Chau had fought on the Viet Minh side against France during the First Indochina War and then joined the South Vietnamese side during the American war. He told her that *Viet-Nam: Sociologie d'une Guerre* by Paul Mus would help her understand what was unfolding in the American war.[27]

She was enthralled. *Sociologie d'une Guerre* was a masterpiece. Mus provided her with the historical and cultural underpinnings to see Vietnam as its own country and its quest for independence. His book was much more than an academic's work; it was infused with insights and nuance from his upbringing in Vietnam.

The son of a French academic, Mus was raised from an early age in Tonkin, the northern region of French colonial Vietnam, where his father opened the Collège du Protectorat. He graduated from high school in Hanoi, knowing Vietnam and the Vietnamese as few other foreigners did. In World War II, he joined the Free French resistance and saw firsthand what it meant for your own country to be occupied by a foreign country. Mus left Europe with a new sympathy for the Vietnamese and their fight for independence. After the war, Mus became a senior adviser to the French high commissioner of Indochina as France faced another war with the Viet Minh.

By then, Mus was the most qualified of the senior French aides and was sent to the jungle headquarters of Ho Chi Minh on a historic mission to reopen negotiations for a cease-fire. On hearing the French offer, Ho famously rejected it, saying: "In the French Union there is no place for cowards. If I accepted these conditions, I would be one."[28]

Mus became convinced that Ho and his Viet Minh had already won the war for the people's allegiance. He became a respected public opponent of the French Indochina War and published *Sociologie d'une Guerre* before the war ended.

Sociologie d'une Guerre wasn't an easy read: it was never translated into English. But Mus's book gave FitzGerald a new understanding of the sophisticated questions that Americans refused to ask.

~ ~ ~

RECOVERED FROM HER illness, FitzGerald set off on one of her most ambitious projects: an article for the *New York Times Magazine* on the village of Duc Lap. But first she had to convince an American commander to allow her to ride on his helicopter to the village. He refused to believe she was a journalist much less writing for the *Times*. Though FitzGerald had shown him her credentials from MACV, he still didn't believe her. This wasn't the first time the American military had given her a hard time, but it was among the most brazen. She had no doubt the problem was her gender.

"Wait," he told her. FitzGerald waited, politely, for hours, while Lt. Col. Harley F. Mooney Jr., commander of a battalion of the United States Twenty-fifth Infantry Division, picked up his military telephone and asked to be patched through from rural Vietnam to New York City and the *New York Times*. When he finally reached the newspaper, an editor confirmed that FitzGerald was writing a piece for the magazine. She then was given a ride on the helicopter.[29]

On the ride to Duc Lap, FitzGerald flew over undulating blue-green rice paddies that appeared to her "like the bottom of an aquarium." She would make multiple trips to the hamlet in order to describe the war at village level, where the consequences of the set-piece battles and lethal politics played out on the most human scale. Missing from official US or South Vietnamese findings was any evidence that their aid and military campaigns harmed or helped the rural villages where the vast majority of Vietnamese lived. Who was protecting them from either the Viet Cong or errant friendly fire of the ARVN or the US? Did they feel loyalty to either side or victims of both? Were the American programs to win the political war working? FitzGerald had selected Duc Lap, a provincial capital just twenty-two miles south of Saigon that was regularly under attack, as the test case for whether the Saigon government had recovered any effectiveness after the string of political crises in the capital.

The village was sufficiently important—a transportation crossroads in the middle of a rich rice-growing region—that the US Army sent a battalion to help the ARVN combat a resurgent Viet Cong in early 1966. It was also part of a larger project, which Daniel Ellsberg was involved in, to uncover and try to eliminate corruption.

As she began her reporting, FitzGerald kept Ellsberg at a distance, writing in her notes that Dan was wrong to "expect a simply anti-government article about Duc Lap." She tried to let the villagers and farmers speak for themselves, which was difficult to do since she didn't speak Vietnamese and had to rely on translators.

In "Life and Death of a Vietnamese Village," Duc Lap became an entire universe. The war was seen uniquely from the villagers' point of view: what had been lost in each phase of the war beginning with the drive for independence from the French; how homes, fields, and traditions were changed or obliterated beyond recognition.

The villagers described the sorrow and anger they felt about the recent programs crafted in Saigon or Washington that forced them out of their homes into barbed-wire enclosures called strategic hamlets. FitzGerald included no quotes from foreign experts. Her method of reporting required sitting patiently with people with a radically different sense of time and different cultural touchstones and sorting out how their stories fit together.

In Duc Lap, the two sides were at a virtual standoff. The men guarding the village fled when the fighting flared up. The Viet Cong taxed the villagers at night while the South Vietnamese taxed them during daylight. Each side drafted the young men until most had disappeared.

The American commander hoped his battalion's visit would shore up support for the Saigon side of the war and break the deadlock. An American military medic set up a makeshift clinic in a hamlet's granary and storage shed where he dispensed medicine and treated people who hadn't seen a doctor in years.[30]

The medical care was meant to offset the damage that had been done earlier when American mortars had landed on the village, destroying homes and killing water buffalo.

In this designated strategic hamlet, the villagers had to stay in their homes or risk being shot by the government troops protecting them. Because the fighting made it impossible for them to farm their rice paddies, food was routinely scarce. A village elder said all he wanted was enough to eat and to sleep in peace without the sound of artillery.

In that atmosphere, FitzGerald wrote, "fear and suspicion rose like a ground mist."

The officials from the Saigon government were routinely corrupt. The village's local administrators stole food, money, and, most alarmingly, the *dinh* or the village's guardian spirit. Village elders told Fitz-Gerald that the people believed the communists would win because the side that relied on a foreign power would lose.

"Worse than the houses burned and the fields left to jungle was the villagers' loss of identity," FitzGerald wrote.

The *Times* published her article in September 1966.[31] The next month the *New Yorker* published a more traditional magazine piece about Vietnam. The contrast was striking.

Robert Shaplen, the esteemed Far East correspondent for the *New Yorker*, wrote "Letter from Saigon," a densely reported analysis of the state of the war as seen from the capital.[32] He reported that the South Vietnamese Constituent Assembly had been elected with the purpose of holding free and fair elections; the French rubber planta-tions continued to make money; and a shake-up of the generals had preceded the Viet Cong's continued assaults during the rainy season while the communists continued their strategy of fighting until the United States gave up. That comprehensive sweep did not break new ground or offer a fresh perspective much less present the reality for rural Vietnamese villagers.

Yet, one year later, the *New Yorker* ran a piece called "The Village of Ben Suc," a devastating article by Jonathan Schell, a young journalist who chronicled how the US attacks and forced migration destroyed the village and banished its inhabitants to muddy camps.[33] It was similar to FitzGerald's and showed the extent to which her vision was helping define the war.

~ ~ ~

FitzGerald was relieved when Ward Just returned to Saigon from Washington. In his absence, she had moved into her own apartment, a carriage house behind a Vietnamese villa where she continued her recovery in relative quiet. In one diary entry she wrote: "I am scared of the loneliness of it. This small town is a lonely place."

In September she had a burst of introspection, about herself, her work, and her romance: "It's so hard to write. I haven't the energy left

over for it after this day of walking up and down Tu Do Street in the
dead, sulk heat . . . Real entropy this place.

"One goes along drifting—not listening, not really listening at all
the way one must as a writer and a person. I haven't listened to Ward
for so long . . . I feel numb, deadened to the point where I hate to spend
an evening alone . . .

"I do not long for another day. I don't want to wake up tomorrow.
So, I read Tolkien and tears come."[34]

She had few close friends she could confide in or relax with, and
none of them were women journalists who could appreciate the
pressures of her life. About four other women reporters lived in
Vietnam at the time, but their lives rarely crossed. She never met
Catherine Leroy. Denby Fawcett remembers seeing FitzGerald at a
distance with Ward Just and once writing in Just's apartment. Nothing more.

The legendary Martha Gellhorn did visit Saigon to report a piece,
but she essentially ignored FitzGerald to concentrate on Just, who was
happy to accompany her around. Gellhorn's marriage to Hemingway
and her stories of the Spanish Civil War and D-Day held Just in thrall.

FitzGerald did report briefly alongside Patricia Marx, a visiting radio reporter who was dating and would eventually marry Dan Ellsberg.
The two women had much in common—Marx had graduated from
Radcliffe two years before FitzGerald and was also an heiress—and
they worked well together.

FitzGerald wrote her final long-form article for the *Atlantic Monthly*,
focusing on the city of Saigon like a local reporter, showing the consequences of war far from the battlefield. She spent weeks investigating
how well the city worked, not as the capital of South Vietnam but as
the municipality in charge of the welfare of 1.7 million inhabitants and
the infrastructure and economy to provide their needs.

Saigon had become overwhelmed by the tens of thousands of new
refugees fleeing their war-torn villages in 1966. The municipal government had no power or funds to care for them, and neither the South
Vietnamese nor the US governments took direct responsibility for
their welfare.

The budget of the mayor of Saigon was miniscule, less than that of a small American city even though the national war budget was endless. He had to beg national ministries for help that never came. He bragged that he once went to the countryside and stole a herd of hogs from the Viet Cong to help feed his city. "I do not have to fight the people; I have to fight the government."

The US embassy admitted it didn't know if American aid money was funding successful projects in Saigon. "If you find out anything, just let us know," one of the coordinators told FitzGerald with a straight face.

Official neglect blighted the city: the sewer system was foul; the water pipes were rusting and corroded and all the water in the city came from just forty wells; the public bus system contained only seventy buses, a third of which were usually out of commission. Public housing was inadequate even before the population explosion provoked by the American war. Public education was even worse.

The Vietnamese elites, Americans, and other foreigners lived in Saigon neighborhoods with piped clean water, sewer, and electricity. Corruption created an impossible gap between the few rich and the massive number of poor people in Saigon.

"Given the overcrowding, the lack of drainage, of sewage and garbage collection, it may rate as one of the least healthy cities in the world," FitzGerald wrote. The thousands of Americans living in the city ignored or shunned these slums "hidden within a tangle of canals, between main streets fronted with respectable houses."

"Gigantic sewers, lakes full of stagnant filth, above which thatched huts rise on stilts, crammed together but connected by only a thin strip of rotting board . . . a small boy falls in and flounders in the filth."

The slum dwellers were former villagers and farmers who turned to begging for a lack of a livelihood and whose children ran in gangs. They were angry. When FitzGerald and Marx visited one slum, they were pelted with stones.

FitzGerald called these slums the new face of Vietnam. They were the ultimate expression of the dysfunctional American war strategy. The contrast with the American extravagance for the military was stark. Just one Defense Department contract to MK-BRJ, a group of

American companies hired to build military construction projects in South Vietnam, cost more than the total Vietnamese GNP. Such an imbalance fed corruption. It was impossible for the Vietnamese professional classes to be both honest and able to feed their families.

FitzGerald's final report anticipated America's ultimate failure in Vietnam. It was entitled: "Behind the Façade: The Tragedy of Saigon."

She considered it her most substantial piece, and it reflected her growing sense that the United States' military strategy was failing. She was tired of the deaths and the torpor of daily life in the war zone. It was a cumulative fatigue. Her notebooks were scattered with exhaustion. "Am too tired to write after another average day in Saigon. Mostly errands. How to transport a potted palm in a cycle moteur. How to be sure the French market has sent the food, how to buy notebooks, telephone 3 bureaucrats, get a new Vietnamese press card . . . et tout, et tout."

With fatigue came friction. Another day she wrote: "Maybe Ward wishes I would go away for a while. Just to see what it would be like."

By September 1966, she realized she hadn't fully recovered from her illness and was at the end of her rope. She made plans to move back to New York. She wrote her father, who was relieved at the thought his daughter would soon be leaving Vietnam.

Desmond FitzGerald welcomed her decision and wrote her a letter of congratulations for her *New York Times Magazine* piece about My Tho and the Mekong Delta, showing he appreciated what his intellectual daughter was trying to accomplish.

"I think I understand your style of working which is not to write until you feel you have a three-dimensional graph on the subject— most commendable and encouraging when one contemplates the miles of newsprint covered with surface scribblings from everywhere," he wrote.[35]

And he included her in his own work on the war: "Like everyone else in Washington, (it must be by statute) I devote a good bit of my time to Viet Nam but I wish that I could swear that it was to great avail. I am about to lose my franchise as a participant in the V N game because I haven't inflicted myself on Saigon for almost a year."

In a last burst of energy, Frankie FitzGerald finished the reporting for several articles she would complete after she returned to the United States. She celebrated her twenty-sixth birthday in October with Ward Just. Their romance was still blazing when FitzGerald flew home the next month, arriving in New York City for a fancy gala on November 28, 1966.

It turned out to be the party of the century—literally. She had been invited with her mother, stepfather, and sister to the lavish Black and White Ball in the Grand Ballroom of the Plaza Hotel hosted by Truman Capote. At that moment he was the most famous author in the country, fêted everywhere for his novel *In Cold Blood*. Katharine Graham, the new publisher of the *Washington Post*, was his guest of honor. More than anything, the party was meant to demonstrate Capote's new wealth and position in society.

He invited over five hundred people, mixing movie stars with artists, high-ranking officials, theater giants, business tycoons, and high-society couples like Marietta and Ronald Tree. The guests wore couture gowns or tuxedos and Venice-style masks, giving the night a twentieth-century version of European decadence. They drank Taittinger champagne and danced to the music of the Peter Duchin Orchestra, breaking for a midnight supper of spaghetti and chicken hash.

The mood was electric. FitzGerald's sister Penelope Tree was discovered that night by Diana Vreeland, the editor in chief of *Vogue*, and launched as an international fashion model.

Everyone was entranced except for Frances FitzGerald. Almost as soon as she arrived, she saw Secretary of Defense Robert McNamara, mastermind of the war, in the ballroom. She couldn't cope at all. She was obsessed by the war and couldn't tolerate a fun-loving atmosphere that seemed callously indifferent to events in Vietnam.

She told her family she wished she had been in a better mood at the party. Yet her mood didn't improve in the following days. New York felt like alien territory. She holed up in her apartment in the city and could think of little else than Vietnam and war.[36]

Regular missives from Ward Just kept her up with the Saigon gossip behind the news and included bulletins on his love for her. "You are more important than the war—do you like being more important than the War in Vietnam? I want to write about the war and be in love with you, and do both equally well."[37]

They made plans for a long vacation in Ireland where they would stay in a castle of a distant FitzGerald cousin and pick up where they had left off in Saigon—writing about Vietnam.

CHAPTER FIVE

Violence, Madness and Fear and Agony

M APS ARE THE BACKBONE OF THE STORY OF WAR.
When the French colonized Vietnam, they divided the country into three regions: Tonkin in the north, Annam in the center, and Cochin China in the south. The Geneva Accords of 1954 ended French control and temporarily divided the country in half along the 17th Parallel. Ho Chi Minh and the communists governed North Vietnam, and Ngo Dinh Diem governed South Vietnam, with a promised national election in 1956 that was rejected by Diem and the US.

War replaced elections, and the maps reflected the change. The temporary divide became permanent, and American and South Vietnamese military added an overlay to the map of South Vietnam. They divided the South into four military regions denoted in Roman numerals: I Corps in the north, II Corps in the center, III Corps around Saigon, and IV Corps in the Mekong Delta. That map was used in military briefings. American soldiers knew South Vietnam through that map. They served in I Corps or III Corps, rather than a specific Vietnamese province. This was a break in US military tradition since the word *corps* normally referred to an organization or unit, not to a specific geographic area.

This pointed to the fact that in Vietnam the front lines never changed. There were no front lines. Battles could be won or lost, but the map didn't change because the US did not conquer and occupy territory.[1] The military regions remained intact, at least on the map. The goal of the war was to protect and win the loyalty of the South Vietnamese people, not territory. How do you represent that victory on a map?

General Westmoreland declared his war of attrition a success. "We'll just go on bleeding them until Hanoi wakes up to the fact that they have bled their country to the point of national disaster for generations," he said.[2] But on April 24, 1967, a battle broke out in I Corps, near the demilitarized zone, that tested Westmoreland's confidence.

An advance party of Marines was sent to scout the hills surrounding their base at Khe Sanh where, unbeknownst to them, a North Vietnamese regiment had taken control. The Marines were ambushed. Only one survived.

Two companies of Marines were ordered to take the hill, actually a ridge named Hill 861 for its height. Just as the Marines reached the ridge, the Vietnamese opened fire, wounding and killing many Marines with mortar shells from concealed positions. The Marines answered back with strafing and rockets fired from Huey gunships and with bombs and napalm from fighter jets. Fog and rain hampered visibility; the hillside paths turned into mud. After several days of ferocious fighting, the Vietnamese disappeared, leaving behind impressive fortifications of deep six-foot bunkers built with thick walls of earth layered with bamboo.[3]

As the Marines would discover, the Vietnamese had withdrawn to the nearby ridges known as Hill 881 North and Hill 881 South.

At that moment Catherine Leroy returned to Saigon from a work vacation in Malaysia. She had been recovering from a lingering bout of malaria and a knee deeply scratched by cactus needles from climbing over a paddy dyke.[4] Leroy went straight to the AP office and asked Horst Faas to get her up to speed. It was April 30, 1967.

He told her to go immediately to Khe Sanh, to the battle that was now being called the Hill Fights. She cadged a seat on a military flight to Dong Ha base in Quang Tri Province and a few hours later was on a supply helicopter to Khe Sanh. From there, she walked to the base camp opposite Hill 860, arriving in late afternoon. She was the only journalist present; the others were stuck in Da Nang.

A colonel was briefing her on the fighting when a bullet whizzed by them. He glanced at Leroy's head and yelled: "Good God, take off your headband!" The Vietnamese were using her bright white headband as a target. She tore it off.

At dusk, Marine Captain Shaan and his company moved out, walking in single file toward Hill 881. Leroy followed. They navigated around a thirty-yard-wide bomb crater and then began the climb up the first section. The bombing had defoliated the jungle and plowed up the earth, leaving an empty landscape of dead wood blackened by explosions and muddied by the monsoon rains.

Just as they reached the summit, the Vietnamese opened fire. Leroy saw several Marines fall dead. Two other units of Marines joined the fight. Against the cackle of automatic gunfire, she heard screams for help.

And then she saw the tableau of what would become the iconic image of the conflict.[5]

The battle had moved on while a lone medic in full battle gear was left behind, crawling up the ridge to reach an injured Marine. Leroy clicked.

The medic, Vernon Wike, a twenty-year-old navy medical corpsman from Phoenix, Arizona, cradled the Marine, took off his helmet, and bent over the body, listening for a heartbeat. He heard nothing. The Marine was dead. The medic's young face twisted in anguish. Leroy kept clicking. Wike never noticed Leroy the whole time she was taking the photographs.

Anguish turned to anger, and the medic picked up the dead man's M16, swearing at the top of his voice: "The bastards . . . the bastards . . . I'm going to kill them!" He charged a fortified Vietnamese bunker, emptied his magazine at whomever was hiding inside, and dropped the rifle. He returned to the hillside to care for the other wounded soldiers.

The sequence happened in minutes.

Leroy photographed with care, shooting only three rolls of film in the poor light, purposefully not wanting to waste a single frame to avoid having to reload the camera. She kept her focus on the medic, as his heroism and humanity played out on a ridge exploding with gunfire and mortars.

Soon night took over, and the fighting died down.

Leroy returned to Da Nang to ship her photographs by military aircraft to Horst Faas in Saigon. Since she had shot at dusk under abysmal conditions, she wrote precise notes to help process the film.

Faas, who had been photographing the Vietnam War since 1962, was amazed by what he saw: "I realized that these pictures were something new, their expressions were new."[6]

Intimate portraits during battle became Leroy's hallmark. Few photographers got closer to soldiers than Leroy, who crawled in the mud alongside them if necessary, aiming for the eyes and subtle shifts in expression. She was a silent presence; soldiers were rarely aware of her.

Faas sent out Leroy's photographs, and they were published around the world. They seemed to capture the war at that moment. The medic's anguish and the valor of soldiers seizing the hill was a confirmation for many that American soldiers were courageous.

Time magazine ran an article on May 12, 1967, about the impact of Leroy's photographs, which had appeared in newspapers around the country, saying they were a reminder of the ghosts of Iwo Jima. Entitled "Photographers: Gnat of Hill 881," the article described the petite photographer as small as a gnat. "But the little French girl is a tough freelance photographer; and for Americans looking at their front pages last week, her A.P. pictures of Marines headed up 881 North evoked ghosts of Iwo Jima and Pork Chop Hill."

To have any Vietnam photographs compared to the heroic World War II images of Marines struggling to raise the American flag after victory on the island of Iwo Jima was nearly unheard of. It underlined how Leroy's photographs of Marines sitting on hills made barren by bombs and artillery, caring for their wounded, and holding their positions were seen as ennobling by an American public that still believed in the American cause and a future American victory in Vietnam. Leroy began to understand what this meant when she received countless letters from mothers of American soldiers thanking her for the photographs and asking after their sons.

The *New York Times* ran one of her photographs on the front page and credited her by name. An issue of *Paris Match* ran several of the photographs, which her parents proudly displayed. Her biggest splash was in *Life* magazine, which published six pages of her photographs in a spread called "Up Hill 881 with the Marines."[7]

With her camera, Leroy made the battle famous and the Marines who fought it down-to-earth heroes. "These are not portraits of a warrior class but of ordinary, frightened and often bewildered young men trying desperately to stay alive, and relying upon each other to pull off this seemingly impossible feat," said Peter Howe, author of *Shooting Under Fire: The World of the War Photographer*.[8]

In two and a half weeks of the Hill Fights, the Marines pushed back the North Vietnamese and held the ridges above Khe Sanh. The cost was high. Americans suffered 155 dead and 425 wounded—the worst losses for a battle of the Vietnam War at the time. The estimated Vietnamese loss was 764 dead.

The victory was not what it seemed. Americans would learn that the North Vietnamese actions around Khe Sanh were in preparation for a far bigger offensive at the start of the coming year.

Leroy went back to the Marine company to give the men copies of what were now famous photographs and to meet the medic. When she gave Wike his photographs, he just said: "Where were you? I didn't see you."

Leroy's prestige skyrocketed. Rival editors in New York were astonished at her scoop. The CBS bureau in Saigon received a cable from headquarters asking: "If an 84-pound French girl can do this, why can't we?"[9]

The Hill 881 photographs demonstrated Leroy's very personal approach to photography and her attachment and identification with her subjects. "The GIs were like my brothers. We were the same age, and

I loved them. Besides, I cannot photograph anybody for whom I don't have any feelings. I would rather stay at home, smoke a cigarette, and drink a good glass of wine."[10]

The photographs from Khe Sanh helped fill her bank account. She upgraded her now badly overused equipment. *Life* alone paid her $5,000. She ordered two new cameras and a pair of shoes and bought children's tunics as gifts for friends in France.

She wrote to her mother how much it meant to have taken those photographs on Hill 881: "I am very happy. After all these long months, this time I was lucky."

Only three months after some of her colleagues had encouraged the military to deny her the right to continue as a war photographer, Leroy had become a hero. General Deane, who tore down official barriers so she could jump, sent her "a charming telegram from the depths of an operational command to congratulate me."

In quieter moments, Leroy realized something essential was missing from her photographs. "No image that you see can translate the cry of the wounded or translate the smell of the corpses. When you see the photos, it is a frozen moment of eternal silence."

She thought she knew where that ungodly noise had gone, where it was entombed, along with the stench of the dead. It was inside her, the photographer. "Those images rest inside of you with the violence, madness and fear and agony—all those things rest in you, remain in you."[11]

Catherine Leroy's first expression of the trauma building up in her was poetic.

～ ～ ～

IN THE MIDDLE of May 1967, Leroy was back in the field to report on Operation Hickory near Con Thien, the first American assault into the demilitarized zone. The United States had considered the DMZ off-limits, a boundary officially delineated in the 1954 Geneva Accords. But General Westmoreland lifted this ban because the North Vietnamese had clearly set up positions inside the DMZ. It was considered another example of the North Vietnamese refusing to play by the rules.

According to the Geneva Accords, the division at the 17th parallel—the DMZ—was "provisional and should not in any way be interpreted as constituting a political or territorial boundary" that would not be necessary after the 1956 elections. South Vietnam and the United States refused to allow the elections, and so the DMZ was still in place in 1967.

In the eyes of North Vietnam, the United States and South Vietnam had refused to respect the Geneva Accords, not them. The North Vietnamese army buildup along the 17th parallel was a strategic preparation for a counteroffensive in the south.

In Operation Hickory, begun on May 18, the Marines came up against the powerful presence of regular North Vietnamese units in the demilitarized zone. According to the official Marine history, the North Vietnamese "directed heavy mortar, rocket and artillery attacks against all Marine positions along the DMZ."[12]

The lieutenant colonel leading the Second Battalion of the Twenty-sixth Marines was wounded in that lethal barrage. Leroy arrived on a supply helicopter with his replacement, landing at the Marine's operational command center in Dong Ha. That night she barely slept. Rockets streaking overhead lit up the sky. Marine artillery flew over her head. Shells burst near the lines. A military photographer jumped into the hole where she was trying to sleep and crushed her.

Early on the next morning, May 19, she was with troops headed toward the front line when a volley of mortar fire ripped through their position. Leroy was wounded, badly.

"I was hit by the first mortar. In my head it was a big sound . . . like a gong. I knew I was hit but was still on my feet. I felt nothing but noticed my right pigtail was all bloody. My three cameras were also bloody . . . they had been hit and probably saved my life.

"It seemed like five minutes before anyone saw me. I was pretty groggy and in bad shape. I couldn't breathe and was bleeding all over. I thought I was going to die."[13]

Leroy had thirty-five holes in her from the shrapnel. A medic cut off her battle shirt and bra—she protested, and he told her this was no time for modesty.[14] For the next hour, she and the other wounded were transported by armored vehicle over a very rough road to Con Tien, where she was laid on the ground beside a Marine.[15] They shared a cigarette and held hands to keep up each other's spirits. With the little strength she had left, Leroy opened her camera and handed over her film to the nearest information officer, asking him to get it to Saigon and Horst Faas. Then she passed out.

When Leroy woke up, she was conscious of motion, a pitching motion. She was lying on a stretcher in the reception area of the USS *Sanctuary*, a floating navy hospital. She remembered only the one moment when a medic lifted the sheet over her and shouted, "My God—a woman—a blond."

After that she lost consciousness again, anesthetized for a three-hour operation. Her wounds were mended; her fractured jaws were wired shut. For the better part of three days and nights, a medic she knew from a previous assignment stayed by her bedside to be sure that she was out of danger.[16]

In Saigon, Faas was relieved. He suffered every time a photographer died in the war. They were all his friends. This time he was able to send the good news of her survival, albeit traumatized, to her family and the AP offices.

Then the perfectionist in him took over. Faas sent Leroy's German Leica camera to Woody Edwards in AP's Hong Kong bureau with instructions to take it to Schmidt and Company for cleaning.[17] He sent the two Japanese Nikons to Sam Jones in Tokyo with a request to take the cameras and lens to Nikon itself for repair and cleaning.[18] More letters asked for payments for her work. In respectful French, he wrote a reassuring letter to Leroy's parents.[19] And in a big brotherly tone, he wrote to Cathy congratulating her on the requests for her work, signing it "hurry back fast and in one piece—love, Horst."[20]

Crucially, Faas also wrote to Wes Gallagher, the general manager of the Associated Press, to suggest that the company pay for all of Leroy's medical costs. He agreed.[21]

The *Sanctuary* was anchored at Da Nang Bay for one week when Leroy received an important visitor. Over the loudspeaker, it was announced that Gen. Lewis Walt, commander of the 73,000 Marines in

I Corps, was boarding. He came to Leroy's bedside with a gift. "I can't give you a purple heart," he said. With some awkward hesitation, he gave her a manicure set. "You might find some use for this."[22]

Leroy thanked him.

With that, the ship sailed to the US Naval Hospital at Subic Bay in the Philippines, where patients could convalesce. One month after she was injured, Leroy was released and cabled Faas from Da Nang saying she was coming home—to Saigon.[23] One week later, the Marines concluded Operation Hickory and their assault on the North Vietnamese in the southern portion of the DMZ. The Marines had driven the North Vietnamese out of their refuge and turned the area into a free-fire zone. They had also removed all the civilians from their homes and farms.

~ ~ ~

IN THE MIDDLE of these intense operations, Defense Secretary Robert S. McNamara, the man considered the architect of the Vietnam War, admitted to President Johnson that the American war wasn't going according to plan.

The war hawk was becoming a dove.

On May 19, 1967, the day Leroy was injured, McNamara sent a long memorandum to President Johnson suggesting a radical new course. He argued against the military's request to increase troop levels to 671,616 soldiers and against expanding the ground war to Cambodia and North Vietnam. Instead, he favored a reduction in bombing of North Vietnam, holding troop levels around 400,000 and narrowing American goals to negotiating a settlement. In so many words, he said he saw no evidence that the US military was winning the war or could ever win the war.

This was heresy.

McNamara began by describing how unpopular the war had become in the United States, citing the growing casualties, the widening war, and the suffering of Vietnamese civilians. "Most Americans are convinced that somehow we should not have gotten this deeply in. All want the war ended and expect their president to end it. Successfully. Or else."

Then McNamara demolished the military's argument that the US was winning, using data from the intelligence services and the military. America's technological advantage, he argued, was proving brutally ineffective. The prime example was the nearly 800,000 tons of bombs already dropped on North Vietnam—far more than were dropped during the Korean War.

"There continues to be no sign that the bombing has reduced Hanoi's will to resist or her ability to ship the necessary supplies south."

International opinion was confounded by the escalating war, too. "The picture of the world's greatest super-power killing or seriously injuring 1,000 non-combatants a week, while trying to pound a tiny backward nation into submission on an issue whose merits are hotly disputed, is not a pretty one," he wrote.[24]

McNamara's verdict could have been lifted from the strongest antiwar pamphlets. The defense secretary then offered a solution. First, he reassured his president the United States had already won. The original intent of the war had been to prevent communist China from expanding in Asia and that had been achieved. The dominos had not fallen. McNamara was correct.

"The time has come," he concluded, to reaffirm America's minimum objectives: "to see that the people of South Vietnam are permitted to determine their own future" with the caveat that "this commitment ceases if the country ceases to help itself."

The administration should take steps to negotiate a peace settlement.

Johnson was furious with McNamara, considering the new position something of a betrayal. The official US position was adamantly opposed to negotiations. The president sided with the military chiefs. Without any qualms, Johnson let McNamara understand it was time for him to go. The change in policy would not become official until November 1967.

All the wrangling over strategy was done behind closed doors. The troops and the journalists in the field would continue to hear the positive spin of progress on the battlefield. Nothing in the press at the time hinted at the deepening pessimism of Washington's leaders, especially in the intelligence community.

The US offensives in the South and bombing of the North intensified. The South Vietnamese army was reduced to the secondary role of pacifying the countryside, and even that wasn't going well, as McNamara had observed.

North Vietnamese propaganda spotlighted how the "colossal army" of the "imperialist" United States had reduced the "puppet troops" of the South Vietnamese to a subservient role.[25]

The mockery from the North for South Vietnam's weakness was more than propaganda. It was a fact. South Vietnam could not fight its own war; it needed the US. Without the American military leading the way, their troops would go down in defeat. The North Vietnamese and Viet Cong also needed help: China provided essential military equipment—tanks, artillery pieces, radar, planes, and weapons—as well as safe havens and basic necessities from shoes and toothpaste to uniforms, and the Soviet Union provided big weapons and military aid, each country trying to counter the influence of the other—but the Vietnamese communists were fighting their own war. No Chinese or Soviet air force bombed South Vietnam; no Chinese or Soviet troops marched south to fight against ARVN.

～ ～ ～

FRANKIE FITZGERALD SPENT July and August of 1967 in Glin Castle, in County Limerick, on the Shannon River, where she began her project on the origins and meaning of the war in Vietnam.

Frankie had had only the haziest idea of her father's side of the family until college, when she met Desmond John Villiers FitzGerald, the 29th Knight of Glin, who invited her to stay. Frankie happily accepted the invitation and decamped to an Irish Georgian castle.[26]

Since her move back to the US, Frankie and Ward Just had kept alive their long-distance romance with letters about love and Vietnam.

At Christmas 1966, Just wrote from Saigon: "Your letters come as great lifts to the spirit. I'm off to Quang Duc tomorrow to write my year-ender. I'm using you and Sheehan as the standard to be bettered. . . . You are much missed here. Much much love and joyeau noel."[27]

Frankie was now his professional equal, praising her in the same sentence with Neil Sheehan.

Two months later he wrote to tell her about the death of Bernard Fall, the great French historian and journalist, and to offer solace. Fall had been a hero of Frankie's whom she met on one of his last reporting visits to South Vietnam. He had covered the French Indochina War and now the American war, and while he initially supported the Americans, he had concluded the US had lost the political war. For FitzGerald, he was larger than life, an intellectual like Mus and a down-to-earth courageous foreign correspondent. Fall had been killed when he trod on a landmine as he was recording a taped dispatch. He was only forty years old. To cheer Frankie up, Just wrote her a ditty from Singapore:

> *I think that I shall never see*
> *(which sight my heart imperiled)*
> *A poem as lovely as this tree,*
> *(her real name's FitzGerald)*
> *A tree who looks like God all day,*
> *Exquisite fruit of the CIA*
>
> *Who fashions dreams of wildest scandals*
> *With one thong of her Hong Kong sandals.*
> *To love her is like landing on an aircraft carrier*
> *Think of the astronaut ecstasy of the one who will marry her?*[28]

Finishing his Vietnam tour in May 1967, Just wrote that "I miss you more than I can say." Immediately after he arrived in Washington, he was sent to Israel to cover the Six Day War. When that conflict ended on June 10, he cabled her from Rome: Rendezvous June Twenty Ninth Paris Love Ward.[29]

Ireland was their first chance to recover the romance of Vietnam. While Paris was delightful, their expectations hadn't matched, exactly. Frankie pushed back from any discussion of marriage—she did not want to become a wife. Just dropped the subject and spoke instead about settling into his new job in Washington. In Ireland, they could relax for two months and suspend knotty discussions while discovering each other anew without pressing daily deadlines. And they were in a country at peace. They wrote their respective books in the deep silence of the castle during the day, with a staff to cater to their needs. They walked in the palatial gardens, and at night they drove to the town of Glin for drinks at the bars and conversations with locals who couldn't care less about Vietnam.

Ward Just thrived in the idyllic setting. His book—a war correspondent's memoir—was taking shape and included an entire chapter on his near fatal injury. His working title, and the book's eventual title, was "To What End: Report from Vietnam." He asked the simple question: What did the United States think it was doing in the war? Despite his best efforts, he couldn't see anything to redeem it. He introduced Fitz-Gerald in his first chapter, "Saigon and Other Syndromes," describing her as a beautiful reporter recently arrived from New York whom he escorts through bars and the cynical hustles of the city.

She talked through the book with Just, helping with his memory, discussing the context of certain events. She had witnessed many of the episodes he recounted; Frankie was part of his war.

Meanwhile, FitzGerald was writing an outline for a very different book, building off her fifteen-page magazine piece on the war to be published that August in the *Atlantic*. Her theme was the depth and danger of American misconceptions about the war and the Vietnamese, and it would be told from the Vietnamese point of view. The book would challenge the American justification of the war and underline the enormous damage it was doing in Vietnam and to the social fabric of the United States.

She was attempting to break into an almost entirely male world. Women rarely wrote serious books on war, especially not wars that were still raging. Books on war were almost exclusively the purview of men.

But FitzGerald was escaping the pigeonhole of a wealthy intellectual dabbling in war and, in some quarters, was being perceived as a serious if young journalist. She now wanted to become a fully respected chronicler of the war in Vietnam.

The romance seemed easy while they were writing. They ate well at the castle. They were regulars at a few pubs. They went to Ballybunion Greyhound Stadium and bet on the dog races.

Then on July 23, the castle's telephone rang with a call for Frankie. It was an official from the CIA station in London. A soft voice said that her father had collapsed and died playing tennis at his country home in Virginia. Frankie wrote that she "felt like my stomach had been torn out."[30]

Desmond FitzGerald was only fifty-seven years old. Frankie's beloved father had often closed his letters: "I miss you very badly, Frankie and always will when we are away from each other, love Daddy." Yet he hadn't visited her in Vietnam. And now he would never read her book. The inspiration for her Asian obsession was dead. She could not stop crying: "I went into a paroxysm of tears."

"Ward let me cry and fed me Scotch and curled up around me in bed. But it was no substitute."

She caught the first plane to Washington. Just stayed behind in Ireland to continue writing. FitzGerald's funeral was impressive. Vice President Hubert Humphrey attended, along with Senator Robert F. Kennedy, Katharine Graham, publisher of the *Washington Post*, and enough CIA officials to fill the pews. Frankie wept throughout. "His death felt like a desertion—so strong were my emotions."[31]

Just wrote her a reassuring note from the castle: "I'm all right here except that it's lonely and quiet and Joan calls me Mr. FitzGerald and gets flustered. . . . Please hurry back, Much love."

Frankie did return quickly to Ireland, but for the rest of their time in Glin, she couldn't concentrate on writing. As always, the women in her family looked after her from afar. Her mother sent a package with all of the obituaries about her father. FitzGerald read and reread a note from her maternal grandmother, Mary Peabody, an outsized figure who had been jailed at the age of seventy-two for taking part in a civil rights protest in Florida. Grandmother Peabody wrote: "All of us share your sorrow over your father's death. We were so fond of him . . . he was working so hard for the U.S. that he will be terribly missed—and he was much too young."[32]

Determined, Just finished writing most of his book and stayed through August before returning to the US. But the intimacy was fading. Frankie knew that "eventually he got annoyed with me. All I was thinking about was my father and not about him."

She was still grieving when, two months later, Just sent her a birthday letter with what he described as an "unusual" announcement. He had married another woman a few days earlier.[33]

Just had ended what was considered the great romance of the Vietnam War with a betrayal carried out like a thief in the night. He had been seeing another woman in Washington and impulsively married her without bothering to break up his romance with Frankie.

FitzGerald was surprised, maybe even shocked, but she disguised whatever she felt with a simple response: "He said he knew her from before."

Just's friends in Washington were also shocked. When Just called Ann and Walter Pincus to ask them to witness his upcoming marriage, they had no idea who the bride was: "We thought it was Frankie, but we didn't know. Ward said, no, it was Anne Harvey. We had no idea."[34]

After the ceremony at a suburban courthouse, the four of them celebrated with a picnic lunch. Just's book was published the next year. He removed Frances FitzGerald's name from the book, leaving only a description of an anonymous reporter clearly based on her. In his introduction, he said he wrote the book in Ireland, "a country I felt would be in every respect the reverse of South Vietnam," implying it was his idea with no acknowledgment that he had been with Frankie as a guest at her cousin's Irish castle.

He had erased Frankie, his wartime love, from his Vietnam story.

~ ~ ~

By 1967, THE war had taken over the American conversation so much that *Vogue* published three of FitzGerald's articles from Vietnam, setting some record for a fashion magazine's concern about the conflict.[35] The most intriguing was "The Power Set: The Fragile but Dominating Women of Vietnam." She begins with two women: "Like butterflies they have floated in and, folding the panels of their au dais [traditional tunics], have settled on the couch."[36]

One of these butterflies owned two bars on the toughest street in Saigon. The other was applying for a loan to buy an ice plant in Da Nang. In war, FitzGerald wrote, Vietnamese women were taking advantage of the vacuum of manpower "to go to the limit of escaping their condition as women." The two businesswomen had become the norm, she wrote, as women during the war "control virtually all of the business in Saigon that is not monopolized by the Chinese."

That last claim may have been an exaggeration, but FitzGerald's interest in the status of all Vietnamese women—beyond the prostitutes and refugees who appeared routinely in other stories—was unique. No other correspondent at the time explored the subject. The few women reporters working in Vietnam were allergic to any assignment that smacked of a women's page feature.

FitzGerald's epic fifteen-page article on the war, "The Struggle and the War: The Maze of Vietnamese Politics," was published in the *Atlantic* in August 1967 while she was in Ireland. Nothing she had written before had such an impact. With this piece she marked out her territory. For the first time an American journalist looked at the war from the Vietnamese point of view. She wrote with a disciplined and deep appreciation of Vietnamese history, culture, and politics. In her telling, Vietnam came alive as a separate country, not just an American battleground, with more than a thousand years of rich history of independence interrupted by centuries under the thumb of China and its Confucian culture and later French colonial masters. She showed how these foreign nations enriched and distorted Vietnamese society and how the Vietnamese tried to recover their integrity.

She described how the Americans had little interest in understanding the Vietnamese as a separate culture outside the American experience and how this led to Americans adopting strategies and policies based on dangerous misconceptions of Vietnam and the war that undermined their own cause.

FitzGerald wrote: "In the context of Southern [Vietnamese] politics the American vision of a popular, non-Communist government looks today, as it did twelve years ago, as improbable as an air-conditioned motel in the middle of a trackless jungle."

By the end of the piece, she convincingly wrote there was little evidence that the government of South Vietnam could survive without the Americans—their money, their military power, and their authority. She predicted with unusual foresight: "the intractable problem for the United States is not the war but the peace."

In other words, with victory out of reach, how could the US leave Vietnam without discrediting the whole costly operation?

The article was noticed. While most war correspondents are lauded for their physical bravery, FitzGerald was exhibiting a quieter moral courage with her willingness to puncture some of the myths and consequences of the American war effort.

Henry Kissinger, still an informal adviser on the war, was impressed. He wrote to her: "Dear Frankie: I have been promoting your article in the Atlantic all over Martha's Vineyard. . . . Shall we try to get together either in Boston or New York? Warm regards. Sincerely yours."[37]

One year later he would take charge of Vietnam policy under newly elected President Richard M. Nixon.

John T. McAlister Jr., a lecturer at Princeton University, telephoned her when she was back in New York to praise the piece. He also asked Frankie if she wanted to meet Paul Mus, the French sociologist whom she had cited in the article.[38] McAlister had studied under Mus at Yale, fought in the Vietnam War, and then returned to become Mus's collaborator on a book about the Vietnamese and their revolution.

Could FitzGerald come to Yale where Mus was a visiting professor? He wanted to meet her.

FitzGerald had no idea that Mus was in the United States.

The normally distant but gracious young woman was starstruck when she visited Mus at his campus office in October 1967. The French professor looked the part of an intellectual. He was European in dress, wearing a proper suit and tie, and in manner. He had a comforting and expansive style, gesturing broadly with his arms, smiling easily, raising his eyebrows, modulating his French accent when speaking English, pleased to switch to his native langue. Plus, he was funny.

FitzGerald listened intently to the legend who had grown up in Hanoi, trekked for days to ask Ho Chi Minh to consider a cease-fire with France, and then became an opponent of the French war. His office was tastefully accented with painted scrolls and silver mementos among the inevitably well-organized bookcases. He was one of the first professors in Yale's Southeast Asian department and knew all too well the level of Americans' general ignorance about Vietnam.

Even though he was partially blind, Mus kept up with news and was impressed by FitzGerald's work, a compliment that pleased her beyond words. She told him how his book, *Sociologie d'une Guerre*, had become essential for her understanding of Vietnam and the war. Afterward, she wrote Mus a long note. He responded in his rococo English to her "kind letter."

"I am not shy to say that its direct personal tones meant much to me. I have much appreciated that kind of harmony, which so naturally establishes itself between . . . us."

Then he urged her to get on with her work: "Look at yourself and at what you have written with unprejudiced eyes, and you will understand our prejudice in your favor. Life is too short, especially at my present time of day to allow for excessive circumspection. Even at the risk of appearing too bold, if we are to be friends as I believe we can become—no delay then!"[39]

From then on, FitzGerald and Mus kept up a correspondence, and she traveled from her apartment in New York to visit him in New Haven when she could.

The *Atlantic* article also elevated FitzGerald to the status of an expert on Vietnam among opinion makers who were growing more and more concerned about the escalating sacrifices and costs of the war. The Carnegie Endowment for International Peace invited her to attend a conference on the war in Bermuda in December 1967. With the Johnson administration openly claiming that victory was at hand, the conference's intention was to discuss and reassess US policy and make recommendations. She flew down and was happy to see Daniel Ellsberg. Other notables included Gen. Matthew Ridgeway, Hedley Donovan, editor of *Time* magazine, and a swirl of former senior officials from the Defense and State Departments.[40] She and Ellsberg sat next to each other, catching up and discovering they were the rare naysayers. "Frankie and I were the only ones who thought we should be getting out, not just cooling down."[41]

They were also the least senior people at the conference and the only two who had lived in the war zone recently. As the conference debated its report, the two argued explicitly for the US to get out of Vietnam. When they read over the final document's modest goals, which included the "aim of moderating the level of hostilities . . . [putting] the emphasis not on the military destruction of communist forces in the South but on the protection of the people of South Vietnam," FitzGerald leaned over to Ellsberg and whispered: "The Carnegie Endowment for International Peace should be renamed the Carnegie Endowment for Limited War."[42]

The Johnson administration rejected the tepid Carnegie recommendations as unnecessary.

FitzGerald signed a contract for her book with the Atlantic Monthly Press and sent in her first chapter. Peter Davison, the director of the publishing house, hated it and said he wanted to cancel her contract. "He said it was terrible. It didn't make any sense."[43]

Appalled and shaken, FitzGerald refused to give up.

After she submitted a few more chapters, Davison toned downed his withering critiques in favor of more constructive comments. He wrote her in November 1968: "We do admire many, many things about these drafts: their psychological subtlety, their discrimination among institutions and political forces, their originality. And we are not seriously discouraged about the contents of the book. It is simply that you have jammed too much too closely together. Give us air."[44]

Mus was her north star. With his help, FitzGerald felt she was working toward an understanding of what her book might become. "After my father's death I started looking for a substitute father and I found one in Paul Mus."

Somehow, through all their intense conversations, FitzGerald did not learn that Mus was in poor health. He had had multiple heart attacks and was following doctor's orders restricting his diet and controlling his exercise. He left New Haven at the end of the spring 1968 academic year to spend the summer at his home in Southern France. He lectured the next year in Paris, and while visiting his daughter in New York in 1969, Mus suffered a stroke.[45] He died a few months later at his home in Murs, France, leaving Frankie bereft of another father figure.

CHAPTER SIX

How She Came Out of That Alive Is a Miracle

CATHY LEROY RETURNED TO SAIGON AT THE END OF JUNE 1967 renewed. "My stay in the hospital was almost just as much a cure for my morale and my nerves," she wrote her mother. "I can still wear my dresses—you'd think I was twelve. I look youthful which should please you a lot . . . and I'm going to have a sensational dress made. I'll send you a photo when it's finished."[1]

The one-time waif was becoming one of the more fashionable women in Saigon, cutting out pictures of new styles from Parisian magazines for her tailor to copy at bargain prices.

In the flush of her happiness, she made an impossible pledge to her mother. "I entirely agree with you. I will go back to work on less dangerous subjects. Believe me, I've thought about the problem."

For a few weeks in August, Leroy was true to her word. It was the "cold and sad" rainy season. She burrowed into her studio apartment one block from the AP and began what became a lifelong attempt to make up for misspent years in school. She read stacks of books, whatever she could find in French shops. She was inured to jibes about her foul language, but she detested any hint that she was ignorant of basic history or literature. She perfected her written and spoken French and went to American movies in Saigon to improve her English.

During this interlude, she initially accepted only soft assignments, safe features: photographing US Special Forces riding elephants on a mission in central Vietnam's high plateaus and illustrating a story about the French community in Vietnam for *Paris Match*.

But the unprecedented battle around the DMZ pulled her back in. The artillery and mortar fire were so intense and the muddy hills and bunkers so foul that comparisons were being made with the Battle of Verdun in World War I. Four months after she was wounded there, Leroy was back at Con Thien to photograph Americans fighting the North Vietnamese. This time, though, she was with trusted colleagues: John Laurence and Keith Kay, the CBS reporter and cameraman.[2]

The McNamara Line, the barrier across the DMZ ordered by McNamara, was supposed to hinder the North Vietnamese and protect the Marines defending Con Thien. But the North Vietnamese were not deterred by the 2,000-foot-wide line with its minefields and sensors. Instead, they pounded the Marines with artillery. For their part, the Marines answered back in kind and called in B-52 airstrikes. The North Vietnamese were relentless, and the Marines were ordered to hold the line against an NVA breakthrough. That battle, under various names, lasted from 1967 through 1968, leaving 1,419 Marines dead and 9,265 wounded.[3]

Leroy arrived in the last days of September 1967 during a short lull. Waiting in the bunkers with Laurence and Kay, she discovered they were under assault by a different enemy—rats. Lots of rats, rats "as big as hideous cats, with red eyes and snot dripping from their noses." She saw them squeeze through mosquito nets to bite Marines.

Inevitably, the shelling soon resumed, and Leroy photographed the Marines who were targeted at times like sitting ducks. "Bodies and wounded men pile up night and day in the [medics'] bunker," Leroy wrote, noting how difficult it was to evacuate the wounded by helicopter without drawing enemy fire.

"And then there are the dead. They are the last to be evacuated in special green plastic body bags with handles. When there is a shortage of body bags, the bodies are simply put into [mail] bags."[4]

Stuck in the bunkers with her, Laurence was struck by Leroy's maturity. Even as she shook involuntarily during the shelling, as she always did, Leroy "was poised, alert and professional." Strikingly, she also trusted Laurence to make the call about when to leave and go back to the base. Leroy was a better colleague after her injury. Their bond would tighten early in the next year.

After fending off her parents' repeated requests to visit them and convince them she had recovered from her injuries, Leroy gave in. She dug into her savings and in October 1967 boarded a plane for Paris, stopping for a few days in Bangkok to decompress. She spent much of the month at home with Jean and Denise Leroy in the still boring Parisian suburb of Enghien-les-Bains. Her return trip took her around the world, stopping in New York and Washington where newspapers were filled with stories about an enormous antiwar demonstration in Washington that month, including two days when protestors had surrounded the Pentagon. Those demonstrations raised questions Leroy hadn't heard before; for instance, was the war racist, as Martin Luther King Jr. insisted and as President Johnson implied when calling Vietnam a "raggedy-assed little fourth-rate country."

Leroy knew she was not pro-war but didn't consider herself antiwar. That would be unfair to the soldiers she covered. She loved them. Yet in her first trip to the United States, she couldn't avoid the intensity of the American division over Vietnam.

In New York she was all business, groomed and dressed as a proper Parisian. She signed a contract with the Black Star photo agency, a major step in a freelancer's life. There was a gaping disequilibrium between the power of the corporate media and the support given to freelancers. Leroy was part of the first generation of photographers who had a chance of earning a decent living, as the agencies were designed to secure assignments for them and ensure they were well paid for their work. Leroy was relieved to be asked to join Black Star.

She also met with Wes Gallagher of the Associated Press. She asked him if he would give back her negatives for an upcoming book. He also lent her money for her airplane ticket. She returned to Saigon from San Francisco—the only American city that reminded her of Europe.

The warm glow from her break in that affluent world disappeared within days of her return to Vietnam.

As soon as she arrived in Saigon, Leroy was admitted to Grail Hospital with a nagging pain in her foot. A surgeon operated on her and removed a large ball of pus and cleaned a serious infection.[5] Worse, while recovering in the hospital, Leroy learned that Horst Faas had been badly injured by a rocket-propelled grenade while he was covering a battle at Bu Dop in South Vietnam's Central Highlands.

A fragment from the rocket tore through Faas's legs so badly he couldn't move. An American medic pulled him away from the fighting, and an armored vehicle driver took him to a clearing where a helicopter flew him away to safety. Surgeons initially feared they would have to amputate one or both legs but patched him up instead. Faas refused AP's offer to fly him to Honolulu or New York for further care, saying he "had total trust in the military surgeons who were dealing with these problems day in and day out."[6]

Faas's serious injury saddened Leroy and gave her pause. Her mentor and patron, the great Horst Faas, was vulnerable. Leroy appreciated her inclusion in his "army" of photographers and had memorized his instructions to get close but not behave stupidly, to be honest and show the innocent victims as well as the dirty war, and to always bring back good photographs. Implicit in those instructions was the belief that a photographer could be smart enough to avoid injury. Lying in the hospital and thinking of Faas, Leroy knew in her bones that was not true.

Leroy celebrated New Year, January 1, 1968, in Da Nang on assignment, at a moment when the official rhetoric about the war was especially disconnected to the reality on the ground.

Publicly, the Johnson administration was optimistic. In late November 1967, General Westmoreland announced the war was entering its final phase "when the end begins to come into view . . . and success lies within our grasp."[7] In December, the US military handed over the defense of Saigon to the South Vietnamese, redeploying American troops away from the city. And in January 1968, Brig. Gen. William R. Desobry said the South Vietnamese military now "has the upper hand completely in the Mekong Delta." Yet at the same time, some of the most influential senators from Johnson's own party disagreed and said the military strategy wasn't working.

On the battlefield, the NVA made a new push toward Khe Sanh and Hill 881. Westmoreland suggested the North Vietnamese were attempting to turn Khe Sanh into a second Dien Bien Phu. Leroy and many other journalists were persuaded by Westmoreland's theory. She told her colleagues about her father's tears when he listened to the radio report of the French defeat at Dien Bien Phu. Inevitably, she felt she had to return to Khe Sanh, where the fighting had turned into a fierce stalemate. The Americans held the high ground and used their formidable air power to prevent a North Vietnamese breakthrough. Leroy stayed there until the traditional cease-fire was declared for Tet, the Lunar New Year, when she returned to Saigon, happy to mix with friends at a party on Tu Do Street.

Sam Bingham, an American freelancer in Vietnam who occasionally worked for *Newsweek*, met Leroy there.[8] He brought his bagpipes to the festivities and an American friend visiting from Hong Kong. With fireworks exploding in the night, the group moved outside to dance, snaking up and down the street to the squawk of Bingham's bagpipes. Everyone was drinking, flirting, and laughing. Romance sparked between Leroy and Bingham's friend. It was that kind of evening. Fireworks continued throughout the night, drowning out sounds of distant explosions that the journalists otherwise would have heard. Because the war had come to find them.

~ ~ ~

FIGHTING HAD BROKEN out all across South Vietnam. The North Vietnamese and Viet Cong had launched a massive Tet Offensive on a scale never before attempted. Some seventy thousand troops were attacking posts from the ravaged DMZ in the north to the rice fields of the Mekong Delta.

In the middle of this audacious offensive, one minor skirmish of little military significance caught the world's attention. A dozen Viet Cong soldiers fought their way into the United States embassy compound in Saigon and held it for six hours. It was a brilliant piece of political theater: it had no military value, but at a stroke it changed the perception of the war because something had happened that should have been impossible, completely impossible.[9]

The American public had been told the end of the war was in sight, that the US had the upper hand. Yet Nguyen Van Sau, an illiterate leader from the Viet Cong C-10 Battalion, was able to organize the assault from an automobile garage near the embassy. In the dark hours before dawn on January 31, Nguyen Van Sau and his men drove a taxi and a battered Peugeot truck to the newly built embassy compound. At 3:00 a.m., the men blasted a hole through the wall, killed the two US military police guarding the entrance, and then held the garden and first floor of the main chancery. When the Americans telephoned South Vietnamese police at a nearby post, they refused to help. The communists managed to fend off the Americans for six hours until the American 716th Military Police Battalion cleared the compound.

General Westmoreland inspected the embassy as soon as it was secured, telling reporters: "The enemy's well-laid plans went afoul. Some superficial damage was done to the building. All of the enemy that entered the compound so far as I can determine were killed." But that was not the point.

The rest of the world saw that the US embassy, the physical representation of the American government in Vietnam and considered American territory, had been attacked and held for hours. And all Westmoreland had to say was the North Vietnamese "plans went afoul."

The American public and officials in Washington were stunned by the news alerts of the offensive. Tet showed that South Vietnam was marbled with Viet Cong and their sympathizers and that the American and ARVN military had failed to pick up advance intelligence on the plans much less stop it. The three American television networks broadcast special reports on the Tet Offensive, and newspapers published long, detailed articles with banner headlines reporting the attack on the embassy.

For the normally risk-averse North Vietnamese, Tet represented a huge gamble: a bold and foolhardy campaign with the nearly impossible goal of sparking a national uprising throughout the South with attacks on five cities and multiple US military bases and villages.[10]

It was the brainchild of Le Duan, the severe, pro-Soviet, hard-line general secretary of the Vietnamese Communist Party, who had argued it was time to go all out for a clear victory against the southern forces no matter how many Vietnamese were killed.

His strategy was to pin down US troops around their bases while the communists made a full attack to "decimate" ARVN troops, all to be accomplished by some 85,000 soldiers from the NVA and Viet Cong (VC). Pamphlets were printed calling for an insurrection against the South Vietnamese "puppet" government.

General Vo Nguyen Giap, the leader of the 1954 victory at Dien Bien Phu, opposed the offensive in the belief shared with Ho Chi Minh that the best approach was to wait until the Americans inevitably gave up and left. But Ho was sidelined with illness, and younger leaders considered Giap too timid—Le Duan essentially outflanked them.

Within the first week it was clear that the offensive would neither spark an insurrection nor decimate ARVN. But it was making a mockery of American claims of victory in the coming year. In the United States, the revelations that Vietnamese communists were able to invade cities and military outposts was challenging official American optimism.[11]

The longest and most costly fight of the offensive was in Hue. Over ten thousand communist soldiers, including two battalions of the NVA, had captured the imperial city on the first day of Tet. They encountered little resistence.

Leroy felt she had to cover Hue. She headed to Da Nang where she found a seat on a military flight to Phu Bai and discovered she was sitting near Bingham, the journalist she'd met a few days earlier playing bagpipes as the Tet Offensive began. They chatted in French.

He was struck by what he considered her "macho" personality, as she explained how she would break away from the journalist pack to explore how to best cover the story.[12]

She left Bingham behind and teamed up with François Mazure, a reporter for Agence France-Presse whom she trusted. They grabbed seats on a military truck convoy into Hue, and when they were dropped off, they disappeared, failing to show up to be paired with American military escorts as required for journalists during the siege. Instead, they changed out of their press battle gear into civilian clothes and crossed over a wobbly front line to walk into a no-man's land. It was reckless. The battle of Hue was becoming the bloodiest of the entire war.

Leroy and Mazure rented a bicycle from a French-speaking Vietnamese man on the road and reached Hue riding tandem. At a market on the city's edge, they were caught in a volley of shooting and realized they had stumbled into communist territory.[13]

A Vietnamese stranger understood their plight and guided them to a Catholic cathedral that had become a refuge during the fighting. The sanctuary was crowded with hundreds of frightened, hungry Vietnamese. Yet the priest, speaking an elegant old French, welcomed them. The people, though, were wary. Leroy's photographs show them crowding around the two Europeans, their eyes filled with worry. Another photograph shows a woman off in a corner lying on a single sheet comforting her baby who had been born in the church that day.

The next morning the priest told them they had to go, that their presence was adding to the danger facing the refugees. Leroy and Mazure understood and left immediately. They made a white flag from a priest's robe and wrote on a large sign: *phap bao chi bale* (we are French journalists). The priest wrote a letter in Vietnamese verifying they were journalists and asking they be respected as neutrals.

As they stepped outside the door, they were walking into the unknown. No foreign journalist had been captured by the NVA in the war, as far as they knew. They had no idea what would happen to them if they were taken.

Just minutes later they had their answer. They wandered past a graceful villa guarded by three North Vietnamese soldiers carrying AK-47s who stared at them.

In seconds Leroy and Mazure were under arrest. The NVA soldiers confiscated their cameras and tied their wrists behind their backs with parachute cord. "More efficient than brutal," Leroy thought. To her surprise she was less afraid now that she had met actual communist soldiers. They were no longer monstrous abstractions.

The priest's letter did no good. The soldiers looked at the paper but did not read it. It was not clear if they were literate. Leroy and Mazure were led inside the compound to the servants' quarters where a Frenchman and his Vietnamese wife were being held as prisoners in what was once their home. The Frenchman was head of the community's electric plant and had been treated well by the NVA. A young North Vietnamese officer came to question the foreign intruders, and the Vietnamese wife explained that these were French, not American, journalists. The mood changed immediately.

The officer ordered the cords removed and then returned the cameras. Feeling safe for the first time, Leroy asked to photograph the soldiers in their bunkers around the garden. The officer agreed. "All of the men were well armed and had a great deal of ammunition," Leroy wrote. "I photographed some of them swarming over a captured American tank. I doubt that they knew how to drive it, but they all grinned at us like soldiers of a victorious army."

That is what the young NVA officer wanted to convey. They were winning. They were liberating Vietnam.

While that scene unfolded, Horst Faas was in the AP bureau, still hobbling on crutches and worried.

"The day the Tet Offensive was at its height there was a story about a woman photographer being captured by the North Vietnamese. I thought—poor, poor little Cathy. This is her end."[14]

In fact, Leroy and Mazure were negotiating their release in a most French fashion. They thanked the officer as if theirs had been a routine interview in a normal day of reporting. Mazure said something to the effect that they had to get back to Paris with their story, so it was time to run along. And then they made their farewells.

Freed, Leroy and Mazure walked into the street and heard constant firefights nearby. They feared they would be encircled and ran back to the cathedral. This time the priest and his refugee flock burst into applause, welcoming them as fellow survivors. They fed them fruits and cake and soup, exclaiming "number one!" in English. Mazure and Leroy were giddy at having survived.

They still had to flee the communist zone, however. Along the way, Leroy photographed a Vietnamese father holding an infant, his wife shepherding their older children: stunned civilians caught in the crossfire with no place to hide. This time they crossed the urban front line successfully, holing up in a South Vietnamese army unit where they helped two wounded American soldiers.

Eventually, they worked their way back to the Marines. Leroy saw her friends John Laurence and Keith Kay of CBS, as well as the photographer Dana Stone, who were covering the unit. She ran up to them, kissing them and shouting: "I am so happy to be alive."

Laurence never forgot Leroy's extraordinary feat. "Cathy's daring bicycle ride into occupied Hue at the start of the Tet Offensive in 1968 and the still pictures she took while there was one of the most courageous acts of any journalist at any time in the war."[15]

The next morning the Marines took up position and began firing at the cathedral in which Leroy and Mazure had taken refuge. Leroy was alarmed. "I ran up to the platoon leader shouting: 'there are 4,000 refugees in there. They aren't VC. They're just people.' And those huge warriors in their flak jackets grinned at me and stopped shooting."[16]

Finally, Leroy and Mazure got back to Saigon and sent their story and photographs to Paris and New York.

Her photographs of the North Vietnamese—the first ever taken of the NVA in South Vietnam—made her famous. They were the cover story of *Life* magazine and featured in *Paris Match*. Her name became known worldwide.

Faas wasn't easily impressed with stories of courage in war, but Leroy's was different: "How she came out of that alive is a miracle. She must have run into the one North Vietnamese who ran a humane and considerate outfit. I myself later saw they really did slaughter thousands [in Hue]—executing teachers, shopkeepers and anybody who had any connection to the South Vietnamese war effort."[17]

Twelve days after her release from Hue, Leroy went back to the now-ruined city to photograph the rest of the siege and its atrocities. The city stank of putrid flesh.

The Marines approved her return even though "she had been hanging out with the enemy so to speak," said Don McCullin, whose own photographs of the battle of Hue were among the best. "The mere fact that she was allowed to stay after being captured was a huge coup in itself."[18]

In war, journalists crossing enemy lines are routinely considered spies.

Leroy was unaware that she was breaking new ground in Hue by photographing soldiers on both sides of a battle. In fact, it was a first in Vietnam and rare in any war. Among the most famous and still unmatched example was Matthew Brady's extensive photography of both sides of the American Civil War. For Leroy, what mattered was capturing as full a view of the war as she could.

Her photographs showed bodies strewn on streets; refugees fleeing to the American side across the Perfume River, impassively filing past cadavers; and newly homeless families carrying what she called the "incredible bric-a-brac of poverty." And they showed a still divided city. The Viet Cong flag flew over the citadel. One kilometer from the Marine base, she met Vietnamese civilians whose faces seemed full of hate, mumbling "American go home—kill me, kill me."[19]

The press contingent in Hue included Brigitte Friang, a veteran French television correspondent who impressed Leroy with her composure and professionalism, "making quite a change from the highly-strung excitement of the other journalists."

The two women arrived together at the command post of the First Battalion of the Fifth Marine Regiment. Leroy photographed the Marines attempting the final assault on the citadel as the sticky rain of the monsoon fell relentlessly on their ponchos.

At one point the Marines asked Leroy to translate for them. A family that spoke only French wanted to tell them something. An older woman picked up an English dictionary and said: "They killed my son-in-law because of this dictionary. . . . He was learning English . . . they killed him in front of us at close range. . . . Then they dug a tomb in the garden and buried him. . . . He wasn't dead yet."[20]

Her son was one of some two thousand civilians executed by the NVA and VC.

One month later, in March 1968, American troops would massacre more than five hundred Vietnamese civilians in the hamlet of My Lai, an atrocity discovered by reporter Seymour Hersh one year later.

Throughout the siege, journalists were injured. Bingham, the young freelancer, lost his right eye. Nearly two weeks later, H. D. S. Greenway, then of *Time* magazine, Charles Mohr of the *New York Times*, and Al Webb of UPI were wounded trying to rescue a wounded Marine. Years later they each received a bronze star with a V for valor.

The elegant city of Hue and its Purple Forbbiden City, which had inspired Frankie FitzGerald during her first weeks in Vietnam, were in ruins; 80 percent of Hue had been destroyed. The tower of the citadel had been bombed by the United States in the grinding battle to capture it from the North Vietnamese. The Marines and ARVN eventually pushed through the citadel's gates and found priceless blue and white porcelains crushed on the floor. The citadel's dismembered galleries resembled scenes from Berlin at the end of World War II. The promenades and villas along the Perfume River had been shooting galleries, their gardens dug up for bunkers.

The Tet Offensive changed the war. The US casualties during Tet set a Vietnam wartime record. In one week, ending on February 17, there were 543 Americans killed and 2,547 wounded in action. By the end of Tet in September 1968, the total US combat deaths in the Vietnam War had reached 20,096.

The North Vietnamese and the Viet Cong casualties were vastly greater. At least 35,000 were killed in Tet and up to 60,000 wounded. It was their worst military defeat of the war.[21]

Caught in the middle were Vietnamese civilians: nearly 165,000 died in the fighting and another million were left homeless.

In a moment of wishful thinking, General Westmoreland compared Tet to the Battle of the Bulge, the last battle before the Nazi defeat in World War II. He genuinely believed that North Vietnam was near its end and about to surrender.

Westmoreland could not have been more off the mark, and influential Americans were worried.

~ ~ ~

THE WAR WAS at a stalemate.

For some of the smartest minds in the Pentagon, this was proof that American leaders, beginning with those in the administration of President Harry S. Truman, had misjudged Vietnam entirely.

"They were ignorant," said Leslie H. Gelb, Pentagon's director of policy planning who shepherded the secret Pentagon report on the war that became known as the Pentagon Papers. The United States had gotten into Vietnam without knowing "a damn thing about the country, culture, history, the politics . . . a war that depended on knowledge of who the people are, what the culture is like."[22]

The Tet Offensive intensified the divide in the Pentagon between military and civilian leaders. The military had claimed to have killed so many Vietnamese that there shouldn't have been enough Southern communists left to fight. After Tet, the US government realized North Vietnam was going to fight to the finish, and that it would exhaust the United States. The Americans began to seriously consider turning the war over to the Vietnamese.

At the start of the Tet Offensive, the American public was behind President Johnson, but as the full dimensions of the communist incursions sank in, the support slipped. A Gallup poll reported "a new wave of pessimism" about the war, with at least half of Americans disapproving of the administration's handling of it. More and more, the public was asking: What is the United States doing in Vietnam?

~ ~ ~

BY THE END of the siege of Hue, Leroy was tired and sad. Bravo Company, with whom she had spent so much time, had been reduced from 197 to 85 Marines. Leroy wrote her mother: "Within one week 400 Marines were injured or killed. Poor guys."

Life magazine's cover of February 16, 1968, featured one of Leroy's photographs of NVA soldiers in their heavily guarded post in Hue. Inside, she wrote a three-page article to accompany her remarkable coverage of the NVA. The *Life* editor's note was a profile of Leroy, describing her extraordinary success covering the war. Its headline "A Tiny Girl with Paratrooper's Wings" would have made her wince— she insisted on being referred to as a photographer, not a girl photographer. But the exposure was priceless.

Marcel Gugliaris, a French writer and Asia specialist, interviewed Leroy in Saigon a few weeks later, asking how she felt during her capture. "Very calm during it but afterwards I was afraid. I panicked. Sometimes it's the next day or one week later—generally it's the next day when I am safe and have nothing to worry about that I panic."

After discussing the risks she took as a photographer and her injuries, Gugliaris asked her why she had chosen this career. "I follow this profession out of love," Leroy replied. "My life in Vietnam is so fantastic. In war I have found something I never had anywhere else—a kind of fraternity, camaraderie, pure friendship of soldiers. The soldiers are my friends. . . . I love them because I march with them, because we have memories in common, because when we meet again three months later we remember the operations—1004, 852 or 881—where so much went on, the most incredible, the saddest, but memories that have become wondrous. We remember the good side, the heroics."[23]

~ ~ ~

CATHERINE LEROY'S WORK in 1967 brought her multiple awards, lifting her to the ranks of the well-regarded professionals. Among her prizes were the National Press Photographer Association's top award for news photographs; the Sigma Delta Chi Award for photography; an honorable mention for an Overseas Press Club Award in news photography; and, most importantly, the 1967 George Polk Award for Outstanding News Photography.

Not only is the Polk among the most coveted prizes, Leroy was the first woman to ever win it for photography. She was also the first freelance photographer to win. It would be twenty-one years before another woman won the Polk, when it was awarded to Mary Ellen Marks.

A few years later Leroy would become the first woman to win the Robert Capa Gold Medal Award for exceptional courage and enterprise—the highest prize for any photographer of conflict.

During the war in Vietnam, as many as six hundred photographers trekked to Southeast Asia to make their mark. None of them accomplished what Leroy achieved as a freelancer. For a woman—the sole woman combat photographer in Vietnam—to do so was unprecedented, historic.

Leroy went to New York to accept the awards.

She arrived in the city on April 2, 1968, two days after President Johnson shocked the nation and announced he would not run for reelection. The Vietnam War had worn him down. When she visited the city's news bureau, they were talking of little else and what it meant for the United States and for the Vietnam War. The antiwar movement had never been stronger.

Two days later, while she was meeting with editors at *Look* magazine, news came over the wire that Dr. Martin Luther King Jr. had been assassinated in Memphis. Immediately, anger and sorrow ripped through the country. Riots broke out in some cities. Curfews were imposed. *Look* asked Leroy to go to Harlem to photograph the crowds of African Americans grieving over the loss of their extraordinary leader, the thirty-nine-year-old winner of the Nobel Peace Prize who had just been savagely murdered by a white racist.

She agreed, of course, and found her way to Harlem. And the people of Harlem soon found her—a stranger taking their photographs, possibly even a foreigner. She was surrounded. Someone asked for her cameras. She felt the hostility. Somewhere in that crowd, a deep voice yelled: "Cathy, what are you doing here?"

An African American soldier who had jumped with Leroy in Operation Junction City recognized her and made his way through the people. Smiling, he invited her to dinner at his mother's home. She had no trouble after that.

Succinctly, Leroy wrote to her mother: "Two days in Harlem. It's war there, too. No need to go to Vietnam."[24]

The day of the awards ceremony, Leroy went to the AP office to retrieve her Vietnam photographs. Hal Buell, the new head of photography, met her and told her he would do what he could to find the negatives. Impatient, Leroy went up to the seventh floor looking for the head of AP. Buell was called and asked to escort Leroy out of the building.

Buell said he was polite at the beginning of their conversation. "This film she was talking about—I said I would do what I could to find it. I remember the set of pictures were very good: the assault on a hill. But she got nastier and nastier, and there's no sense in dealing with someone like that."[25]

By the time of the award dinner that evening, Leroy was in a foul mood. She had packed two evening dresses: a white silk gown studded with pearls and a softer, green silk one, both tailored for her in Hong Kong. She wore the green dress for the dinner.

Early in the evening, Leroy was called to accept her George Polk Award for her AP photographs of Hill 881. One of the few women celebrated that night, her blond hair gleaming, Leroy walked to the stage, her diminutive figure in the fitted dress contrasted with the men who had picked up the other awards. There was applause until she opened her mouth.

Instead of expressing gratitude to the Associated Press, the company that had nurtured her career when others would not, the company that had seen her through battlefield injuries and nominated her for multiple awards, she went on a small rant. The crowd cringed.

In front of the leaders of American news companies, she complained that AP had a lackadaisical attitude toward freelancers and had lost some of her photographs. At her moment of triumph, Leroy managed to insult her best patron and ally.

That charming French accent sounded sour and petty.

She walked back to her seat, oblivious to the icy reception her remarks received. When the ceremony ended, she sauntered over to the post award dinner hosted by AP only to find herself barred from the table, a petty reaction to match her petty speech. She was told that the head of AP did not want to see her. Her relationship with Horst Faas never fully recovered.

Writing to her mother, Leroy said she was worried about "getting a big head" someday but put all the blame for her blunder on AP. "Everything would have been better if I hadn't had some unpleasant surprises with AP. They lost a good many of the negatives of one year of my work. And after a speech I gave at the Overseas Press Club where I described their lackadaisical attitude towards photographers like me (they were there, so was all the New York business community) now they don't want to give me back the others. . . . This episode completely drained my morale. I am feeling really depressed."[26]

Leroy knew how to be gracious, so what was she thinking? Seemingly, after her encounter at the AP offices, she convinced herself that AP was cheating her out of her own photographs. (AP eventually gave her the negatives, as Buell had said it would.) So she had allowed herself to give in to her stubborn, sullen side—the implacable teenager who bridled at authority and had dropped out of school and then for the rest of her life was embarrassed at her poor education; the young woman who became a chain smoker even though she had suffered debilitating asthma as a child; the young photographer with a granite-hard chip on her shoulder.

Although she was loath to admit it, Leroy was punch-drunk from recurring nightmares and depressions. She was eating poorly and smoking too much. In another era, she would have been diagnosed with acute post-traumatic stress.

~ ~ ~

LEROY HAD ONE more major magazine spread on Vietnam, one where she pushed her distinctive style to the limit and anticipated the future of war photography.

"This Is That War" was published in *Look* magazine on May 14, 1968. It was a dramatic ten-page spread that used five of Leroy's color photographs. Each image either filled an entire single page or was spread across double pages. The photographs commanded attention. The magazine was trying to make a statement and chose Leroy's photographs to underscore the message.

When sending her proofs of the initial layout of her "excellent" photographs, *Look* went further. The editor asked her to write 140 to 200 words about the Vietnam War in general, captions that told a story.

The text Leroy wrote to accompany those pictures was as unusual as the pictures. "We all belong to the same war. We all have the same God. We're all in the same adventure. This is that war."

For the image of a distraught mother holding her toddler son whose head is half-covered in bandages, she wrote: "The town was destroyed. I saw thousands of new refugees with no food, no home, hate in their hearts."

It was titled "The Ravaged."

Under a photograph of an injured American soldier dripping blood, his face drawn in agony, she wrote: "'I lose men,' the commander said. 'I lose so many men.'"

Her commentary had the undertone of a farewell: "The Americans here are boys of 20, with the idealism of their age, but they are fighting a war without glory. They all look the same from the 1st Cav to the Marines, and they are united without discrimination by life and death. The Vietnamese are not united. I believe about 20 percent are Viet Cong—20 percent are strongly anti-Communists—the rest are being crucified in a land of steel and fire, with their only political feeling a hope to survive. Who can blame them? The wounded and dead in dirt and debris—the villages and towns ravaged, destroyed. Thousands of refugees with no food, no home and hate in their hearts. This is that war."

The *Look* editors followed Leroy's spread with an unexpected announcement. The essentially right-of-center editorial board had decided it was time for the United States to leave Vietnam "quickly and honorably."[27]

"The Vietnam War has been a mistake, destroying something precious in the word 'America.'"

Coming from a magazine that printed Norman Rockwell illustrations, the antiwar editorial complementing the photo-essay was revelatory.

Susan D. Moeller, the author of a classic history of war photography, put it this way: "Leroy grabbed the images in a way that not only brought the viewers up close and personal but she is interacting with what she is seeing rather than standing outside as a dispassionate observer. She is engaged.

"It was arguably the most impressive photo-essay to date in the war because of the angle of Leroy's vision and the range of what she included in it."[28]

Moeller said Leroy had the advantage of a small woman able to take photos without getting in the way. "She interacted and engaged with her subjects," said Moeller. "She was doing things you weren't taught to do and others weren't doing."[29]

Future photographers followed Leroy's distinctive style—intimate and seemingly spontaneous, catching a moment in a war that eschewed classic heroics. Her portraits were of soldiers in all moods, of a pilot giving orders one minute and crying the next, of the stoic faces of Viet Cong prisoners beaten in front of her, and of a dog on the front line, his paws over his ears: "She saw everything. She went everywhere. She had the eye."

~ ~ ~

RETURNING TO VIETNAM in May after New York, Leroy failed to recapture the momentum she had built. *Look* gave her several big commissions, including a feature on ARVN paratrooper operations. She slowed down enough to begin dating an American military adviser to the paratroopers.

"Yesterday I was with the principal commissioner of Saigon, the general chief of staff of the paras, my boyfriend the American para advisor . . . and we drank like only the Vietnamese can do. I hit the bottle of Cognac with disconcerting speed (I who couldn't drink before)," she told her mother.[30]

That affair did not last. Leroy stuck to her decision to relax, renting an expensive apartment on Tu Do Street between the river and the Continental Hotel. She bought lamps, rattan bookcases, and potted plants. She added to her wardrobe and swam in pools. But she wasn't meant for an easy life in the middle of a war zone.

After her trip to the United States, she had come to the conclusion that the war would continue indefinitely. She had no confidence in either Richard Nixon, the Republican candidate for president, or Hubert Humphrey, the Democratic candidate. "I'm really afraid the war won't draw to a close for a long time yet," she wrote. "Whether it's Nixon or Humphrey doesn't make any difference, in my opinion."

Leroy continued to make business decisions that undercut her independence. Without understanding her contractual obligations to Black Star, she signed on with another agent who promised to help her make a film about Vietnam.

Her contract with Black Star was up in December 1968 with no sign that the agency wanted to renew her unless she clarified her commitments to the two separate agents.

"It led to a big confusion," said Dominique Deschavanne of Contact Press Images who later curated her work. "She didn't listen to advice."[31]

She jumped from project to project in Saigon. She earned $900 photographing a Vietnamese priest but felt "embarrassed to make so much money taking so little risk."

She spent one week in October on an aircraft carrier. She negotiated with a French television news program to make a Vietnam documentary. It was scattershot and not especially rewarding artistically or financially.

"I am very tired and I still haven't taken a vacation," she wrote her mother in one of her last letters from Saigon. She was losing her appetite for going out in the field. "In Vietnam, most of the time it was extremely boring: exhausting and boring. You walked for miles through rice paddies or jungles, walking, crawling in the most unbearable circumstances and nothing happening. And then suddenly all hell would break loose."[32]

In Saigon she was again surrounded by gossip about her love life, which seemed to fascinate and intimidate her male colleagues and competitors. Dirck Halstead, another photographer, typified the male view of Leroy at the time: "She had a formidable libido. To Catherine, a rifle platoon translated into a smorgasbord."[33]

Men were dashing war correspondents; women were whores.

By December 1968, after nearly three years in Vietnam, Leroy was worn out. In the final months, she worked until late at night and woke up exhausted. She came to the conclusion that "after all life in Saigon is not much fun."

Leroy moved back to France, telling herself it was time to be close to the decision makers in Paris and New York who could listen to her pitches and give her assignments.

Her parents paid for part of her airplane ticket. She arrived in time to celebrate Christmas 1968 with them.

⌒ ⌒ ⌒

IN PARIS, SHE was restless. She had trouble focusing. She had trouble crossing the city's boulevards without risking being run over. She had trouble sleeping. "In fact I couldn't sleep for many months when I came back to Europe. I had nightmares of impending assaults by North Vietnamese soldiers."

She made new friends, but her mind was elsewhere. The war back in Vietnam was escalating, but Cathy couldn't bear to look at her war photographs, and she hated discussions about the war with Parisians no matter what their opinions. Her left-bank liberal friends sounded self-righteous and parochial. "There was a lunch that was given in my honor upon my return, and they all started to have this big political discourse [on Vietnam] and I felt that I was being attacked. I was in such a fragile mental state that I started to cry, stood up, and left. I took it very personally."[34]

Marijuana became her best friend.

It wasn't until the summer of 1969 that Leroy felt able to move forward, to get on with her life. She allowed herself to remember some of the better parts of Vietnam as well as the nightmares. "I was so frightened sometimes, so frightened. I really never thought I was going to get out of this alive. But when it was all over, and when I was alive . . . the release of fear gives you a rush, high of just being alive. You're alive like you've never been alive before."

～ ～ ～

IN AUGUST SHE accepted an assignment and flew from Paris to New York to photograph a music festival in Bethel Woods, New York.

Leroy put aside her camera the first day of the Woodstock Festival. She looked out at the thousands of her peers in the open fields of a New York dairy farm and decided this was for her. "I dropped it," she said. "I blew off the [*Look* magazine] assignment."

She was not going to be a voyeur at the 1969 festival of "peace and love." She danced and laughed in the mud and the mayhem, feeling unfettered for the first time since leaving Vietnam. Onstage was Jimi Hendrix, the Grateful Dead, Janis Joplin, Sly and the Family Stone, Jefferson Airplane. Grace Slick singing, "Don't you want somebody to love? Don't you need somebody to love? Wouldn't you love somebody to love? You better find somebody to love."

In the masses, Leroy found dozens of Vietnam veterans, her people. They looked nothing like the fresh-faced young men she had photographed just a few months earlier. Former Marines wore their hair down to their shoulders. They smoked pot in the open and seemed adrift, happily adrift and lost. Leroy shared war stories with them. They said they felt cornered, uneasy. There had been no parades to welcome them home. Old-style veteran groups denounced them as hippies and losers and had little to do with them. The antiwar crowd was usually welcoming. But at a few peace rallies, the veterans were called killers. And the military—the military was maybe the worst at not understanding what the Vietnam veterans needed, why they felt so "fucked up."[35]

Leroy dropped out and traveled with the veterans for several months after the festival, "substituting the lack of adrenaline from war by taking drugs and drifting." By year's end, she had bounced back and returned to Paris and photography. She directed a film about the destruction of the city's beloved Les Halles fresh food market. After the 1970 Black September attack, she flew to Jordan and photographed fighting between Palestinians and Jordanians. She was trapped after one battle and walked thirty miles in the desert with Palestinian fighters, searching for safety.

But she did not forget the veterans from Woodstock.

CHAPTER SEVEN

Three Deaths

K<small>ATE</small> W<small>EBB</small> <small>AVOIDED THE</small> 1968 T<small>ET PARTIES IN</small> S<small>AIGON</small>. A young Australian freelance reporter, Webb was something of a loner. She was frugal, living in a single room, lodging above a Vietnamese shoe shop in the central working-class district of Saigon. Dining with well-known newspaper reporters who were friends of Frances FitzGerald was not her style or in her budget. She similarly shied away from the outrageous parties of photographers like Tim Page or Catherine Leroy. She did like to drink beer, though, especially with wire service reporters while listening to their war stories. She read books by Bertrand Russell to relax.

On the morning after the Tet parties, she woke long before dawn and dressed in her reporter's uniform and boots to catch a 4:00 a.m. flight to Pleiku in the Central Highlands on temporary assignment for United Press International. She went outside to hail a taxi and was unhappy to find the streets empty. She did not own a radio or a telephone and had no idea that the Tet Offensive was underway.

To her surprise, an American military jeep sped by. Instinctively, she yelled out to the driver, asking where he was headed. Urgently, he yelled: "the American embassy."

Realizing that something was happening, Webb threw her pack over her shoulder, forgetting her helmet, and ran along the uneven paving, past the wooden houses and homely storefronts toward the usually serene enclave of the US embassy. She ran toward a noise that was now unmistakably gunfire and not New Year's fireworks as she had first thought. By the time the embassy was in sight, Webb was crawling on her knees to stay under the tracer bullets that were crisscrossing the sky over the nearby Presidential Palace. An antitank rocket had torn open the front door of the chancery. The Tet Offensive of 1968—the year of the Monkey—was at its height.[1]

Webb was the first wire service reporter on the scene, but she had no way to send a story to the UPI office, far away on Ngo Duc Ke Street near Saigon Port. The AP had beat her by an hour. Its first report was on the wire at 3:15 a.m., based on telephone interviews from the bureau chief, who never left his home six blocks away.

Webb, just one block from the embassy, watched as a small arms battle played out inside the compound. Journalists joined her, some lying in the gutter, all stunned that the communists could be attacking the US embassy. Webb took notes, careful and thoughtful notes. She was a twenty-four-year-old New Zealand–born Australian who carried a British passport and had never been to North America. She had traveled through Europe and Southeast Asia with her family, but the United States was foreign to her. In the six months she had been in Vietnam, she had studied the Americans and the American way of war and politics with the same curious intensity she applied to the Vietnamese and their country.

A military policeman gestured to her to move back against a wall; she had gotten too close. He pointed to the military snipers firing M16 rifles from behind the trees and neighboring buildings.[2]

"Their rifles were pointing in all directions," she noted.

Then she watched as another US military policeman ran back after throwing a grenade at the compound.

"He went behind a jeep—not to dodge—but to cry," she wrote. His commanding officer told Webb that the policeman had already lost three men from his platoon in the fighting and was limping because of a grenade fragment that had torn into his leg.

Webb spotted Marine guards attached to the embassy. "I moved behind a Marine closer to the embassy gates. I wanted to get the Marine's name, and hometown. It seemed ridiculous to ask for it at this time."

She monitored their movements, listening to their walkie-talkies.

"They called out, 'there's a Marine dead on the roof up there.'"

"Another voice said: 'get help over to that jeep.'"

"Another replied: 'it's no good I tell you, they're dead . . . there's one guy sitting there, he's alive.'"

When the attack was over and the communists killed, she and the other reporters were allowed to enter the embassy compound: "It was like a butcher shop in Eden, beautiful but ghastly . . . the green lawns and white ornamental fountains were strewn with bodies. The teak door was blasted."[3]

Just as Catherine Leroy's photographs of Khe Sanh became the defining image of that battle, Webb found the words that would be the durable epitaph for the Tet Offensive. The phrase *a butcher's shop in Eden* captured the shock.[4] The meticulously landscaped new embassy of the greatest power on earth had been invaded, however briefly, by communist soldiers of a preindustrial nation and defiled at the moment that the United States was declaring victory.

Webb's article was printed in newspapers around the world and the phrase repeated and reprinted countless times in articles and books.[5]

For Webb, her scoop was a godsend. UPI finally agreed to hire her as a member of the local staff. When she had applied months earlier, Bryce Miller, the Saigon bureau chief, had rejected her summarily, saying, "What the hell would I want a girl for?"—loudly, in the middle of the office.[6]

Hearing Miller's curt dismissal, Paul Vogel, a Vietnamese-speaking reporter in the bureau, decided to help Webb find work. He introduced her to Vietnamese newspaper editors who happily accepted her articles, paying her no more than they paid Vietnamese in the local currency. Webb dove into her assignments, covering Vietnamese politics and maneuvers, assembling a web of Vietnamese sources who trusted her. All the while, she begged foreign editors for better paying assignments.

But Webb discovered she was ineligible for those freelance gigs because she lacked official accreditation to cover US soldiers on the battlefield. At MACV, she was told she couldn't apply for accreditation without certification from a foreign media outlet that she was either an employee or was on assignment. It was a perfect catch-22. Webb was literally hungry for work. She was eating mystery rice dishes and soup from sketchy street stalls.

The only woman editor in Saigon came to Webb's rescue. Ann Bryan, the editor of *Overseas Weekly*, was known to have an open door for young reporters. She was not easily intimidated. Earlier, she had successfully sued Defense Secretary Robert S. McNamara to over-turn a ban on her paper, and she had helped push back General West-moreland's proposed ban on women on the battlefield. Bryan gave Webb assignments and then filled out the necessary paperwork for her to become an official reporter on MACV's list, with the full rights that implied. The credentials were a lifesaver for another reason. Webb's tourist visa was running out; as a newly accredited reporter, she could stay as a resident in Vietnam.[7]

Her work for Bryan led to piecemeal assignments from UPI. Most of these were requests for "hometowners" from smaller newspapers across America who wanted feature stories about local boys serving overseas. The UPI staff reporters happily handed over those assign-ments to Webb, whose reporting was so thorough one soldier thought she was investigating him for an offense he had committed back home.[8]

At UPI, Miller began to appreciate Webb's abilities. When former First Lady Jacqueline Kennedy visited neighboring Cambodia in No-vember 1967, he commissioned Webb to be the number-two reporter on Kennedy's semiofficial trip. In many ways, Webb was ideal.[9] French was still the second language of Cambodia, and Webb was fluent. She traveled on a British Commonwealth passport, a major asset since Cam-bodia's Prince Norodom Sihanouk routinely refused to allow American

journalists into the country. Cambodia was officially neutral, and Sihanouk was terrified of the American war spreading into his country.

Ray Herndon, UPI's Singapore correspondent, was to be the lead
reporter and would cover the news of the day. Webb covered the awe-
struck crowds who followed Mrs. Kennedy; she described her elegant
wardrobe when she visited the prince at the royal palace in Phnom
Penh and fed elephants from a balcony. She was alongside when Kennedy traveled to Siem Reap to tour the temples of Angkor Wat.

In a sign of what was to come, Herndon quietly left the official
party and investigated secret Vietnamese communist sanctuaries inside
Cambodia's eastern border. He and AP reporter George McArthur
found a battalion-sized NVA base that was used to target American
soldiers in Vietnam. Sihanouk said the base was Cambodian and used
to train guerilla fighters. Within one year, the US would secretly bomb
that area.[10]

Webb also wrote freelance articles on South Vietnamese politics
that were so well sourced they were censored in the South Vietnamese press. She teamed with a BBC reporter to interview Truong Dinh
Dzu, the popular peace candidate challenging Nguyen Van Thieu in
the South Vietnamese elections. Dzu was expansive in his critique of
Thieu, and to Webb's horror, he was charged and convicted of libel for
his remarks in the interview. He was sentenced to hard labor but later
released.

But even with extra assignments, Webb was living what she called
her "hungry shoe-string" life, still eating street food and at times for-
going real soap.

Only after the Tet coverage did UPI hire her and officially put her
on the local staff. The perennially second-place wire service needed
her talents full-time; Webb became the first and only woman in the
bureau and was paid just enough to quiet her worries about money.

Coverage of the massive Tet Offensive was grueling and difficult in
part because it was so unexpected. As a full-time local staffer, Webb was
assigned to the Saigon area to cover the evacuation of dependents of
the diplomatic corps and America's stepped-up bombing of the North.

Webb finally did fly to Pleiku in the Central Highlands, where casualties were high on both sides and the NVA was executing Vietnamese considered puppets or Americans whom they deemed imperialists.

As Tet wound down, Webb was put into rotation to cover combat. It was a historic first for any wire service in any war. It was never officially noted, but from the moment her byline appeared in American newspapers, Webb became a role model and talking point for American women agitating to be sent to Vietnam. The AP held to its policy of no women in war zones until 1972, when, like the *New York Times*, officials thought the war was nearing its end. However, the AP forbade the women reporters to cover combat.

Webb struck her UPI colleagues as fearless, even though she claimed the contrary. Her first time reporting from the field was outside Cu Chi with the Twenty-fifth Army Infantry Division. "It was one of those long walks in the sun with a couple of mortar attacks, a couple of people dying of heat exhaustion. . . . These kids [American soldiers] were mostly 17, 18-year-olds off the street. What struck me about that was how inexperienced most of the troops were."

Then she wet her pants when a mortar landed nearby. When she was asked if that battle was the first time she had seen anyone die, she answered no: "I'd seen quite a lot of people die before that."[11]

That was an exaggeration that obscured the grim truth of three deaths that had led her, circuitously, to Vietnam.[12]

~ ~ ~

WEBB WAS BORN into a prominent New Zealand family. Campbell West-Watson, her grandfather, was a Cambridge-educated English cleric sent to New Zealand, where he became archbishop and was honored by Queen Elizabeth.[13]

Webb's English-born mother, Caroline West-Watson, was raised as a teenager in New Zealand but returned to England for graduate studies at the London School of Economics, a rare woman student at the time. She was intrigued by modern politics and traveled as a New Zealand delegate to a conference in Kyoto to discuss Asia's incipient independence movements. She attended debates on similar issues at the League of Nations meetings in Geneva. Then she got married.[14]

The 1932 wedding of Caroline West-Watson to Leicester Chisholm Webb, a promising young journalist and college lecturer, was a major New Zealand society event. Webb was already marked as a future leader. Educated at Canterbury College in Christchurch and Cambridge University in England, Webb was a lecturer in history at Canterbury and wrote his first book on government in New Zealand. During World War II, he worked at the Economic Stabilization Committee, and in peacetime he was appointed head of the New Zealand Marketing Department. Somehow, he managed to continue writing on contemporary issues.[15]

In the small world of the region, Webb's work was noticed by neighboring Australia. He was recruited to head the new political science department at the Australian National University in Canberra.

Catherine Merrial Webb, always known as Kate, was born in 1943, the third of four children born to Leicester and Caroline Webb and their second daughter. Theirs was a rarified household: their mother read Latin for pleasure, and their father was regularly interviewed on the *Notes on the News* national radio program, discussing national and international affairs. In photo albums the four children—Nicholas, Rachel, Kate, and Jeremy—play in English-style gardens, ride ponies, and glide on rowboats, squinting into the harsh Australian sun.

Church and Sunday school were de rigueur, and education was an absolute priority. Kate excelled in academics, the best of her siblings. Languages and the social sciences came easily. Her passion, though, was drawing and painting, one reason she was considered eccentric. She was also the good child, the least likely to act up.

Although their parents held back on physical affection—no hugs or kisses—they inculcated their children with their deeply held views. At dinner, their mother and father explained why Australia and New Zealand needed to accept that their larger community was Asia and how they should support independence for their Asian neighbors and not side with the European colonial nations. Just as often, their father would discuss the meaning of the ecumenical religious movement and its belief in the dignity of all peoples and races. They were progressives by the standards of the times, although her daughters noticed that Caroline suffered for having given up her career to raise the children and support her husband.[16]

In 1956, Leicester Webb was given a year's paid sabbatical to study the politics of postwar Europe. He and Caroline budgeted carefully to bring their two daughters with them for a rare educational opportunity. Their two sons had to attend a local Australian boarding school in their absence.

The Webb itinerary was enviable: Naples, Rome, Paris, London, and Oxford with a side trip to Germany for Kate and her mother. At thirteen years of age, Kate had decided she wanted to read German philosophy in college, which required learning the language. Leicester focused his European research on the strength of communism in postwar Italy. Kate concentrated on art, sketching, and keeping an epistolary journal, writing letters to an imaginary friend she christened Raoul. In her first letter from Naples—Napoli—she wrote about the "poverty, people in ruins, shacks and grass huts all piled up." In Rome "Daddy hurried off after breakfast to work in the library and Mummy, Rachel and I caught a bus for San Silvestro." The three went on to the Roman Forum, but the highlight was the Borghese Gallery—"600 lire to get in and there were really lovely pictures by Titian, Raphael, Caravaggio . . . I was awfully thrilled to see a really lovely Botticelli . . . but the real cracker was a brown ink and silver paint sketch by Leonardo."[17]

Paris meant a ride up the Eiffel Tower—"a most wonderful experience ever"—and cafés where Kate sketched waiters with platters of food and French diners eating with animated reverence. As she did at home, Kate went on long evening walks with her father while in Europe, asking him questions and soaking up his full attention.

The Louvre was her touchstone. She wrote to Raoul: "Rachel and I skipped the Italian stuff. Hundreds and hundreds of famous artists rolled before us . . . there were miles we didn't see. . . . Suddenly we were in an impressionist room. Wow!!! I just about went nutty. There were

Daumiers, Van Goghs, Gaugins, Lautrecs, Manets, Monets, Renoirs, Cezannes, Degas and billions of others. Each was a masterpiece."

Young Kate had an appreciation of the impressionists far ahead of the more conventional tastes of 1957. In her drawing of the impressionist room Cezanne was given pride of place.

England was a whir of castles, the London Underground, and Westminster Abbey. In Germany, she daily worked on translating *Aida* with her German tutor, Frau Ringel, before her nightly bath. During a pilgrimage to Goethe Haus, she learned her favorite philosopher had been very rich.

And then the perfect year abroad ended. Her sister, Rachel, stayed on in Italy as an au pair, and the rest of the family returned to Canberra.

Kate entered high school with hopes of plunging into art and painting. The girls in her new class, who were uniformly bubbly and outgoing, viewed Kate as out of place with her intensity and seriousness.

Kate stuck to art but at the price of becoming an outcast and loner. She worked hard at school, avoiding her classmates, whom she considered shallow. Even at home, she was becoming an introvert.[18]

Luckily, she found a friend in Vicki Fenner, a neighbor who rode on the same bus to school. Vicki was the daughter of Professor Frank Fenner, a prominent microbiologist and a colleague of Leicester Webb at the university. The two girls began walking home together and discovered they were both deeply alienated from school. Soon Vicki and Kate were reading poetry about the futility of life. With hormones raging, they dug deeper into the darkness. They fed each other's despair until they saw no way out.

They decided that suicide was the answer.

One Sunday afternoon, Kate slipped into her home and stole her father's hunting rifle and some ammunition. She met Vicki at a storm drain in their Red Hill neighborhood. Vicki stood in the water, leaned against the barrel, and fired directly into her forehead, collapsing after one shot. Her face was cratered and covered in blood. Kate looked on in shock. Then she turned and ran.

Her brother Jeremy was at home when Kate came crashing through the kitchen door, "screaming yelling, distraught, ripped apart."

"Papa took control immediately," he said, "and made Kate describe what had happened. Papa zoomed down to Vicki's father and told him. He kept saying no—that's not possible. They went off up the hill to see Vicki and Kate stayed with mother. Kate was now in complete shock, not saying anything. An ambulance was called. The police detectives arrived."

Vicki Fenner died in a hospital two hours later.

The police charged Kate with homicide. She had provided the weapon and ammunition knowing her friend intended to commit suicide. Leicester Webb nearly collapsed in the witness box testifying on Kate's behalf during the initial hearing.[19]

He hired first-rate lawyers who argued that Kate had tried to stop Vicki at the last minute, asking her to reconsider, saying: "Think, think."

Her lawyer argued this proved Kate had turned against the idea of a double suicide since Kate had also refused to write a suicide note. Vicki had. She left a suicide note in her bedroom for her parents saying: "Life is not worth living."[20]

An Anglican bishop testified in favor of bail for Kate, saying she needed to be with her Christian family who loved her. A detective said Kate had told him she was "acting in good faith and assisting a friend." The judge granted fifteen-year-old Kate her freedom on a bail of 200 pounds, while the family fought the murder charges.

Kate stopped speaking to anyone. To her brother Jeremy she became the "ghost who walks."

Caroline Webb wrote urgently to her daughter, Rachel, in Italy. "Come home right away to help your sister, maybe she'll talk to you."

Rachel arrived to find her parents in a standoff, refusing to talk to each other. "It was really vicious. Our whole family life was turned upside down. Father had stopped working to defend Kate."

After six weeks of unrelieved tension, the court dropped all charges against Catherine Webb.[21] But the damage was done. A grief-stricken Professor Fenner wrote a wrenching letter to the family blaming Kate for his daughter's death. Over the years he softened, and in his memoirs, Fenner said that he agreed with the court's opinion. Kate was not to blame. But that didn't mitigate his loss. Vicki's death, he wrote, had been "the most tragic episode" that he and his wife had experienced.[22] By then Fenner was the most highly decorated and awarded Australian scientist of the twentieth and twenty-first centuries.

The family rallied around Kate and tried to devise strategies to comfort and heal her. An Anglican nun was brought to counsel Kate, who had effectively remained incommunicado. The nun failed to convince Kate to open up, so she switched tactics and had Kate design and sew curtains, to bring out her creative spirit and bring her back into the world. Kate was given no other medical care or counseling.

She didn't want to speak about Vicki Fenner, but the story was on everybody's mind. So Kate stayed away from everyone. The whole city seemed to know about the suicide and had an opinion about Kate. Her friend Marianne Hill convinced Kate to go to the movies; Kate arrived wearing an outlandish black hat that she refused to remove lest she be recognized.

Somehow, her parents, sister, and brothers quietly steered Kate back to high school and real life. She left home to begin studies at the University of Melbourne and began to let go of her fears. Compared to stuffy Canberra, the college atmosphere was cosmopolitan, almost electric. She ate yoghurt for the first time and learned to love modern music. She made lifelong friends; she scandalously rode on the back of motorcycles. She majored in philosophy and became attached to the philosophy of libertarianism as well as the professor who taught those courses. She was happy.

She was visiting school friends when she was awoken late on the night of June 23, 1962. The police telephoned with the impossible news that both of her parents had been killed in a traffic accident on a highway in Tasmania.

Kate was weeping uncontrollably when she arrived at her sister Rachel's home. "We were all like stunned mullets. We weren't a hugging family. We managed to hold it together."[23]

The university sent chancellors to Rachel's home to help organize their parents' papers and sort out an infinite number of issues, keeping the two sisters busy.

On the day of their parents' funeral, much of Canberra came to a standstill. The cortege for the caskets of Caroline and Leicester Webb stretched for miles. The pews of St. John's were overflowing, but the family barely heard the eulogies. They were so profoundly in shock. After the burial, Jeremy moved in with Rachel and her young family, while Kate went back to university in Melbourne. Rachel was worried about her sister. It had been only four years since Vicki Fenner had killed herself. But Kate insisted she wanted to return to classes.

In what became a dark habit, Kate sought refuge in her work. She drank so much coffee to stay awake she fell ill with caffeine poisoning. Nonetheless, she graduated with honors, earning a philosophy degree. She thought art might offer rewarding employment and enrolled in the Julian Ashton Art School in Sydney, the ultimate metropolis in Australia. From the start, she was disappointed, telling Rachel she felt the teachers were oriented toward the men and ignoring her. She left midway through her course after she broke a stained-glass window and needed to earn money to pay for the damage.

Rachel stepped in with a practical suggestion for Kate: she should contact Douglas Brass, an old friend of their father who was the editorial director of the popular *Mirror* newspaper owned by Rupert Murdoch. Brass was happy to help the youngest daughter of Leicester Webb. He told Kate she was hired as a secretary. Kate couldn't type. Brass went one better and offered her a position as a news cadet, essentially ferrying news copy from one desk to another and learning the ropes by watching reporters in the newsroom. Women were rarely allowed into the newsroom, even as apprentices. Instead, women reporters were usually confined to the women's section, where they still wore white gloves to work.[24]

Journalism was familiar to Webb. Her father had begun his career as a reporter and had many friends in the field, including Brass. The newsroom was exciting and comfortable. As a cadet, she was sent out on the street to do the legwork for staff reporters, mostly on the police beat. Webb paid off her art school debt but decided art school was a bore compared to her life at the *Mirror*.

She was helping with the police beat when Lyndon Johnson made a state visit to Australia in October 1966. Australia was one of the few American allies supporting the US in Vietnam and had sent two battalions to fight in the war. Most Australians were thrilled—Johnson was the first sitting president to visit the country—and waited hours to greet his motorcade. There were opponents of the war, especially among the young who saw no reason to fight an American war. Several hundred students waving antiwar placards broke through a police barricade and blocked the streets. Some threw red paint at the presidential limousine. The activists were carried away by police and condemned as militants. Webb, who had been sent out to follow the huge crowds, became intrigued by the angry students and the war.

Back in the office, Webb read the wire service stories from Vietnam and asked a foreign editor why the newspaper hadn't sent its own reporter to Saigon since Australia was at war. No need was the answer. The paper could use the wires. So she offered to go herself, to general laughter. In one of her next visits to Sydney, Rachel was surprised when Kate told her she was scheming to go to Vietnam. "Kate felt she needed to see what the fuss was about."

Rachel didn't take her sister seriously, but the next word from Kate was in the form of a letter postmarked from Saigon. She had bought a one-way ticket to Vietnam without telling her family and arrived with her Remington typewriter and no source of income.

Rachel wondered how an increasingly bloody war would affect her sister who was already so damaged by three sudden deaths.

CHAPTER EIGHT

We Were Laughing

K ATE WEBB ARRIVED IN SAIGON WITH COTTON SUNDRESSES that she ironed obsessively and sturdy sandals.

Within a year, she had swapped the dresses for tight white jeans and loose cotton shirts. She cut her dark shoulder-length hair into a full pixie style. She paid for her own combat gear to wear in the field and from a distance looked like a young man. This was no accident. Webb was determined to fit into the male press corps and the soldiers they covered. She had no idea that the transformation had the opposite effect on men: they found her mesmerizing. She was unmistakably voluptuous. The army shirts couldn't camouflage her breasts, leading the GIs to give her the nickname Highpockets.

Her primary ambition to cover the Australian deployment was a nonstarter. The Australian military refused to allow her or any other woman anywhere near their forces on the battlefield. No exceptions. The prohibition lasted throughout the entire war.

Instead, Webb had to compete against the hundreds of reporters to cover the American and South Vietnamese troops.

When UPI finally hired her in 1968, Webb was allocated the bureau's junior position—as a gofer for Dan Southerland, a reporter who would eventually become the head of Radio Free Asia. Webb covered beats the American reporters considered second tier, like the baffling political machinations of South Vietnamese leaders and the ARVN, the South Vietnamese military.

This suited Webb. She yearned to uncover the context for the war. Reporting daily stories on the military situation or about American aid wasn't enough. Instead, she sought out the historical and political movements that drove the people and armies. She tried to fit what she learned into the worldview she had developed over the years listening to her parents discuss modern Southeast Asia and her own philosophy studies.

Two things seemed evident to her: the war in Vietnam was an extension of the independence movement to overthrow French colonial rule and the Vietnamese would decide the outcome, not a foreign power.

Otherwise, she wasn't sure what to make of it. She tried to fit Vietnam into the mold of the Malayan Emergency of the 1950s and often wondered out loud why the Americans weren't as successful as the British had been in stamping out a communist insurgency.

The question driving Webb's reporting was: Is South Vietnam capable of defending itself and establishing an independent and somewhat democratic government? If the answer was no, then the corollary question was: Why hadn't the United States used its money and might to build up a competent Saigon government—or was that an oxymoron?

On the battlefield, she routinely gauged the effectiveness of the South Vietnamese military. ARVN soldiers, she wrote, "are tough. Some of them were taken out of jail with the choice of execution or join the army, and some of those men made extremely good officers." Since ARVN soldiers were fighting for their country and even had relatives on the other side, she believed they were more committed than American soldiers who were rotated out after one year.

Covering ARVN required a high tolerance for danger. Southerland sent Webb on night patrols with small units of the ARVN, something he rarely did. Webb knew there was "no back up if you were wounded, no Medevac helicopters, and little chance of a story that would interest American newspapers."[1]

Once she used her ten-day vacation to live with the First Infantry Division of ARVN. Spending all that time with the Vietnamese, she noticed signs other reporters missed, like the significance of garlic. If garlic was suddenly in short supply in a market, Webb wrote, it was likely that a Viet Cong element was nearby. Why? Garlic was the cheapest and most transportable form of vitamin C and essential to Vietnamese cooking. Chinese merchants were happy to sell garlic to the Viet Cong on the black market at a tidy profit.

In May 1968, another offensive known as a second Tet broke out, and Webb was assigned to cover street fighting, again, one of the most dangerous assignments. She reported: "It is pretty terrifying. . . . It's the confusion that is tricky. You haven't got your normal guerilla pattern or fixed piece battle pattern outside . . . where you're looking for ambush sites and mines, the absence of kids or cows, the usual quiet. In street warfare it's a Chinese kitchen, all confusion. Noise is magnified. You can't see around a corner. You don't know who is in a house, whether there is someone above you dropping a grenade. And you can't react because you don't know if you'll be jumping into someone else's line of fire, the angles are so crazy."[2]

Webb developed a loner's mystique within the press corps. She got along with everyone but remained aloof. She was friendly with other women—she saw Leroy in the field occasionally—but she had no close female friends other than her Vietnamese landlady.

She liked drinking after hours with colleagues—all men—but then would disappear. In an unpublished novelistic memoir, she wrote about avoiding unwanted sexual advances from the men. One character warns her: "Beware, kid, he letches after you like the rest of us."[3]

By keeping a distance, Webb made no enemies. Even though she was a fiercely competitive reporter, her colleagues looked forward to working on stories with her. She was welcome just about everywhere. Gene Roberts and other reporters at the *New York Times* enjoyed seeing her appear at the door of the *Times* office.[4] While her exterior affability was genuine, it was also a shield. Underneath, Webb questioned her work and struggled to manage the pain and despair that

often consumed her. She tried putting it in verse, in a poem she titled
"War Groupie":

> *Beware—it's not done to care*
> *Unless, of course, it's your own child*
> *War Groupie, adrenaline freak!*
>
> *Swallow despair, mask horror,*
> *Post-operative nausea, lest the metal*
> *Hooks smash your heart.*
> *Beware. It's not done to care.*[5]

It's quite possible Webb wrote this while drinking her nightly quota
of beer or Scotch. She became a heavy drinker, which made her morose.

Her news stories from the field were notable for the dimensions
she added that were missing from standard-issue wire service reports,
often because she was the only person there. She was not afraid to use
strong personal narratives.

In the battle for Saigon in June 1968, Webb assigned herself to
the South Vietnamese military command post. She was nearly killed
when a US helicopter accidently fired on the post, killing the Saigon
police chief and five other high-ranking South Vietnamese Army officers, as well as injuring the mayor. Her account of the day continued
in what was becoming Webb's signature style:

"I had been sitting on the steps of the command post with Col
Phouc and Col Tru and we were laughing about always meeting on the
street. We had been there about fifteen minutes and Col. Luan joined
us, wearing a new pair of boots."

Webb left to check on nearby fighting, when two minutes later the
rocket hit. "There was an explosion. Smoke was billowing from the
building. I saw the bodies but could not tell the difference between the
dead and wounded because they were caked with white plaster dust
and blood. Rangers and police loaded them onto Jeeps, shielding them
with their own bodies."[6]

She omitted to say she rushed back and aided the wounded before writing her account.[7]

In "Life and Death of a Helicopter Crew," she used the personal backstories of the crew to allow her readers to appreciate the poignancy and significance of their deaths:

"Tay Ninh, Vietnam—There are times when the Vietnam War makes a reporter's fingers shake while holding a pencil. My pencil wobbles as I write the story of two young helicopter gunners I knew briefly as Smitty and Mac. I saw them go to war many times. Now I have seen their bodies come back and that is why this is a hard story for me."

Webb's goal, she wrote, was to go beyond "that impersonal language of an Army war report, words saying a chopper crashed and burned, all four crew members killed in action."[8]

She had spent days with the two men, traveling with them into action on their assault helicopter, riding high above the jungle where "wind tears at your clothes and flattens your face."

As the sole woman covering the military story full-time, Webb stood out. She was profiled with Catherine Leroy and four other women in a 1968 *Women's Wear Daily* article called "Women Cover the News, Too."

"There is a new breed of newspaper woman covering this war," wrote J. W. Cohn. "These girls in Vietnam ask no favors and want none. They cover the same assignments as the men reporters. They face the same dangers. . . . They write and they think like men. In the field they even dress like men. The last thing they want to do is write the 'woman's angle.' . . . Yet back in Saigon over a martini at the Caravelle Hotel bar, dressed in a simple cotton dress, these girls are just as feminine as any girl 'back home.'"

Cohn called these six women the "news hens" who had joined the "news hawks" in the Saigon press corps. His piece demonstrated the wide chasm in 1968 between traditional expectations of women and the new expectations women had for themselves.[9]

They all put on their game face for the world: they had all found their way to Vietnam, showed they were as good as the men and still found time to remain attractive.

One woman said she retained her femininity by only wearing blouses—not military gear—in the field. Another said it was a very good ego boost to be one of a few women among hundreds of men, and one said she was leaving Vietnam to get married because "you can't be a wife and a journalist and do both well."

Leroy and Webb, however, didn't play along with this scenario. Leroy used her voice to denounce the effect of the war. "This is a great calamity for everyone and especially the Vietnamese. The whites, including the French, have a great responsibility for this war. . . . As far as politics are concerned, men are mad and I am living in a man's world."

She conceded she loved fashion—she was French—and said that with her miniskirts and tight trousers, she had become Saigon's Twiggy, the posh British model of the go-go era.

Webb refused to answer any question whatsoever about being a woman. Instead, she warned about the underlying problems of the South Vietnamese. She complained about how loose regulation of US aid and supplies had encouraged corruption. "Everyone is taking part in it—Americans, Filipinos, not just the Vietnamese." She lamented that the United States was so late "to give M-16 rifles to Vietnamese troops. How long could you expect them to stand up to the Communists' AK 47s with the M-1 popgun."

The readers of *Women's Wear Daily* probably didn't know what to make of Webb's analysis of military hardware.

Webb hated being called a girl reporter; she felt it was a way to dismiss her accomplishments. Men were never described as boy correspondents, she would say; they were simply correspondents. She deflected attempts to draw distinctions between men and women. Whatever hardships and barriers she had faced and continued to face as a woman, she never referred to them.

She knew that if she alluded to any such issues, she would be greeted with taunts that women needed special favors to make it in a man's world. She did not want to be accused of using women's liberation as a crutch, which was how her male colleagues viewed feminism. To be called a women's libber was an insult: women's liberation was for those who couldn't make it unassisted. David Halberstam said admiringly of a woman reporter in Vietnam that she made it on her own, that she "didn't get her job through Gloria Steinem."[10] Webb pushed back against any suggestion that she relied on anything other than her own talent and work. She wrote she did not want to be known as "a six-foot, fat, pistol-whipping women's libber." Whenever she was asked, Webb replied: "I don't believe in women's liberation."[11]

She suffered the humiliations and biases of women of her era privately, until she finally had enough in 1976, one year after the war ended, when a new boss at UPI demanded repeatedly that she have an affair with him. When she refused, he made her life difficult. She complained to bosses in New York, but she only said she couldn't get along with him, reluctant to explain why.[12]

～ ～ ～

ON MAY 13, 1968, at the start of the American summer from hell, President Johnson ordered the beginning of tentative Vietnam peace talks as he had promised when he refused to run for reelection. Diplomats met at the imposing conference center on Avenue Kleber in Paris. Slowly, a deal took shape. By the middle of October, Johnson had agreed to halt all bombing of North Vietnam in exchange for Hanoi's pledge to engage in true peace talks with the South.

The press corps in Saigon knew that a breakthrough in peace talks could put Humphrey, the Democrat candidate, in the lead in the US presidential election scheduled for November and possibly end the war.

On October 30, 1968, six days before the election, the talks mysteriously halted. The South Vietnamese diplomats abruptly walked out. Secret files revealed many years later that Richard Nixon, the Republican presidential candidate, had convinced South Vietnamese president Nguyen Van Thieu to hold off on peace and wait for his election. In return, Nixon promised Thieu a better deal than the one offered by Johnson.[13] Nixon won the election.

It would take another seven years and more than twenty thousand additional American deaths before the war ended—with a victory for

Hanoi. By then, the Vietnam War had divided the United States as no conflict had since the Civil War. Nixon's eventual peace agreement in 1975 was nearly identical to the one proposed by Johnson.

~ ~ ~

SOON AFTER NIXON'S election, when the war was at a stalemate, Jeremy Webb arrived in Saigon for an extended stay with his sister. Kate's younger brother had flown from India after following the hippie trail from London to New Delhi. He wanted to test his skills as a novice reporter. Kate was happy to help him, essentially giving him the run of her apartment while she spent much of her time with Bob Stockton (not his real name), a handsome American soldier and Green Beret.

Jeremy could not believe his sister was in love, swooning along the boulevards of Saigon with Stockton, who seemed equally in love with her. They made a striking couple huddled in cafés, she with her deep brown eyes laughing at his tales of war.

Jeremy followed Kate on her journalist rounds, and soon UPI issued him press credentials. For all of Kate's talk about fitting in, it was clear to her brother that she still wasn't part of the pack. "She'd have a beer with them, she always likes a beer, but she wasn't socializing with them. She had intense conversations with her colleagues, but she had closer friendships with Vietnamese."

In her mind, Kate told Jeremy, she was covering the underreported story of the South Vietnamese. She went to the hospitals regularly to measure the ramifications of battle in Vietnamese life. She kept pushing UPI to cover the ARVN. She wrote about American soldiers losing their moral reference points, pointing to the practice of fragging, or attacks on a commanding officer. Jeremy was impressed that questionable characters showed up at her apartment and admitted to corruption. "Kate thought people wanted to talk to her partly because she was a woman."[14]

She was uncovering corruption at ever higher levels of the Vietnamese government when she was shot at near her home in Saigon in late 1968. The clumsy would-be assassin missed. "I got a couple of pot shots fired at me a couple of times and at one stage UPI took me out [of Saigon] temporarily because there was word of a contract man coming to get me."

She felt more at ease in the field, even when she was interviewing and reporting under dangerous situations. When it was time to file, she was adept at using the clunky field phone to call in the story to Saigon. Her calls zipped through the military relays in part because the soldiers were surprised to hear her extremely soft female voice. Once her call reached the bureau, though, her signature whisper was a problem. The UPI subeditors would routinely shout: "Kate, speak up, I can't hear you."[15]

During the summer of 1969, officials in Washington privately conceded that the war was lost or at the least that Americans could not win. Nixon began planning a phased withdrawal of American forces, a process he called Vietnamization. The war would gradually be handed over to the South Vietnamese. His first withdrawal was 150,000 troops.

Webb was excited about covering the story of the South Vietnamese taking control of their war. It dovetailed with her understanding of how this war would be won or lost. She shared all of this with Bob Stockton.

Jeremy saw Kate relax with Stockton and enjoy the sophisticated side of Saigon. The couple strolled down the tree-lined avenues hand in hand. They dined at fine French restaurants—the Champs-Élysées on the rooftop of the Caravelle Hotel and the Aterbea. They crossed into Cholon to eat at Eskimo, for the best Chinese food in the city. The Chinese quarter had calmed down since the Buddhist uprisings, when FitzGerald and Daniel Ellsberg had been surrounded by a mob. Webb even went to movies, pleasures she had previously denied herself in favor of obsessive working habits. Jeremy noticed the effect Stockton had produced on Kate: "She spent so much time with him. He was so impressive."

Stockton befriended Jeremy, and Jeremy in turn told Kate that he liked Stockton better than the boyfriends she had in Australia because he made her "terribly happy."

Stockton's tour in Vietnam was coming to an end during the summer of 1969. He asked her to marry him. It wasn't his first proposal; Kate had previously refused when Stockton was stationed in Vietnam, and there was no immediate chance of his return to the US. She was dedicated to her career. Webb felt she was riding a wave, "surfing in and out, sometimes a little ahead, sometimes a little behind the headlines. Front page adrenalin kept [me] on the crest."

But after a year of dating, of emerging from her deep loneliness and feeling joy in Stockton's companionship, she gave in and said yes. In the end, she "was relieved to have finally surrendered" to a man, even if it meant she would be moving to the United States and giving up all that mattered professionally to become an army wife who put her husband's career above all. There would be no room to establish herself in a country where she was a foreigner and within a profession where women were having to file lawsuits to be given jobs half as exciting as hers in Vietnam.

Webb resigned from UPI and packed her bags in the autumn of 1969 for the move to Fort Bragg, North Carolina.

When she and Stockton arrived in the United States, Kate called her sister, who was living in New York where her husband was posted as a diplomat at the United Nations. It was the beginning of the General Assembly, and Rachel was surprised to hear from her sister.

"We're here—we're getting married," Kate said over the phone. Rachel asked to speak to Stockton. She told him one thing: "You have to treat my sister well." She was worried, as always, about Kate. Stockton said he would.

When Webb arrived at Fort Bragg, she walked into a full-blown nightmare. Stockton was married. He had lied all the way through their affair. Worse, Stockton pretended nothing was wrong; he said they would marry after his wife agreed to a divorce. He kept Webb hidden in a hotel room, where she waited, going over their time in Vietnam, asking herself how she could have been so oblivious.

For days, Stockton went to his job at the base as if all was well and then returned to the hotel late at night, wearing his dress uniform. He would tell her to be patient. But soon Kate heard him on the telephone telling his wife he was away on field exercises. She knew it was over.

Soon enough, Stockton said good-bye to Webb. He had chosen to stay with his wife and was abandoning Webb in a foreign country with nothing.

She felt as if she were dead. Not sad or broken, simply dead. Rachel wanted to help, but "there was not a lot of communication with Kate at that point."

She had one goal: return to Vietnam and the world she had been persuaded to leave behind. She pleaded with UPI to give her work, anywhere, so she could earn enough money for a plane ticket back to Saigon. They found her a job in Pittsburgh where she spent a long northern winter. She befriended Vietnam vets in bars, which she knew was strange. The cold was intolerable after years in the tropics. The stories she wrote were pedestrian. Bored, she studied Chinese with a private tutor. She steeled herself to survive, nothing more. After the three deaths early in her life—Vicki and her parents—Webb had created what she called her method of living through sorrow. "I just cut off each part of my past life. No regrets." Now she attempted to cut off Stockton, and she drank to help the shell harden. She described this phase as searching for "my quiet soul." In fact, she was hiding from her own despair.[16]

Escape came when the war exploded again.

In May 1970, President Nixon ordered the American invasion into Cambodia. He went on live television to announce the incursion, as he called it, saying it would be short and lead to the end of the Vietnam War. He said this would be accomplished by American and South Vietnamese troops finding and destroying the headquarters of Vietnamese communism inside the Cambodian border.

Students across the United States were angry, appalled, furious; Nixon had been elected to end the war, not expand it. They carried out the largest student protest in American history. Expanding the war to get out of Vietnam sounded like double-talk. At Kent State in Ohio, national guardsmen fired live ammunition into a crowd of protestors.

Four students were killed, and nine were injured. A searing photograph of a young woman crying beside her murdered friend became the symbol of American youth outrage. A few days later, policemen killed protesting students at Jackson State in Mississippi. On the campus, the Vietnam War had turned National Guard soldiers and policemen against their own.

UPI sent Webb from nearby Pittsburgh to cover the Kent State disaster. She reported with a sense of urgency and wrote her way into the good graces of the wire service. Two weeks later, she was on an airplane to Phnom Penh, Cambodia, taking the number-two job in the new UPI bureau. She was a local hire and had to pay her own ticket, which she did without complaining. Where better to recover than the war and witnessing more suffering?

The student protestors were right to be suspicious. The war in Cambodia lasted five years and ended in catastrophe. Kate Webb, who covered the debacle, became a legend.

Catherine Leroy about to jump with the 173rd Airborne in Operation Junction City, South Vietnam, February 22, 1967. © Bob Cole. Courtesy Dotation Catherine Leroy.

French photographer Gilles Caron caught an unguarded Catherine Leroy upon their return from a helicopter offensive, Vietnam, December 1967. © Fondation Gilles Caron

Frankie Fitzgerald.
© Getty.

Frances FitzGerald reports from the National Liberation Front in South Vietnam, 1973. (Her colleague is David Greenway of the Washington Post.) Courtesy Frankie Fitzgerald.

Kate Webb. © Getty.

Kate Webb at a news conference on May 1, 1971, the day she was released from captivity by the North Vietnamese in Cambodia. She is wearing her Chinese good luck medal. © AP.

Catherine Leroy photographs her jump during Operation Junction City, South Vietnam, February 22, 1967. Photograph by Catherine Leroy. © Dotation Catherine Leroy.

Evacuation of a mortally wounded Marine, Hill 484, South Vietnam, October 1966. Photograph by Catherine Leroy. © Dotation Catherine Leroy.

The Vietnam War, c. 1967. Photograph by Catherine Leroy. © Dotation Catherine Leroy.

Fleeing civilians during Tet Offensive, Hue, South Vietnam, February 1968. Photograph by Catherine Leroy. © Dotation Catherine Leroy.

US Navy corpsman Vernon Wike helps a dying Marine on Hill 881 near Khe Sanh, South Vietnam, April/May 1967. Photograph by Catherine Leroy. © Dotation Catherine Leroy.

US soldier during a search and destroy operation, South Vietnam, c. 1967. Photograph by Catherine Leroy. © Dotation Catherine Leroy.

CHAPTER NINE

Where Does the Story End?

O N HER OWN IN NEW YORK, FRANKIE FITZGERALD REMAINED a journalist and wrote occasional articles about Vietnam while she completed her book. A particularly meaningful piece was her review of *Last Reflections on a War* by Bernard Fall for the magazine *Commentary*. She lauded the collection of his essays published after his death and demonstrated why his voice mattered.

Twice a refugee, Fall "took nothing for granted," she wrote. His books and articles reflected his sympathy for soldiers, both the guerillas fighting for their independence and the French fighting for their lost world. The Americans, Fall wrote, seemed lost with their "abstract theories unrelated to the local situation."[1]

But writing in New York City with its temptations and distractions was proving close to impossible even for the highly disciplined Fitz-Gerald—especially with her social and family obligations and the perpetual shadow of her mother. She applied for and won a residency in the fall of 1969 at the MacDowell Colony, the renowned artists' retreat in rural New Hampshire. She wanted nothing more than absolute silence and found it in her cottage surrounded by woods and meadows.

She likened it to a "beautiful desert island . . . silence and time for the most unadulterated form of concentration."[2]

FitzGerald had returned to a life of privilege.

She met her next beau at MacDowell, the author Alan Lelchuk.[3] So much for unadulterated concentration. Lelchuk was writing his first novel—*American Mischief*—and was considered a bright young talent and something of a protégé of Philip Roth.[4] A Brooklyn-born intellectual, Jewish, bearded with a mop of long, unruly hair, Lelchuk was nearly the absolute opposite of Ward Just. Yet as she had with Just, FitzGerald fell for Lelchuk within a few days of meeting him. She agreed to move to Cambridge, Massachusetts, at the end of her MacDowell residency and live in his dilapidated apartment at 6 Centre Street, about five blocks from Harvard Square. Lelchuk welcomed her with the warning that he was not a man of money: he was living on the low salary of an assistant professor at Brandeis University. They shared expenses. "We moved her out of New York in my station wagon and she lived in my apartment with my make-shift furniture. She got the big study; I used the little one. All I cared about was my desk."

FitzGerald had made her escape. Her new lifestyle was the closest she ever got to counterculture, though FitzGerald did want the apartment painted. She chose the colors, and Lelchuk hired some students to do the work, surprised at the difference the paint and some basic house cleaning made.

Physically, Cambridge had changed little since FitzGerald graduated seven years earlier. Harvard Square, Lowell House, and Memorial Hall still defined the university as they had for decades if not centuries. Socially and politically, though, it was a different world. FitzGerald had landed in a city and community that now considered Vietnam of paramount importance.

The antiwar movement had taken hold on campuses across the country and Harvard was no exception. As early as 1966, Harvard students had protested the presence of Defense Secretary Robert McNamara when he refused to publicly discuss the war when he visited. After he addressed a small, private group, hundreds of students blocked his exit. As a compromise one student was allowed to ask a question: Why is the United States killing so many Vietnamese civilians? McNamara answered cryptically: "I was tougher then. I am tougher now." No one understood what he meant.

The editorial board of the *Crimson* student newspaper wrote an apology to McNamara for the disruption.

The next year, as the American involvement grew, any sheen of good manners among the antiwar students disappeared. They blockaded a representative of Dow Chemical Company, which was responsible for producing poisonous napalm for the US military. After the 1968 Tet Offensive, the campus grew more militant still. The university administration agreed to student demands to add Afro-American studies to the curriculum and to reduce the status of the military's campus Reserve Officer Training Corps (ROTC) program to an elective.

In the spring of 1969, just before FitzGerald moved to Cambridge, antiwar students broke into University Hall, and expelled eight deans, and spent the night rifling official files and occupying the building. The next morning Harvard president Nathan Pusey called in the police and state troopers. Jean Bennett, a student inside the occupied building, said each of the troopers "seemed a giant; each cradled a hungry baton."

After twenty-five minutes of "clubbing and bloodshed," the students were evicted. Nearly two hundred were arrested. Frank Rich, a student who would become an award-winning critic and writer, witnessed the eviction. "The arrival of police in military formation, helmets glinting in the Yard's lights, was terrifying. The screaming, the trampling, the blood on the steps that followed would set off not just a strike but months of angry debate and aimless seething among students and faculty."[5]

To their critics, these Harvard students were elite cowards protected from the draft who refused to fight for their country. The students argued back that they were protesting because they didn't want anyone to fight in the Vietnam War.

The women in the protests were now truly Harvard students. Unlike FitzGerald's class, young women at Radcliffe now received degrees from Harvard College. A few Radcliffe women wore white armbands on their graduation robes to signify opposition to the war.[6]

FitzGerald's class was among the last to be connected to the hidebound era of the 1950s, when the college had banned wearing pants, much less jeans, on campus and encouraged limited aspirations. One of FitzGerald's classmates wrote that her goal upon graduation was to "give lovely dinner parties with wonderful conversations." Living close to campus, FitzGerald was fully aware that she was breaking with the expectations of her gender and class again.[7]

With the work ethic of her Puritan ancestors, FitzGerald devoted her days and many of her nights to her book. She didn't skimp on cigarettes or exercise, jogging on the streets of Cambridge in all weather. And she told herself that her goal was doable and made sense: "The war kept going on and on, and I kept getting more and more furious, and I thought I would have to write a book about it. It wasn't a career choice. It was a desire to tell people what the place was like, what the Vietnamese are like, and what the US was doing in Vietnam. That's all."[8]

Besides Peter Davison, the publisher, her manuscript was edited by Robert Manning, who had been the editor and champion of her seminal *Atlantic* magazine piece, and Michael Janeway, an old friend and one of FitzGerald's classmates who moved in the same social circles.

Writing a first book is daunting no matter how talented or organized or imaginative the author. FitzGerald's routine was circumscribed. She worked at her desk in her home study. She did research in the Widener Library at Harvard. She went back to her desk to write letters to experts. Then she repeated the routine.

FitzGerald identified China, Vietnam's first overlord, as the main impetus behind Vietnam's centuries-long struggle for independence and as the country that would always be at the forefront of Vietnam's worries. She positioned the Americans as the latest in a parade of powerful foreigners disrupting the lives of the Vietnamese. It was a dramatic departure from the way anyone else saw the war. Her historical reach was unheard of at the time when even American experts, as well as journalists, chronicled the Vietnam War as primarily a conflict that grew out of the 1950s clash between the West and communism, with a head nod toward the battle of Dien Bien Phu and the defeat of French colonial rule. Her editors at the *Atlantic Monthly* were worried.

Lelchuk was not. Even though he knew next to nothing about Vietnam, he regularly read her pages as they came out of her typewriter. "First rate quality. She is extremely smart and wrote beautiful prose. But she would get these nasty notes from her editors and didn't know if she was doing well."

Lelchuk, who was busy writing his novel, told her he was appalled by their harshness. "I said this is wrong and dumb. When she got hammered, I would say they're wrong. You're better than they are. . . . I think the way they treated her at the Atlantic Press was male chauvinism at its finest: without proclaiming she's a woman and she can't do this, they wrote to her in a way they wouldn't write to a man."[9]

Another letter from Davison epitomized Lelchuk's point.

He wrote: "So far in our working together on this book, I have suggested that you keep working and regard the completed material as first-draft only. I now begin to see I was wrong. The present material is pre-first draft; it has not yet got to the point where an editor can do anything with it. It is so rough, so lacking in clarity, that all we can do is throw up our hands.

"Frankie, you have to solve the problem of articulating the Vietnam problem, both in the organization and the style of your book. I think you have a lot of work to do before solving it. If you believe you should keep forging ahead before you solve it, simply to cover the area you want the book eventually to cover, by all means do so; but when that is done, I am afraid you have another task ahead of you that is at least as daunting. . . . Yours ever, Peter."[10]

This was Davison's assessment two years after FitzGerald began the book. Lelchuk was furious and told her she should change publishers. FitzGerald listened. She considered Lelchuk very supportive: "I sort of went under his wing." But she stayed with Davison. She doubted any other publisher would be interested in her book no matter what Lelchuk said. She felt loyal to the editors who were working hard on her manuscript, no matter how disparaging their comments. "They were very involved with the war. They had this one book under their control. Really, they were close to me."

After the death of Paul Mus, FitzGerald asked John McAlister to be the Vietnam expert to review her manuscript. He wrote that he was disappointed "that the brilliant and profoundly impressive FitzGerald style" was missing and detailed in five pages how he thought it could be recovered.[11] In a subsequent letter, he was supportive and offered to help her organize the material. He always added friendly notes. "Excuse me for being so grim. Hope to see you soon. Love, John."[12]

She also turned to Professor Richard Solomon, a China specialist at the University of Michigan, who commented on her draft pages, suggesting she "do more with a description of how the foreign presence (American) dislocates the indigenous (South Vietnamese) power situation."[13]

With each critique, FitzGerald reexamined and sometimes reshaped sentences and chapters. She clarified and reorganized large chunks of the material, but the substance and the overall narrative arc never truly changed. Like nearly every writer, she was willing to rewrite drafts until she uncovered the polished manuscript she knew she could write.

That didn't mean her doubts disappeared. Over the ensuing months and years, she routinely wondered if her book would ever be published or would be noticed if it were.

FitzGerald was under other pressure. Henry Kissinger, who had become the national security adviser for President Nixon, telephoned her several times. He said he heard she was writing a book on the war and wanted to explain his policies. With Professor Popkin, she visited Kissinger in January 1970. She hoped to convince him to end the clandestine CIA Phoenix Program that targeted civilians rather than soldiers in the hunt for supporters of the Viet Cong. US and South Vietnamese soldiers were permitted to torture during interrogations and to assassinate Vietnamese civilians suspected of ties to the Viet

Cong. By the time of her visit, some twenty thousand civilians had been murdered.

She made her argument to Kissinger in person and received the predictable answer: "Of course, he didn't agree."[14] Four months later, she wrote to him after the US invasion of Cambodia. Again, she argued against US policy. Kissinger answered:

"Dear Frankie: Thank you for writing. It is not the time now to discuss what happened. But when this is over I would like to see you and talk and see what healing is possible. Warm regards, Henry A. Kissinger."[15]

Even in Boston she dutifully fulfilled family and social obligations. Her mother came to visit, and Lelchuk felt he was under scrutiny, that Marietta Tree was judging whether he was worthy of her daughter. He later remarked, "There was always a kind of tension for Frankie, spoken or unspoken, about being a socialite's daughter and being an intellectual."[16]

At Christmas Lelchek and FitzGerald flew to her family's villa in Barbados where Lelchek met Ronald Tree. "The social demands were constant," he recalled.

Somehow FitzGerald completed her manuscript. It had grown to four hundred well-written and well-argued pages divided into three sections—the Vietnamese, the Americans, and the Saigon government—followed by a conclusion.

When FitzGerald wrote the conclusion in 1971, the war still seemed endless. Instead of reaching a settlement at the Paris negotiations, as he had promised, Nixon had expanded the war into Cambodia.

"In the first three years of Nixon's administration fifteen thousand Americans were killed. . . . [South Vietnam] lost more men than they had lost in the three previous years . . . there were more civilian casualties than there had ever been before—that is, Laotians and Cambodians as well as Vietnamese." FitzGerald asked in the book: "How is that possible?"

⌐ ⌐ ⌐

HER PUBLISHER TOLD her she needed a title. FitzGerald went to her bookshelf and pulled out her copy of the I Ching, looking for inspiration.

"What I did was to open a page of the Chinese Book of Changes at random and I found Fire in the Lake: the image of revolution and of coming of spring."

She had previously explained the fire in the lake symbol in a *New York Book Review* article.

"That was it for me."[17]

She sent the final draft to an expert who finally gave her full-throated encouragement: "Let me say that I think you write beautifully, I love many of your very linguistic images, the book is full of valuable insights that I haven't had the time to applaud in jotting down comments. I hope 'Fire in the Lake' will be read by many, especially in Washington."

That rare early praise would prove to be prescient of the book's general reception.

But before she sent the manuscript to the publisher, FitzGerald, like the rest of the country, was shocked by the publication in the *New York Times* of a three-year-old secret history of the war based on highly classified government documents. The first installment was published on June 13, 1971. The Nixon administration asked for an immediate halt to publication, saying it threatened national security. The *New York Times* refused and published two more days of the study, along with supporting documents, that laid bare decades of lies told to Congress and the public by successive American presidents, beginning with Harry S. Truman. The White House obtained an injunction against the newspaper to end further publication.

The *New York Times* had to comply, but other newspapers, including the *Washington Post*, stood by the *Times* and began publishing parts of the Pentagon Papers themselves. The White House was furious and pushed the case to the Supreme Court. Arguments were heard a mere two weeks later, on June 26. The Supreme Court ruled in favor of the newspapers, and the full report with supporting documents was printed.

Two days before that decision, Daniel Ellsberg publicly admitted that he had leaked the secret history to the *New York Times* and surrendered to the FBI in Boston. FitzGerald's old friend had been behind what became a pivotal event in the politics of Vietnam, strengthening the opposition by disclosing that officials knew there was little hope of winning the war.

Ellsberg had helped write the secret report at the request of Defense Secretary Robert McNamara. Working on the study and watching the subsequent invasion of Cambodia helped convince Ellsberg that the American war was unwinnable and wrong. He and his wife, Patricia Marx, visited FitzGerald in Cambridge in 1970, where he told her of his change of heart and his despair over the war. But he didn't say a word about the secret Pentagon Papers.

At that point, Ellsberg still had hopes that Congress would force the Nixon administration to end the war. He had helped author memoranda for Kissinger on options to withdraw. Nixon and Kissinger rejected that advice. Eventually, Ellsberg decided to leak the Pentagon Papers. "In releasing the Pentagon Papers I acted in hope I still hold," he wrote then, "that truths that changed me could help Americans free themselves and other victims from our longest war."[18]

Although she had no direct role in his release of the papers, as one of his first journalist friends to articulate the reasons why the United States should withdraw from Vietnam, Ellsberg said FitzGerald helped challenge his thinking over the years.

The summer of 1971 became the summer of the Pentagon Papers.

President Nixon was so upset by the release of the papers that, as a direct consequence, the White House set in motion schemes and methods, which eventually led to the Watergate crisis, forming a secret group called the plumbers that broke into the office of Ellsberg's psychiatrist to find dirt on him. The plumbers would later break into the Watergate offices of the Democratic National Committee.

FitzGerald examined those thousands of pages, documenting the secret history of US involvement in Vietnam, to determine whether she needed to alter her own book. She did not.

Finally, she handed in the completed manuscript in June 1971. After years of strain, doubt, and determination, her burden was lifted. She ended her life of isolation in Cambridge and moved back to New York. She also ended her romance with Lelchuk. He said their passions had cooled, but he would have continued on. She "felt bad about it."

Then she escaped to Paris. From there she flew to Saigon in September on a magazine assignment and asked her editor to send the edited manuscript to the Hotel Continental. She had missed Vietnam. She traveled with an interpreter who spoke excellent French and visited villages and provinces that had been off-limits in her much earlier stay. She was stunned by the level of destruction. "It broke my heart to see what had taken place. . . . The ugliness is stunning. The parts that were so beautiful in 1966 are now a wasteland of cast-off American equipment and barbed wire."[19]

While reporting on the new blight of Vietnam, FitzGerald began a wartime romance with Kevin Buckley, the *Newsweek* Saigon bureau chief and a man almost typecast to be her lover. Buckley had also been raised in New York City. They were both Ivy League: he graduated from Yale in 1962, the same year Frankie graduated from Radcliffe. They were a matched set: darkly handsome Kevin, sleek blond Frankie.

To add to the aura, Buckley was one of the original members of the informal Yale Saigon Club begun by Ambassador Ellsworth Bunker in 1968. All graduates of Yale—diplomats, aid workers, journalists, and clergymen—were welcome to these club dinner parties at the ambassador's residence.[20]

But like FitzGerald, Buckley's background did not preclude him from writing critical pieces questioning the conduct of the United States in Vietnam. Buckley was working on a monthslong investigation of US military atrocities when he met FitzGerald in 1971.[21]

The courtship began while she was traveling around South Vietnam. On a day when FitzGerald was expected back in Saigon, Buckley left her a short note at the front desk of the Continental Hotel; a clerk put the message in the cubbyhole with her room key.

This was the same front desk where countless journalists looked forward to finding cables and messages waiting for them and where Catherine Leroy was given mail privileges to receive letters from home.

Buckley's note read:

"Frankie—I have nothing to do this weekend. I want to see you and hear about lobsters and everything else from Nha Trang. Please phone or come by when you get back. If it's this evening, come up for dinner if possible please."[22]

By the time she returned to New York to correct the proofs of her book, they were trading letters. In one letter she invited Kevin to the family home in Barbados, ending it abruptly saying:

"Have just this moment had a call from Michael J. to say that I must finish the galleys tomorrow, not the 25th. So sadly, I must return to that immediately . . . I love you, Frankie."[23]

～ ～ ～

KATE WEBB'S RETURN to the war zone was a reprieve, an escape from the stultifying life in Pittsburg and the brutal betrayal of Bob Stockton. She arrived dressed with attitude, a woman starting again and rejecting any pity. Her hair was now fashionably long, grazing her shoulders. She wore an Yves Saint Laurent miniskirt and high-heel sandals that showed off her slender legs. Even her underwear was couture: Italian silk in purple and fuchsia, gifts from her sister, Rachel.[24]

She landed at Phnom Penh's Pochentong Airport in July 1970, nearly one year before FitzGerald returned to Saigon. Farmers were ploughing their rice paddies, and armies were preparing for battle. The graceful capital was largely untouched by war; barbed wire had yet to snake around the city as it did in Saigon. Heavy barricades were few. The Royal Palace stood sentry on the esplanade where the four arms of the Bassac and Mekong Rivers crossed on their way to the sea. Twisting spires of Buddhist temples punctuated the skyline, and flame trees shaded the boulevards. Food stands set up along the tiled city sidewalks sold her favorite sour plum soup. The handsome art deco Grand Market, built by the French between the World Wars, spread its protective arms over farmers and artisans selling their wares—the sarongs and silks Webb preferred.

The French colonial veneer added the glamour Webb remembered from her reporting trip three years earlier when she had covered the visit of Jacqueline Kennedy. Now the city's French quarter had become press headquarters.

The Cambodian front of the Vietnam War was too dangerous, too new, and too unpredictable for full-time journalists to be resident in Phnom Penh. Instead, news organizations sent reporters living in Saigon, Singapore, or Hong Kong to Cambodia for one or two weeks and occasionally months. To ensure these correspondents and photographers had a bed and a place to work, many news organizations rented rooms and studios at the Hotel Royale on a permanent basis. Reporters nearly took over the hotel, the red-tiled grande dame of Phnom Penh, catty-corner from the Cathedral of Notre Dame. News organizations rented the hotel's air-conditioned rooms, large studios, and bungalows to house a rotating staff of reporters. Webb moved in full-time.

As a rare resident, Webb rented a two-bedroom garden bungalow shaded by flowering trees. It also boasted French-era plumbing and a creaking ceiling fan. The first thing she did was cut off her hair again— what she called her GI cut—and pull out her khaki pants and cotton shirts. The Yves Saint Laurent was saved for embassy occasions.

The atmosphere at the Royale was a cross between a private club and a permanent crisis center. Walking up the broad steps of the genteel yellow stucco hotel into the cool entry, journalists loitered at the front desk waiting to see who had heard what news. In one direction were the duplex studios with wire service correspondents. Just off the lobby was the well-worn dark teak staircase to the rooms. Straight ahead was the swimming pool and beyond that Le Cyrène restaurant, all gathering spots for journalists at day's end after stories were filed.

White-jacketed waiters dragged ice blocks wrapped in coarse raffia rope across the lawn to Le Cyrène, where they chopped the ice into spears for beer and gin and tonics, the favored apéritifs of the journalists. At dinner, journalists ate well from a menu of fresh crayfish and lobster. At least once they ordered *omlette norwegienne* for dessert, just because baked Alaska seemed so out of place in a tropical war zone. Arguments spread across tables.

The first reaction of many newly arrived journalists was that they had arrived in the pages "of a Graham Greene novel."[25]

France was still a cultural force in Cambodia, albeit a fading one. French was the country's second language: English was rarely heard. Ordering morning coffee at Le Café de la Post, locals called out to *la boyesse*, the colonial term for a waitress derived from the English, who addressed waitstaff as boy, and altered to the feminine French form. French wives patronized tailors who could sew duplicates of ensembles pictured in pages torn from *Paris Match*. French cafés offered the equivalent of comfort foods: couscous, curry a l'anglaise, and spaghetti bolognaise—with a dash of marijuana if you knew the owner. The French left their mark in things large and small, designing Cambodian landmarks—the royal palace and the royal museum—and filling Cambodian government positions with French bureaucrats. Foreign-language newspapers, books, and magazines were in French, rarely English.

War had come so quickly, without a buildup, that Cambodia was slow to accept the dangers and the need to mobilize as did the foreigners. Routine life in the city disguised the upheaval in the countryside. It was easy to be delusional.

Unlike in Vietnam, the foreign reporters covered the Cambodian campaign of the Vietnam War face-to-face with Cambodians and without American intermediaries. The American diplomatic presence was small. There were no American troops fighting, no massive military infrastructure to navigate the war, and no crowds of contractors and hangers-on.

In this atmosphere reporters fastened on to the absurd and the dark. The palindromic leader Lon Nol would ask for guidance from his favorite Buddhist monk and sprinkle "magic sand" around the city's perimeter to ward off the enemy. Cambodian soldiers in Lon Nol's army marched off to battle wearing scarves covered with prayers and sucking amulets of the Buddha. Prayers and drawings tattooed across their chests and arms were works of beauty meant to protect them from the evil enemy. Ominously, Lon Nol ordered the massacre of ethnic Vietnamese who had lived peacefully in the country for decades to delineate who he thought was the enemy. Reporters discovered corpses floating down the Mekong.

The city was referred to in countless newspaper articles as a "charming Asian backwater" grown ugly by war. Its beauty had blossomed when Cambodia was the oasis of peace in Indochina, the only country officially declared neutral and shielded from the violence by the 1954 Geneva Accords. Cambodia was also the only country left undivided.

Norodom Sihanouk, the elected Cambodian leader, considered neutrality the only chance for his country to survive the war being waged in neighboring Vietnam. That mattered little to the Eisenhower administration. To undermine that neutrality, the United States used its financial and military muscle to try to pull Sihanouk into war, conspiring with Cambodia's neighbors and Cambodian dissidents. In 1958, Eisenhower signed a secret directive to "encourage individuals and groups in Cambodia who oppose dealing with the Communist bloc and who would serve to broaden the political base in Cambodia," authorizing repeated "covert operations designed to assist in the achievement of US objectives in Southeast Asia."[26]

This Cold War mind-set, begun with legitimate fear after Joseph Stalin's takeover of Eastern Europe, was outdated and did not apply so neatly to Southeast Asia.

Sihanouk was aware of American designs. His country was in the geographic center of the larger Vietnam conflict. Thailand, its neighbor to the west, had opened its airfields to US fighter jets. Laos in the north was at war and part of the Ho Chi Minh Trail. South Vietnam, the neighbor to the east, was the front line.

Both sides saw Cambodia as a key to victory.

China and the Soviet Union courted Sihanouk to prevent him from siding with the United States. In return, China promised to stay out of Cambodia's internal politics, which meant providing no support for the overthrow of Sihanouk by the small Cambodian Communist Party known as the Khmer Rouge. The Chinese and North Vietnamese kept their word as long as the prince was in power.

Sihanouk was less successful with the United States. He feared any military relationship with the US, especially after Washington approved the overthrow of Cambodia's ally Ngo Dinh Diem. In response, Sihanouk renounced all US aid in 1963. The prince's strategy worked as long as he could balance the unforgiving pressure from both sides, offering each concessions, allowing the Vietnamese communists of the North and the noncommunists in the South to use Cambodia's border region to attack each other.

Through the 1960s, as the American war escalated dramatically in Vietnam, Sihanouk became known as "the prince who walked the tightrope." He was a recognized leader of the world nonaligned movement. His outsized personality, intelligence, charm, and humor made him welcome in international forums. Few other Asian leaders were as popular on the global scene. His prestige gave Cambodia an outsized voice.

Maintaining political peace within Cambodia was tricky. Sihanouk had formidable advantages that blinded him to his weaknesses. A dazzling politician, Sihanouk had won every election since independence by skillfully outmaneuvering, buying off, and sometimes even executing his rivals. Even though he abdicated the throne to run for election, he remained a member of the royal family with all the prestige it implied as well as his status as the father of the independent nation. He was nearly revered in the countryside; he called the villagers "his people," passing out gifts on regular forays to the provinces. However, he did little to improve the near-feudal conditions of much of rural Cambodia, a state of affairs his opponents would exploit.

Dissent began to grow in the cities, where elites, intellectuals, and the business community were growing tired of the prince's rule and its attendant corruption. Younger Cambodians, especially those educated overseas, chafed under Sihanouk's old-fashioned autocratic rule and his need to be at the center of Cambodia, even starring and directing in his own movies. Some wanted a truly democratic government; others wanted modern development.

Yet the majority appreciated the quality of life under Sihanouk. Education was prioritized. Racism was rejected. And the middle class was expanding. The arts flourished under Sihanouk's patronage. He resisted the rampant development in countries like Thailand, where he felt the culture was disfigured and the poor no better off. Above all, Sihanouk was popular because he kept Cambodia at peace while its neighbors were engulfed in war.

The turning point came in 1968 when the United States' pledge to find peace only led to more war.

When Kate Webb covered Mrs. Kennedy's visit in 1967, few reporters realized Sihanouk was attempting to smooth US-Cambodian relations as the Vietnam War took another deadly leap, putting his country at greater risk.

Once President Johnson began peace negotiations with North Vietnam in 1968, Sihanouk had hoped that the war could be ended before it was too late. If a peace accord had been signed then, the political tension inside Cambodia would have relaxed, and the Khmer Rouge would have remained insignificant.

But the peace efforts failed, in part because Nixon had a different plan to end the war and it did not include continuing Johnson's initiative. Instead, Nixon opened secret discussions between Henry Kissinger, his national security adviser, and Le Duc Tho, a top North Vietnamese official. Those were the only talks that mattered. Kissinger probed for North Vietnam's breaking point and even suggested Nixon was prone to "madman" behavior and might order a nuclear attack if they didn't accept American conditions for peace.

Simultaneously, Nixon began a secret bombing campaign on Cambodia's eastern border in 1969. The Pentagon was convinced that destroying Vietnamese communist sanctuaries inside Cambodia would turn the war around, or at least buy Washington time for an honorable withdrawal. Code-named Menu, the air campaign lasted fourteen months. The US flew more than 3,500 B-52 raids over neutral Cambodia, rationalizing the escalation because North Vietnam had already broken Cambodia's neutral status. Villages were scattered in the area, but MACV did not release figures on the numbers killed. The Cambodian government filed protests against the bombing to the United Nations but to no avail.[27]

~ ~ ~

THE NEW PRESSURES from Nixon's war escalated Cambodia's internal political crisis. Cambodia's elite were frightened by Sihanouk's openness to the North Vietnamese communists who were encroaching more deeply into Cambodian territory. They were shipping supplies to the Viet Cong through Cambodia's port and then trucking the aid overland. The prince himself became more desperate in his search for a balance that eluded him.

Exhausted, Sihanouk took his first vacation in three years, leaving for a French spa in March 1970. While he was away three officials—his defense minister, a royal prince, and the head of the National Assembly—led a coup d'état and overthrew him, declaring Cambodia a republic, the Khmer Republic.

For the first time in fifteen years, Sihanouk was no longer in charge. The new leaders immediately ended the country's neutrality. Lon Nol, the former defense minister and the leading voice of the new government, ordered the closure of the embassies of North Vietnam and the Viet Cong within forty-eight hours and the withdrawal of their troops. The US congratulated the new regime and offered generous aid. Most Cambodians presumed the United States had promised Lon Nol support before the coup.[28]

Fighting broke out on Cambodia's eastern border when Vietnamese communist troops refused to retreat. Lon Nol publicly appealed to any country to help rid Cambodia of the Vietnamese communist menace. On cue, President Nixon answered and in May invaded Cambodia, without giving the Lon Nol government advance notice. In this haphazard fashion, Cambodia became the last country brought into America's war.

Sihanouk's worst nightmare had come to pass. Nixon pushed the American war into Cambodia and thereby opened the door to the Khmer Rouge.

~ ~ ~

DESPITE THE TURMOIL, Webb felt at home in Phnom Penh. The insistent heat, the slow smiles, and the metallic scent of insecticide spray were as familiar as the morning military briefings, where successful operations dissolved into routs from one day to the next.

By the time she arrived in late July 1970, the American military strategy had already backfired. Bombing the Vietnamese communists on the eastern border had not pushed them back into North Vietnam. Instead, they had moved deeper into Cambodia, capturing half the country. The Khmer National Armed Forces, known as FANK in its French acronym, were outclassed. Bloated with new student recruits, many inadequately trained on the capital city's golf course, FANK soldiers fell back or were mowed down in province after province. The American forces withdrew by the end of July and returned to Vietnam, leaving FANK on its own except for American air support.

The superior North Vietnamese army remained to fight FANK, which allowed the neophyte Khmer Rouge time to train and recruit.

The resulting chaos hit journalists hard. As front lines disappeared in the relentless advance of the Vietnamese, journalists were caught in the middle. No theater of the Vietnam War proved more dangerous than the Cambodia campaign. In South Vietnam, US military helicopters ferried journalists to and from battlegrounds and US military hospitals cared for them if they were injured. The huge American presence provided the intelligence and information that kept most journalists from making fatal mistakes.

Congress mandated a small US presence in Cambodia. Lawmakers had never authorized an American expansion. The Gulf of Tonkin Resolution—the casus belli in Vietnam—only gave permission to fight there. Nixon countered that his role as commander in chief allowed him to send in American troops. Furious, the Senate passed the Cooper-Church Amendment, which forbade any new commitment of US troops to a wider war beyond Vietnam without the consent of the US Congress. Nixon withdrew ground forces by the end of July, making the issue moot. Then Congress passed a law forbidding US military even to advise Cambodians in the war.[29]

As a result, journalists were on their own. For transport they rented Mercedes sedans once used for tourists at the temples of Angkor Wat. They relied on military intelligence from the Cambodian military, delivered in French, since there was no MACV. The American and French embassies were helpful, but they could barely keep up with the rapidly moving war. One misunderstanding could send journalists down the wrong highway straight to an ambush and their deaths.

The casualty rate rose astronomically. Twenty-two foreign journalists were killed or were missing and presumed dead in the first four months of the Cambodian campaign. That nearly matched the casualty rate of twenty-four journalists killed for the entire six years of the Vietnam War. Cambodia became known as the shooting gallery.[30]

In a single week, nine journalists working for American television networks were killed, including Welles Hangen and Yoshihiko Waku of NBC News, who were captured and killed by the Khmer Rouge, and George Syvertsen and Tomoharu Iishi of CBS News, who were captured and killed after their jeep hit a mine.[31] Among the photographers who went missing and were presumed dead were Sean Flynn, the photographer son of Errol Flynn, Dana Stone, and the Frenchman Gilles Caron, all of whom had worked with Catherine Leroy in Vietnam.

Journalists took the obvious precautions: they traveled with buddies, gathered as much intelligence as possible, drove only during daylight, checked with villagers along the highways, and turned back at the first sign of a newly emptied village. But in the hothouse of the Hotel Royale, ghoulish rituals prevailed. Journalists took one another's photographs in case they were needed for an obituary. They counted off in the morning before they left and counted again when everyone had returned.

Webb became a fanatic about preparations. She hired the best translators—always the French speakers. She had the car packed early, before the ground mist had evaporated. Maps in hand, she stuck to her plans, resisting suspicious gossip, reported what she could, and returned to the bungalow to write her day story. By dark, she was sitting around the hotel pool with her colleagues—drink and cigarette in hand.

Webb's boss was as careful as she was. Jesse Frank Frosch arrived in Cambodia from UPI's Atlanta bureau. He had served as an army intelligence officer in Vietnam, studying and appraising the North Vietnamese and Viet Cong military. As an officer, he had raised red flags about the initial army reports out of My Lai, warning his superiors that the body count was far too high for a village that was home to mostly women and old men.[32]

As a journalist, Frosch had similar instincts as Webb. They were almost the same age, with deep if different war experiences and an appreciation for the tactical details of military operations. They also loved the region.

One time the two were stuck on the perimeter of a rice paddy near the Mekong River, waiting for a boat to ferry them across to report on an ongoing battle. American jets streaked across the sky toward the fighting.

They watched as the planes struck targets hidden in dense scrub jungle. Several planes swung back west to their bases in Thailand, and one plane began dropping napalm. Webb and Frosch heard shrieks and giggles coming toward them. Small children had jumped off their water buffalo and were running across the rice paddies toward the bright colors of billowing clouds of fire and smoke from the napalm explosion. "They are running, laughing at that pretty napalm," Webb said with alarm. The two of them chased the children, racing to stop them. Frosch didn't want to frighten them so he laughed when tackling them to the ground, turning the rescue into a game of rice-paddy rugby. Webb did the same and the children returned to their buffalo, Webb shaking her head at "the terrible innocence of those children running towards the napalm, laughing with joy at the pretty colors."[33]

Lon Nol launched his first major offensive against the North Vietnamese in August 1970. Named Chenla I after one of Cambodia's former empires, the offensive's goal was to recover a vast region east and north of Phnom Penh. FANK troops pushing down Highway 6 were successful until the North Vietnamese retaliated with their heavy guns. FANK then turned north on Highway 7 toward the provincial town of Kompong Thom.

Both sides knew this first offensive could determine how the war would be fought and won.

With such pressure on the outcome, Webb and Frosch took turns writing the main story in Phnom Penh, while the other reported from the front line. On September 19, they reported that some four thousand Cambodian troops were pitted against six hundred North Vietnamese in a match clearly weighted in FANK's favor. Yet the Cambodian commander was quoted saying he delayed the fighting because "we wanted American warplanes to bomb the VC a little longer." FANK made only incremental gains.[34]

Cambodia had become the dominant regional news story. The wire services—UPI, AP, Reuters, and Agence France-Presse—were under intense pressure to cover the news well and quickly. Whenever they failed to be the first with a headline, they received a "rocket" from headquarters, asking them why a rival wire service had beat them and to match the scoop. To be more competitive, UPI had temporarily assigned Kyoichi Sawada, their best photographer, to cover Chenla. A Japanese citizen, Sawada had won a Pulitzer for his photograph of a Vietnamese mother desperately swimming across a river with her children to save them from a firefight.

By October, thick monsoon rains were interrupting the offensive. During a lull in the northern push, Frosch and Sawada decided to check out reports of new fighting south of Phnom Penh. They drove down Highway 2 on the morning of October 28 toward Takeo and the Kirirom Pass. By evening they had not returned. By morning there was little hope.

Webb refused to join the search party. Khauv Bun Kheang, UPI's office manager and right-hand man, went by himself, steering through the rain. He saw the abandoned car first, badly shot up and crashed on the highway. He climbed out, waded into the flooded paddy field, and found the bodies of Sawada and Frosch, lying facedown. He turned them over and saw their chests riddled with bullets. They had been killed execution style.[35]

At the teletype machine, Webb could barely pound the letters: R-e-g-r-e-t t-o i-n-f-o-r-m y-o-u."[36]

She sent more details to UPI headquarters. Then raided ice from the local Coca-Cola factory to preserve the bodies in Phnom Penh's morgue.

A woman in Indiana and a woman in Tokyo were awakened with the news that they were now widows. Two children in Indiana had lost their father.

Webb was named the new bureau chief in Phnom Penh, automatically vaulting her to the status as a senior reporter of the Cambodian War. She was now one of the most influential voices on the war. Her UPI dispatches set the news agenda. As far as anyone knew, she was also the first woman to ever head a news bureau in a war zone, but that went unmentioned.

Instead, Webb, unmoored by the death of her colleague, lamented that her promotion had required Frosch's death, that she had "stepped into the shoes of a dead man."

FANK eventually lost the Chenla offensive, although the government considered it a draw. The North Vietnamese largely repulsed the advance in the north and east and then, to emphasize their prowess, infiltrated the capital and blew up most of the fleet of aircraft of the Cambodian Air Force. That didn't stop Lon Nol from holding a lavish parade in Phnom Penh to celebrate his troops' "victory" and plotting a second offensive to be named Chenla II.

~ ~ ~

EACH NIGHT, LIKE clockwork, birds announced sunset with singing and squawking as they roosted in the city's thick canopy of trees. Streetlights lit the main boulevards and strings of electric bulbs went on for the last customers at the open-air markets. Families ate their evening meals around oil lamps during the coolest hours of the day. Skinny dogs and scrawny cats scratched in the dirt for scraps.

Then at nine o'clock, the city was shut down under the decree of a permanent military curfew. All the streets emptied. Armed soldiers and police took up positions behind nighttime barricades.

This was the bewitching hour when Phnom Penh belonged solely to Cambodia's elite and the foreign community. The curfew didn't apply to them. They traveled freely, and their official credentials saw them waved through roadblocks. The magic wand for journalists was their *carte special pour les journalists de passage*, or press card.[37]

More nights than she would have wished, Kate Webb was out past curfew to attend an official event. Embassies around town sent her embossed cards inviting her to dinners and buffets where she would be the rare attractive unmarried young woman who knew more about the state of the battlefield and some of the politics than the diplomats. As UPI's representative, Webb did her duty even though she wrote in her diary she felt like Alice in Wonderland walking through the looking glass when she stepped out of her filthy fatigues, showered, and slipped into a custom-tailored dress made from Cambodian silk: her *tenue de ville*, as requested on the invitations.[38]

Webb balanced the foreign embassy evenings of wine and cognac with occasional visits to the local opium den, Chantal's. She had been a founding patron, along with two British journalists, Jon Swain, who left for Saigon, and Kent Potter, who would be killed in a helicopter crash over Laos in early 1971.

Chantal's became the equivalent of a high-end speakeasy, where visitors imbibed opium and quietly let their hair down. When they knocked at the door of the wooden house on stilts, they were met by Chantal, an outgoing, softly plump Sino-Cambodian woman trained by Madame Chum, who had operated the city's oldest fumerie. Chantal's welcomed all foreigners if they passed her personal test of respectability. No Cambodians.

Once inside, everyone changed into sarongs: French rubber plantation owners, conservationists of Angkor-era temples, officials of European embassies, Asian diplomats, writers, and foreign journalists. Lying on bamboo mats with their heads on pillows, the normal social pecking order abandoned, guests spent the night gossiping about the war and temporarily erasing the craziness locked in their heads. An assistant knelt beside each mat with a pipe, carefully cooking a plug of opium over a small oil lamp and pushing it, bubbling, into the pipe for smoking. No fan of opium, Webb usually drank whiskey. She came to listen to the conversation, which at times was salacious, such as a discussion about a French diplomatic wife who had a female lover, and often silly, such as the rumor that the Khmer Rouge tied grenades to roosters and let them loose in the marketplace. The French could be counted on to explain away the war with their old colonial tropes. "The Vietnamese are the fierce ones, like vin rouge: the Cambodians are vin rose and the Lao—obviously vin blanc."

Chantal would poke her head around the corner and shush the laughter in French: *Silence ici la*. Too much noise and the neighbors might complain, and the police would arrive asking for big bribes, since opium was illegal in wartime.

One night, Webb brought along a new friend: Sylvana Foa, a graduate of Barnard College who dropped out of Columbia University graduate school. Foa had made a detour to Cambodia after being denied entry to Hong Kong for her research and had shown up at the UPI office looking for work in November 1970. Webb liked the smart young woman and gave her a hand around town. After Foa published a respectable piece in the *Christian Science Monitor*, Webb gave her advice that jump-started Foa's career. She told Foa to leave Phnom Penh and go to Saigon where she would find work immediately. With Webb's recommendation, Foa was hired as a stringer for *Newsweek* the day after arriving in Saigon at the end of 1970. Later, she would be back in Phnom Penh and return the favor to Webb.[39]

~ ~ ~

PRESIDENT NIXON AND Henry Kissinger had planned the invasion of Cambodia with one overriding concern: to withdraw American troops and exit Vietnam in an honorable fashion.

With the North Vietnamese fighting the enlarged war, Kissinger believed that the Cambodian communists would fall in line when the time came and accept whatever peace was reached with North Vietnam with the approval of China. He did not consider the possibility that

Cambodia would act independently and dangerously upset his calculations for Indochina.

The first surprise came from Prince Sihanouk. After years of neutrality, he took sides and joined the communists, becoming the titular head of the Khmer Rouge. Sihanouk, who considered himself a descendant of the great Angkor emperor Jayavarman VII, could not separate his destiny from his country's. China offered him a chance to fight back against those who had overthrown him and return to power as head of his former enemies, the Khmer Rouge.[40] The two were joined in an unholy alliance called the National United Front of Kampuchea or FUNK in its French acronym. FUNK brought together royalists and democrats loyal to the prince and the Khmer Rouge who despised him. Dark jokes were made about FUNK versus FANK.

By giving Sihanouk pride of place in the alliance, the Khmer Rouge used his name and prestige in a recruitment campaign across Cambodia's villages, calling on the farmers to join the prince against his usurpers. In a single stroke, the relatively unknown Khmer Rouge became the strongest opposition army under the patronage of Sihanouk. The prince held court from his Beijing villa, welcoming diplomats searching for peace and answering questions from reporters who were told Sihanouk's was the only voice to speak for the Khmer Rouge. The prince remained where he felt most comfortable, as a potent figure on the world stage.

It's unclear what Nixon and Kissinger thought Sihanouk would do: Go into gilded retirement in France? Kissinger largely ignored the prince since he considered China the puppet master pulling the strings of the Cambodian communists and because the North Vietnamese military controlled the Cambodian battlefield. When the Chinese advised him to cultivate the prince as leverage in peace efforts with the Khmer Rouge, Kissinger dismissed the idea. He learned too late that China alone could not bring the Khmer Rouge to the peace table.

Kate Webb's articles from Phnom Penh were essential to understanding why Washington's strategy wasn't working. She had deep sources in the foreign diplomatic community, but she excelled with her Cambodian contacts. Cambodian government and military officials, important professionals, politicians, journalists, and the business community trusted her, giving her access and information reflected in her articles.

Senior correspondents around Asia noticed. One of the first stops for visiting journalists was the UPI bureau to sit down with Webb and ask how the war and the politics were shifting. She generously briefed her colleagues, including men who had belittled her work in Vietnam. Her main advice was not to confuse the Cambodia conflict with Vietnam's war. They both were part of the American war, but the Cambodians were fighting to defend themselves against the Vietnamese.

She also told them that she had little firsthand knowledge of the Khmer Rouge who were fighting behind the North Vietnamese army.

Webb's reporting paid off when she broke one of the biggest stories of 1971. She discovered that Lon Nol, Cambodia's prime minister and commander in chief, was partially paralyzed from a stroke he suffered on February 8, 1971, and the government was keeping it secret. The Cambodian government feared for the country's fortunes if the enemy learned that Lon Nol was incapacitated. Who would take over? What would the Americans do? When Webb filed her story, UPI asked for a comment from Washington. The Nixon administration refused to confirm the story and tried to kill it. Webb argued for forty-eight hours with her bosses, saying the story was true and had to be printed. She won. Once UPI published the news of the partial paralysis of the head of Cambodia, every other news organization followed. For days the *New York Times* published her accounts of Lon Nol's recovery and its effect on the war.

The danger in Phnom Penh never let up. One night, North Vietnamese surrounded the Cambodian base where Webb was trapped with the commander of the local unit. The commander called for airstrikes as mortars were landing closer and closer. The American bombers arrived, but the pilots couldn't communicate with the Cambodian forward air controller. They spoke English; he only spoke French. The Cambodian colonel asked Webb to translate to give the proper coordinates to the pilots. She agreed, but only if the colonel put his pistol to her head and threatened to kill her if she refused. Then she called in the strikes.[41]

~ ~ ~

WEBB RARELY TOOK a day off because "Sundays don't belong in Cambodia or in any war." She rarely wrote home to her sister and brothers. She showed little interest in having a serious boyfriend—Bob Stockton had done enough damage—until one man managed to slip past her guard, a Cambodian journalist named Ly Eng.

Tall and well educated, Eng drove a battered mini-sports car and took his work seriously. He was a reporter for the Cambodian newspapers *Koh Santhapheap* (Island of Peace) and *Domneung Peel Prik* (Morning News). Webb had many friends within the Cambodian press corps and had already admired Eng's work, especially a political cartoon about American aid feeding corruption in the government.

She asked a Cambodian journalist to point him out at a news conference and was pleasantly surprised to learn that Eng was the urbane Cambodian she had already noticed. She introduced herself, and soon the two were reporting together, cross-checking their stories with each other's sources.[42]

In the Phnom Penh press corps, Webb and Eng were breaking several unspoken rules. They treated each other as equals in an environment where Cambodian journalists were habitually considered second class, at best. Those who worked for the foreign press corps as translators, news gatherers, and photographers were well treated but not as equals; foreign journalists were rarely friends with their Cambodian colleagues.[43] They were paid $1.50 a day and were never given credit in print for their reporting and rarely for their photographs.

Webb knew that any romantic involvement with Eng, an Asian man, would break a different taboo, one that dated at least as far back as colonial days when the "white man's burden" included protecting their women from native men. The reverse was not the case. Plenty of Webb's male colleagues had Vietnamese or Cambodian girlfriends; some became their wives. More than a few men frequented local brothels, bragging about it afterward.

To those who pressed Webb closely about her relationship with Eng, she said they were friends, drinking buddies. But in her private writings, Webb referred to this "tall, skinny man with impatient eyes and a shock of fine hair" as her "midnight lover. A lonely woman with a lonely man."

When men in the press corps noticed Webb arriving with Eng at the hotel late, long past normal working hours, they started referring to Eng as Webb's "tame Cambodian."

When his Cambodian colleagues saw Eng with Webb, they presumed it was romantic and considered Eng a Romeo for dating *the* Kate Webb. Eng said, yes, they were and then he concocted elaborate fantasies about their amazing sex and then repeated them to Webb. "I told them we are lovers and I tell them what wonderful things we do in so many details." Their love affair was much more sporadic than Eng's boasting implied.

The gossip poisoned their friendship. They did not fit in anywhere as a couple. When she brought Eng to the opium den, they were thrown out because Chantal did not allow Cambodians into her private foreigners' club. Eng's family home was their one meeting place where Webb was treated like a sister, the beloved Mademoiselle Kate. She and Eng never openly became a couple. In one of her notebooks, Webb later wrote: "Ly Eng, for me, the end I never saw. . . . The bottom line as a woman—we argued. He said if you love me you will come with me. . . . I said I'm not into suicide."[44]

So Webb reverted to her old ways of avoiding her emotional life: work and more work.

With Webb outperforming many of her competitors, it had become difficult for news organizations to claim women didn't belong on the battlefield. The *New York Times* had relented and sent its first and only woman to cover the Vietnam War in 1970. Gloria Emerson, a talented and eccentric fashion reporter based in Paris, "was allowed to go to

Vietnam because the war was supposed to be over so it didn't matter if a female was sent." She went on to win a George Polk award for her coverage.[45]

When François Sully, the *Newsweek* correspondent who reported on Cambodia, was killed in a helicopter crash, Kevin Buckley, the magazine's bureau chief, sent Sylvana Foa from Saigon to become its resident stringer in Phnom Penh. With her arrival, Webb finally had a female friend in the small permanent press corps.

On the night of April 6, 1971, Webb sat alone again staring at a map of Cambodia, mulling the military maneuvers and drinking warm beer. The next morning Webb went over her schedule: a business dinner at the Hotel Royale, the arrival of the new Burmese ambassador, the morning announcement of a new government offensive. She decided to take a quick look at the offensive and drove down Highway 4 south toward Kompong Speu to see if FANK had a fighting chance. The Japanese photographer Toshiichi Suzuki came with her to take pictures.

The next morning, her Datsun car was found on the highway, abandoned, with no sign of Webb or the five other journalists also covering the front. The search began. No one wanted the saga of Kate Webb to end in a ditch in the desolate Cambodian countryside.[46]

CHAPTER TEN

Against the Odds

In a sudden ambush, North Vietnamese fired steady blasts from their AK-47 rifles, killing most of the Cambodian unit Webb and the others were covering. The journalists scrambled across the highway and hid while the North Vietnamese came out and counted their dead. That night Webb and the others cautiously wound their way through trees, as insects bit them and brambles scratched at their skin, searching for a way out. The next morning, their luck ran out.

Just before noon, Webb, Tea Kim Heang, Chhim Sarath, Vorn, Charoon, and Suzuki walked straight into two young North Vietnamese soldiers. Everyone was surprised. All six journalists were wearing civilian clothes and one was a tall foreign woman. The soldiers ordered them to squat and took away their belongings—wallets, Webb's bag, binoculars, notebooks, camera, and her good luck Chinese charm hanging from a golden chain.

They were given a metal bucket of water to drink. Webb passed it to the others first. It was empty when it was given back to her. "That the others hadn't left me anything, and what it meant, shocked me . . . there was a huge loneliness in my head that never left me."

Their captors tied their wrists behind their backs with baling wire, tape, and vines and marched them single line. Tall tree branches were stuck in their wrists as camouflage. At the first rest stop, their shoes were taken away and thrown into the trees. They were given rubber sandals and ordered to march.

They followed a very slender young North Vietnamese soldier, their feet in pain. At night they slept in bunkers, Webb in her own, the five others together. She realized that explaining they were *bao chi*—journalists—was of little help. "If a North Vietnamese captured on a battlefield in South Vietnam had said he was a journalist a fat lot of good that would have done him."

They were told they would be questioned by the North Vietnamese but separately. Webb was last. She had watched as the others were called away, had heard shots fired after each one, and then waited. None had returned. When they came for her, Webb was taken to a table, seated opposite a soldier who was roughly sixty years old. She gave her name, and when asked for her rank, she answered she was a journalist, a civilian without rank. This first long interrogation was a series of questions, often repeated: Who won the battle on Highway 4? Why were you down on Highway 4?

When Webb answered she had been there to find out what was happening, her interrogator asked her, "Why would you risk your life to find out what was happening?"

She began to feel more like a journalist and less like a prisoner. She thought through her chances for release and realized she had to convince the North Vietnamese she was neutral, not an American, and that her identification that plainly stated she was British (based on her passport) was official. It seemed to work, and from then on she was known as *co Anh*, or "the English girl" in Vietnamese.

When the interrogation was over, Kate was ushered to a clearing where the other journalists were waiting for her. No one had been harmed much less killed.

She tried to stay sane as the North Vietnamese had them march through Vietnamese-controlled Cambodia toward a military camp. One morning she rose at dawn before the other journalists and squatted next to ten NVA soldiers eating their breakfast of rice and tea. She pointed to a bar of soap nearby and then to herself. The soldiers understood and pointed toward the river. For the first time since her capture, she was allowed to bathe and for a few hours felt much better.

They marched by night to avoid detection, through jungles and over mountains, wading through streams and across paddy fields. When they passed through traditional Cambodian villages like silent shadows, Webb held her head high hoping someone might notice a Western woman captive and spread the news. During the day they slept fitfully.

Interrogations followed the marches. One interrogator snapped at her when she seemed to disregard his instructions. Something about his anger seemed familiar. She recognized in him the eyes she had seen "too many times in the faces of American, Vietnamese and Cambodian soldiers. The anguish of having to fight on and reduce oneself to an animal with no time to mourn or save friends; all that ground into a passion to strike back at the cause of it all. And I'd seen that hate worked out on prisoners, even the dead, when the first bullet wasn't enough and a GI just kept pumping lead into the still body, till a buddy led him away or the clip was empty."[1]

Toward the end of one march, Webb was so exhausted her "legs felt like bones with no muscles and the jungle was like a black-and-white movie undulating past."

She kept placing one foot in front of the other, propelled by the memory of an orange. She focused on it obsessively: "Bite into it, and the sweet juice runs down your throat. Make a little hole in it, and the juice squirts out."[2]

During their second week as captives, the reporters were placed in a permanent camp.[3] Their socks had worn out, and their feet were badly cut, with open sores. A young North Vietnamese guard sewed up the sores with needle and heavy thread, spacing the punctures to allow the pus to leak out. Next, a field medic soaked wads of cotton with Mercurochrome to sanitize the wounds before wrapping them in thin calico field dressing. Webb's badly mauled feet were infected so she was given crumbling penicillin pills. Watching the medic minister to her, Webb thought he "seemed so terribly young. It was like being treated by a very serious Boy Scout. I wondered what he'd think of the movie M.A.S.H."[4]

They gave him an obvious nickname: Medic. Among the North Vietnamese soldiers was also Cook, Gap Tooth, Dad, Carpenter, and the Twins. Carpenter helped build huts for the two foreigners and another for the four Cambodians. Webb thought they looked like a cattle thief's hideout, but Suzuki said they were typical of North Vietnamese peasant houses. They spent two weeks there, in a place they baptized as Phum Kasat, or press village.

Suzuki was a lifeline. He had covered the war from Hanoi for Nihon Denpa television and spoke fluent Vietnamese, with the accent and vocabulary of the north. He knew the social order of the North Vietnamese and their unspoken rules. As a result, he was able to behave respectfully, which the soldiers appreciated. One night a guard invited him and Webb for some "special tea." Suzuki knew exactly what they meant, smiled, and followed them, warning Webb the tea would be country-style rice wine. It was high-octane wine presented in a half coconut shell. They each took a sip until they had drained the fiery liquid. Her throat burned, but afterward Webb had her first good night of sleep since her capture.

On rare nights she heard the melancholy sound of a flute until bombing resumed in the hills and blocked the music. She discovered Carpenter was the mysterious flautist. When their paths next crossed, she found herself wondering, "How come the world is designed that you're on one side of the fence and I'm on the other?"

Sleep was often interrupted by nearby fighting and bombing. In one of her darker moments, Webb imagined dying from a bomb dropped by an American pilot, maybe even one she knew. Another pitch-black night she thought she was hallucinating when she went outside for air and saw an enormous creature lumbering toward her—an elephant ridden by two NVA soldiers and dragging an artillery piece.

Webb was anxious about her health. She was losing weight, her head throbbed, and blood was in her stools. The one thing she didn't worry about was mistreatment by the guards. None of them attempted to take advantage of her or the others. They never asked for favors—or worse—in exchange for cigarettes or food. She considered their behavior the result of "incredible discipline."

The long interrogations exhausted her. They usually involved the same questions asked repeatedly by the same interrogator: What were you doing behind enemy lines? Why were you on Highway 4?

"We find it unbelievable that you would go down the highway, which is very dangerous, alone in your car, just looking for the truth," he said.

"Sometimes I think my job is crazy myself," she replied.

He reminded her she was a prisoner of war and could be shot at a moment's notice. She refused to accept the designation of prisoner of war since she wasn't a soldier. The interrogator showed a sense of humor. "Then consider yourself an invited guest."[5]

The political game got serious when a North Vietnamese political officer was dispatched to record statements written and read by Webb and Suzuki for Radio Hanoi. Webb composed three neutral paragraphs saying she had been treated well and that "the withdrawal of American troops was an important step toward allowing the peoples of Indochina to determine their own future." The officer was not pleased. She sounded pro-American.

Suzuki and Webb were depressed afterward, fearing their words could be used as propaganda. Suzuki met her outside the hut and handed her sticks and small stones. To lift her spirits and his, he made an unusual proposal: "Let me teach you the tea ceremony that every Japanese girl learns." With delicate precision, they practiced the tea ceremony every day, using the sticks and stones to pretend to pour water, whisk the tea, and serve each other. Webb imagined herself in a kimono. The ritual allowed them to concentrate on art, forget their deprivation, calm their nerves, and keep their sanity.[6]

To the anguish of their families, Radio Hanoi never played the statements that would have confirmed they were still alive.

～ ～ ～

KATE'S SISTER, RACHEL Webb Miller, and her husband, Geoff, were back in Canberra where he was posted to the main office of the Australian Foreign Ministry. He was given the news the family had all feared: another journalist was missing in Cambodia and it was Kate. He called Rachel, pregnant with their third child, to tell her Kate was in the most serious danger of her life. Rachel called their brother Jeremy, who was in a Sydney pub, and their other brother Nicholas.[7]

The media was notified, and Kate Webb's disappearance became front-page news in Australia.

"OUR GIRL IS MISSING IN ACTION" was the *Sunday Mirror* headline, taking pride in the fact that Webb had started as a cadet at their paper. Their coverage, though, read like an obituary.

"Kate Webb is missing in action in the Asian War. . . . She saw more action than most men but although she was offered a big—and safe—job with UPI in Washington, she insisted that she must stay in Asia until the war ended. . . . Her old colleagues on the Sunday Mirror are hoping against hope that Kate Webb will turn up safely."[8]

Rachel was miserable. She hated the "horrible waiting game, living in limbo. In every article the assumption was that [Kate] wasn't going to make it." How much more could Kate suffer?

UPI was in constant touch, reporting all of their search efforts. Foa called Rachel from Phnom Penh to reassure her that Kate's friends had not given up. Prince Sihanouk announced from Beijing that he had ordered his forces to find Webb and free her. The Khmer Rouge responded that they neither held Webb nor any other foreign correspondent. The Australian embassy in Phnom Penh sent regular reports.

On April 20, thirteen days after her disappearance, the *New York Times* reported that the corpse of a young woman had been found and was believed to be the twenty-eight-year-old Kate Webb. The news article ended: "The death of Miss Webb brings to at least 10 the number killed in Cambodia since Prince Norodom Sihanouk was ousted in a coup in March 1970. Seventeen are listed as missing."[9]

The accompanying obituary described Webb as an intelligent, soft-spoken woman with a "masked toughness." It thoughtfully captured much of her personality and her accomplishments.[10]

Not all of the obituaries that followed showed such respect.

Pat Burgess, a well-known Australian war correspondent for the *Mirror*, wrote the equivalent of "I told her so." He had recently reported with her in Cambodia and wrote in an obituary that he told her that she was taking too many risks covering Operation Chenla. The world wouldn't care, he wrote, "no more than three paragraphs in the world press." He also thought her sorrow over her dead colleagues was out of proportion. His was impressed, however, that "she had remained feminine."[11]

An obituary in the *Daily Mirror* began: "Kate Webb was the most unlikely war correspondent in the world. When I first met her in 1964 she was doing interviews with television stars."[12]

The popular *A.M. Radio in Singapore* broadcast a full-throated eulogy, remembering Webb for "reaching the top in a predominantly male profession without ever losing her femininity. She chose the toughest testing-ground a girl could imagine, the Viet-Nam War . . . her humanitarianism and her search for truth were uncompromising."[13]

Rachel refused to believe Kate was dead even when the news came that a female corpse had been found. She demanded more evidence. "We asked them to send us the photographs of the dead woman's teeth who was supposed to be Kate. Our dentist looked at them and said 'no,' this is not a European woman. But the *New York Times* had already run an obit."

As the days went by with no news, the family realized "the odds of her getting out were pretty small." They held a memorial service for Kate as missing not dead at St. John's Church, Canberra, where they had held their parents' funeral.

Jeremy Webb, now a full-fledged journalist in Australia, was so frustrated he volunteered to go to Cambodia. The family forbade it. And they waited.

~ ~ ~

FOUR THOUSAND MILES away, in the jungles of eastern Cambodia, Kate hadn't given up either, but she also resisted hope. She had even asked why she hadn't been handed over to the Khmer Rouge. The North Vietnamese soldier the prisoners had nicknamed Dad firmly shot down that idea. "You would not be so comfortable with them," he said. "They are not civilized and do not have the facilities."

He looked at Webb as if she had gone off her head. She backtracked and said, "I wasn't saying I wanted to be handed over."[14]

The journalists were falling apart. Webb had chills, what she called a "cold fever," and could no longer tell the difference between thunder and a B-52 bomber. Charoon, the shy Cambodian journalist, described his deep depression: "It is raining in my heart."

On April 27, Gap Tooth, one of the guards, told them new clothes had been brought to camp, which meant they were about to be released. Released. Dad confirmed it. The date would be May 1, 1971, May Day, the biggest communist anniversary. Webb insisted they wear their civilian clothes. If they were released wearing black pajamas, people on the other side could confuse the Cambodian journalists for Khmer Rouge soldiers.

That was also the moment Webb started her monthly period, and the bleeding was heavy. White parachute silk was found to act as sanitary pads. One bit was saved to be used as a flag of neutrality.

At dawn on April 29, the excited guards woke them up and gave them back the clothes they had worn when they were captured as well as green cotton carrier bags. Inside were official papers saying that they had been released. They returned Kate's necklace with the gold Chinese charm. She had worn it throughout the war, grabbing at it in foxholes and firefights, convinced the charm had kept her alive.

In what Webb considered a Mad Hatter's tea party, once more feeling like Alice in Wonderland, they munched on candies and bananas while a soldier took photographs. Webb asked for the last time for information about the other missing journalists: especially Gilles Caron, Dana Stone, and Sean Flynn. Dad said he had no knowledge of journalists captured in the area and gave her this message: "Journalists should not travel with Lon Nol troops; anything can happen in battle."

Their final meal was chicken. The soldiers lowered their guns and encouraged the reporters to eat their fill. They had to be strong for their journey home.

The sun was setting, and Webb's feet were bleeding as they began a two-day walk to the other side, led by several guards. On the second night's walk, Webb felt doom-laden: "We've been too lucky; something's going to go wrong; it doesn't feel right: we're going to get bombed or shot."

The next morning, May 1, the journalists shook hands with Dad and Mr. Lib, who told Kate he would miss her and her soft voice. They were let go close to Highway 4, where they had been originally captured, near the village of Trappeang Kralaing. They were in no-man's land, crossing to the other side and hoping to be treated as friendlies. When they found that cursed highway, they saw soldiers marching over the crest toward them, so small they looked like little lead soldiers. "Lon Nol soldiers!" they shouted and ran into the highway calling out that they were press: "*Neak kasset*—press!"

The officer in charge knew Webb; she had covered his unit. His eyes widened when he saw her. "Miss Webb, you're supposed to be dead! It is Miss Webb, isn't it?"

Kate couldn't talk; she was afraid she would cry.[15]

⁓ ⁓ ⁓

FRANK SLUSSER WAS the general desk editor on the 4:00 p.m. to midnight shift at UPI headquarters in New York on May 1, 1971. He heard someone shout over to Jack Brannan, who was running the foreign desk: "Jack, Jack! Look at the Asia wire." Slusser ran over to join him as he picked up the wire copy, smiling.

"What is it, Jack?"

"Kate's alive."

Kate was alive.

Jerry Ballestrari, the teletype operator, ran the news bulletin on the AAA wire—the most urgent. He was so excited he used the old style of double-spacing the bulletin. Slusser could barely keep up with the reactions. "The walking-out-of-the-jungle news was electrifying . . . soon, the phones through the office were ringing, even some from AP guys who had met her and were happy she was alive."[16]

Kate was free and suddenly for the first time everyone loved her.

In Canberra, Rachel wept with relief.

The next morning, she and Geoff woke to a national celebration. They reached Kate by telephone in Phnom Penh and couldn't stop laughing and crying. She was Australia's biggest news story of that day and for many days to come.

The most extravagant was the *Sun-Herald*, which left its large tabloid-sized front page blank except for one enormous headline:

REDS FREE SYDNEY GIRL
BACK FROM DEAD

The other newspapers stripped the headlines across their front pages as if a war had ended:

The *Sunday News*:

FREED NEWSGAL ON CONG: TOUGH MEN, HIGH MORALE

The *Sunday Mirror*:

OUR GIRL KATE IS ALIVE AND WELL

The *Sydney Morning Herald*:

VIETCONG ARE HUMAN BEINGS—AND TOUGH

The *Age of Melbourne*:

'DEAD' REPORTER TELLS OF VIET CONG KINDNESS[17]

The family was overwhelmed. His friends took Jeremy to the Journalists' Club in Sydney to drink to Kate's health. "From then on, I was Kate Webb's brother."[18]

~ ~ ~

THE CAMBODIAN MILITARY sent a helicopter to fly the journalists to Phnom Penh, giving the press corps time to assemble.

At the airport, Webb could barely walk, held on one arm by a beefy journalist and the other by Mr. Khauv, the UPI office manager who had become her closest colleague. She held a truncated news conference that led to headlines like: "Communists are human, too." Afterward, she motioned Foa over and whispered: "I'm desperate for tampax." Foa obliged.[19]

After hugs, flowers, brandy, and more tears, Webb stopped at her bungalow to pick up her suitcase. She stared at the solid tree in the side yard. She was home, she realized, and free. "There was a stillness inside me I had never felt before or since."

A French planter sent his car to take her to his empty apartment where she drank glasses of iced orange juice, slaking the thirst for oranges that had preoccupied her during her jungle trek, and took multiple baths until the water was clear.[20] The next day, Webb flew to Hong Kong to be put under a doctor's care while she wrote a multipart series on her twenty-three-day captivity. And she was treated for malaria.

She wrote like a demon. Within two weeks, the articles were printed in newspapers around the world. The headlines were more dramatic than the articles: "Return of the Dead." "Back from the Dead." "Day of Terror, Night of Flight."

Webb's series was a sharply observed and nuanced diary of her captivity that reflected both sides. Her ordeal was horrendous: a miserable diet, illness, and foot injuries from marches that nearly killed her. But there was nothing sensational: she had not been raped or tortured. She had not uncovered a secret Pentagon-like headquarters.

Even her suffering was tempered by North Vietnamese jungle hospitality. Her daily gruel of tea and rice with fatty pork was the same that the North Vietnamese ate. When she fell ill, they called for their medic, however poorly trained. She did feel mistreated during the hours of interrogation. The daylong sessions were "tough and worrying" because she had to listen and respond to strident communist ideologies not knowing if her answers would put her or the others in jeopardy.

She wrote as a storyteller, without a hint of self-pity, turning her captivity into something like a political fable with North Vietnamese guards who became characters, some of whom she liked and some she didn't. She told of evenings with the guards telling jokes and swapping cigarettes; of days watching them perform their drab duties in primitive conditions with discipline. They never appeared as caricatures of the evil enemy.[21]

With her doctors' blessing, after twenty days Webb flew home to Australia for rest with her family and discovered she had become a national figure.

As soon as she got off the airplane, reporters surrounded her. Her brother Jeremy had to steer her through the crowd like a bodyguard. At an impromptu airport press conference, she seemed taken aback, speaking slowly, hesitantly, searching for words. She made mistakes and called the North Vietnamese the Cong, something she never did in her reports.

Jeremy warned his sister that she had become "a media tart everyone wanted." Despite her apparent fatigue, Webb appeared on television and sat for newspaper and radio interviews. She had fun crashing the men-only bar at the Sydney Press Club, organized by a columnist who wrote up the adventure. She sat on a stool, legs akimbo, wearing white jeans and a short-sleeved white pullover, a glass of wine in one hand, cigarette in the other, surrounded by five grinning men in suits. No one dared turn away Kate Webb.[22]

But in two long personality profiles, Webb allowed the stress to show. In an interview with Australia's *Woman's Day*, Webb broke her own strict rule and agreed to talk about her broken engagement. Without mentioning Bob Stockton by name, she transformed his humiliating treatment of her into "a beautiful thing . . . a war-time style engagement after meeting in a fire base mortar bunker . . . it fell through, and it fell through hard. But it fell through honestly—it's a good thing we realized beforehand—before we married."[23]

She also chastised the interviewer for asking if she had female colleagues. "It's only in Australia that it's unusual for women to be in Indochina." This was an outrageous statement. Kate knew that, in fact, Americans and Europeans were at least as surprised as Australians that women were reporters of the war.[24]

Kate was in such perpetual motion in Australia that Rachel missed the signs that all was not right with her sister. Before she could react, Kate was gone, flying to Washington, DC, for more press conferences and interviews and then to New York for UPI. There she arranged to have an evening with friends at Gough's Chop House, a newspaper bar near the *New York Times*.

Gene Roberts and Doug Robinson, two *Times* reporters she admired from her Saigon days, met her along with other friends. Roberts was taken aback when he saw Webb. "She was in such bad shape it was kind of a marvel she managed to make it to New York. It really was appalling. I remember walking into the restaurant and she looked jaundiced. I was surprised she could pick up a glass."

He and Robinson went back to the *Times* office and made a phone call to the newspaper's medical department, and soon Webb was in New York's best medical facility for tropical medicine.[25] She was diagnosed with cerebral malaria, put in a coma, and placed in an ice bath. Webb later said, dryly, she became a "living martini" in the coma. She did not tell her family until she recovered and was released weeks later.

Over UPI's better judgment, Webb returned to Phnom Penh in mid-1971. They wanted her based away from war zones in countries where she could fully recover. But Webb insisted.

Foa noticed a change immediately. "It was a mistake. The rockets freaked her out, and we had lots of rockets every night. One night we were hanging out in her suite and we got a lot of incoming. I said I was going out to see what was happening, and she threw herself on the floor and held on to my ankles until I agreed to stay. I guess she knew then that she should not have come back so soon. A few days later, she asked me to cover for her as she needed to go to Singapore for a few days."[26]

They often covered for each other, but this time Webb more or less disappeared for weeks, completely incommunicado. Foa kept up the pretense that Webb was hard at work, putting her initials "kw" at the bottom of copy and putting Webb's byline on an article if it was good.

When she returned to Cambodia, Webb became obsessed with missing journalists. She was still working hard, still went to the field, all the while writing a book about her captivity. UPI knew about her absences and her shattered nerves, and finally decided they had no choice but to transfer her out of Cambodia. She was posted to Hong Kong in early 1972 with the promise that she could occasionally report from Vietnam and Cambodia. Foa replaced her in Phnom Penh.

That same year her book, *On the Other Side: 23 Days with the Viet Cong*, was published. She was horrified that the subtitle referred to the North Vietnamese as the Viet Cong and disappointed by the sales. But that mattered little. The reviews were often reverential. Kate Webb was now a legend, a woman combat reporter who survived more near-death experiences than many soldiers. And she told the story intelligently and in unexpected ways that altered how the war was seen.

~ ~ ~

WILLIAM SHAWN, THE legendary editor of the *New Yorker*, received an advance copy of Frankie FitzGerald's book. He knew her journalism and read *Fire in the Lake* carefully. When he was finished, he considered it of such profound importance that he bought first serial rights and planned to publish an unusual five-part series from the book. Such a series would make an unmistakable statement. Not since the magazine devoted an entire issue to *Hiroshima*, John Hersey's account of the devastation following American use of atomic bombs, had the *New Yorker* given so much space to one reporter's story of an American war. The "Hiroshima" issue had sold out within hours. It was reprinted and read by millions and became the subject of countless articles and commentaries.

Now Shawn was giving the privilege to substantially reappraise another American war to a *woman* war correspondent. Moreover, her reappraisal differed significantly from the reporting by Robert Shaplen, the magazine's Asia correspondent who had covered the Vietnam War from the start. Shawn even created a new category or rubric for the series, "Annals of War," which is still in use decades later.

In July 1972, the *New Yorker* published the first of five parts of *Fire in the Lake* by Frances FitzGerald, giving Americans a wholly new view of the war. With each successive installment—"Fire in the Lake," "Sovereign of Discord," "Cave on Karl Marx Mountain," "Johnson's

Dilemma," and "Survivors"—FitzGerald centered the war on Vietnam, its history and culture. The role of the Americans in the war came into a new focus, viewed as dangerous outsiders by the Vietnamese in the countryside, even colonialists. The Americans' answer of using unprecedented force and ham-fisted policies was not creating a new democratic-leaning society in the South; it was having the reverse effect of undermining the legitimacy and any durability of the South Vietnamese government.[27]

Her key thesis was there was no moral, political, or practical reason for the United States to have waged the Vietnam War when the US had no chance of victory.

The *New Yorker* series ended one week before the book's August publication, generating so much respectful publicity it was an instant best seller.

The reviews were uniformly excellent. The *New York Times Book Review* called it "an extraordinary book . . . by its very depth and by its admirable style—cool empathy, restrained indignation, quiet irony, devastating vignettes—help us realize the monumental scope of what went wrong and what we did wrong."[28]

Even the academic press applauded. Writing in the *Journal of Asian Studies*, David G. Marr, a historian of Vietnam, called it a "thoughtful book written in quality prose" that while written for a general audience "touches on subjects likely to concern specialists of Vietnam for years to come." He praised her treatment of the weakness of the Diem regime and rise of the National Liberation Front, although he found her description of the Vietnamese national character "disastrous."

Pointedly, Marr praised FitzGerald for bridging the chasm between scholar and journalist.[29] In fact, as late as 1970, there was no tenured professor of Vietnamese studies in an American university. John K. Fairbanks, professor at Harvard who was considered the founder of Chinese studies in America, said the lack of American scholarly expertise on Vietnam was an "academic Pearl Harbor."[30]

Timing played heavily into the extraordinary reception of *Fire in the Lake*. Americans were exhausted by the endless war and wanted to know who the Vietnamese were who seemed to be winning.

Taylor Branch, who would win the Pulitzer Prize for his trilogy on Martin Luther King Jr., captured that feeling in his review for the *Washington Monthly*.

"Writing authoritatively from her experience in Vietnam . . . Fitz-Gerald makes the culture vivid, the people alive and believable. She accomplishes on the vast stage of Vietnam what few writers can achieve in describing a single incident . . . how American dollars and arms ripped through the Vietnamese society, tearing up its people with firepower, and tearing up its values with whorehouses and refugee slums and Polaroid cameras.

"This comprehensiveness seems like a reward for FitzGerald's sticking to Vietnam, for not bubbling off to Washington to take the pulse of national leaders who were thousands of miles from the effects of their policies . . . the best single volume on Vietnam."[31]

Fire in the Lake came out at the same time as *The Best and the Brightest*, an examination of Washington's early entry into Vietnam by David Halberstam. The *New York Times* journalist who won a Pulitzer Prize for his coverage of Vietnam, Halberstam was considered the savant of the early Vietnam press corps. His long-awaited book dissected how the "whiz kids" at the center of the Kennedy administration—the best and brightest of the title—pushed the US deeper into Vietnam with "brilliant policies that defied common sense."

To the shock of the journalistic establishment, *Fire in the Lake* won the top awards that year. FitzGerald, the young woman many of her colleagues had dismissed as an overprivileged dilettante while she was in Vietnam, won the Pulitzer Prize, the National Book Award, and the Bancroft Prize for history. It was the only book on Vietnam to win those three top prizes.

In a sense, Halberstam's book came in second to FitzGerald because it seemed to confirm what Americans had come to accept, especially after the release of the Pentagon Papers: that Washington officials became involved in Vietnam for misguided reasons, hid unwelcome facts evident on the ground, and stuck to the devastating conflict out of hubris.

FitzGerald was overwhelmed. She had had so many doubts about her book she had never dreamed of winning these accolades.

There was grumbling among her journalist colleagues. The common complaint, as voiced by Dan Southerland of UPI, was she had relied too much on Paul Mus.[32]

FitzGerald's book introduced Americans to the whole story, to Vietnam and the Vietnamese, as well as the American officials and American soldiers, explaining from Vietnam itself why the US was not winning and the unspeakable, tragic consequences.

And she had written for the general audience. "Not a scholar's book," she said, knowing that some academics would "huff and puff" over her generalizations meant to give the full view of war to Americans.[33]

Those complaints were lost in the tsunami of praise in the same year that the *Washington Post* won the Pulitzer Prize for its Watergate coverage. FitzGerald felt a kinship with Bob Woodward and Carl Bernstein who, as young reporters, had faced enormous skepticism as they uncovered the lies and crimes of President Nixon. Her blistering critique of Nixon's war policy was unappreciated by the White House as well. "Henry Kissinger told me he was very offended by my book."

Newspapers ran personality profiles of this high-achieving young journalist. Many treated her like a unicorn and were written by women for women or style sections. They focused on her family background as if being a WASP heiress explained her success. A classic example was a 1972 *Washington Post* profile by Myra MacPherson that began coyly saying FitzGerald had "all these handicaps" of privilege and wealth and important parents when she arrived in Saigon. Because of these "handicaps" the press corps didn't take her seriously. An anonymous male reporter was quoted saying he expected FitzGerald "to be everything I wouldn't like but she turned out to be great." And so it went. MacPherson fixated on FitzGerald's social status and showed no interest in her singular achievement of breaking through in a male world so that she could offer a new vision of how to cover war. MacPherson's employer, the *Washington Post*, had never sent a woman overseas as a foreign correspondent, much less a war correspondent, and had not had a single female byline from the Vietnam War as late as 1972.[34]

Later, after she had covered the women's movement and the legacy of the Vietnam War, MacPherson came to regret her profile of

FitzGerald. She felt "a little ashamed" that she didn't even think to ask FitzGerald how she, as a woman, had become a war correspondent in Vietnam, what hurdles she faced, and why so few women were able to follow her. MacPherson simply presumed that FitzGerald's wealth and prestige magically opened up doors closed to other women.

MacPherson, like Kate Webb, also did not want to be labeled as sympathetic to women's liberation. "In those days, there was this whole thing about trying to be one of the boys. There was a stigma attached to women's lib. You didn't wear it on your sleeve."[35]

David Greenway, the Vietnam War correspondent with a similar high WASP and Ivy League lineage as FitzGerald—he had been christened by FitzGerald's great-grandfather in the chapel at the exclusive Groton School—knew better than most that her family's stature and Radcliff degree were useless to her. "If Frankie had been a young man, she would have automatically been hired by *Time* as I was. But she was female."[36]

For FitzGerald, her new prestige and success meant that for the first time she could support herself as a journalist and author. Her bank account was fattened with the $25,000 payment from the *New Yorker* series and royalties from *Fire in the Lake*. She was in demand. And in Kevin Buckley she had a boyfriend who was happy to celebrate her success. Their romance fizzled out after a few years, but they became lifelong friends.

What FitzGerald couldn't have realized then was how her work would inspire generations of journalists and historians to see war far beyond the battlefield, to examine the culture and history and clash of civilizations as seriously as the armed conflict itself. Among the many reporters who looked to her decades later was Anthony Shadid, the Pulitzer Prize–winning foreign correspondent for the *Washington Post* and the *New York Times*, who cited *Fire in the Lake* as his touchstone when he began covering wars in the Middle East thirty years later.[37]

In a "lessons learned" study on Vietnam, the CIA credited Fitz-Gerald with identifying "the basic misunderstanding and miscommunication between Vietnamese and Americans . . . which made the whole enterprise risky in the extreme."[38]

Her book had an immediate impact on historians even though she wrote it as a generalist. Fredrik Logevall, the Pulitzer Prize–winning historian of wartime Vietnam, said *Fire in the Lake* was "absolutely of seminal importance—a profoundly important book."[39]

When he first read it in college, it "was an intellectually thrilling experience," he said. "It had a huge influence on me as a beginning scholar of the war."

Years later he saw flaws and problems in the book but believes some of the later criticism was motivated by jealousy. "Yes, I think there is jealousy. What we know about academic and journalist envy. There is sexism going on, too.

"This book needs to be judged for its time and its importance at the time. Her book filled a void and was an extraordinary influence. It is a classic."[40]

CHAPTER ELEVEN

Saigon Signing Off

RICHARD NIXON PROMISED PEACE IN VIETNAM AS HE PREPARED for his 1972 reelection campaign. Nixon argued that he had made great progress toward negotiating "an honorable end to the Vietnam War" and had even brought home half a million American soldiers from the war under his Vietnamization program. Reelect him, he said, and let him finish the job. Ignore the antiwar pacifism of his opponent Senator George McGovern, the South Dakota Democrat.[1]

McGovern openly opposed the war and called for an American withdrawal from Vietnam in exchange for the return of American prisoners of war. He also supported amnesty for American draft dodgers. In the climate of the time, McGovern, a taciturn Midwesterner, was successfully tarred as being ultraliberal and unpatriotic, a champion of "amnesty, abortion, and acid." Nixon led in all the polls.[2]

The antiwar veterans whom Cathy Leroy befriended at Woodstock did not trust Nixon. They planned a demonstration they called Operation Last Patrol at the Republican National Convention in Miami in August 1972, part of a massive antiwar rally aimed at disrupting the convention as it nominated Nixon.

The veterans got in touch with Leroy, and she decided to film their event. For her, their protest was a tragic continuation of their service to the country, a coda she could never have imagined when she first photographed the young Americans in battle in 1966. Their message was simple: no other soldiers should be sacrificed for a lost cause.

She flew in from Paris and teamed with Frank Cavestani, one of the Vietnam veterans at Woodstock. Cavestani claimed he had held a bottle of bourbon for Janis Joplin while she performed on stage.[3] Even though she was the only professional photographer or videographer of the two, Leroy shared credit with Cavestani as directors and for cinema photography. Cavestani was an actor and had never been a professional photographer.[4]

The filming began on August 15, 1972, as thousands of the Vietnam Veterans Against the War left in convoys from cities around the country—San Diego, Salt Lake City, Chicago, Detroit, New York—all headed to Miami. Leroy was with the crew in San Diego. With their long hair, mismatched shirts, and antiwar signs, the veterans resembled hippies on a quest. The discipline they showed in keeping the cavalcades moving reflected their military training.

The film, *Operation Last Patrol*, begins with Leroy's still photographs from Vietnam showing the face of the war that these men fought. Then an intimate, casual monologue by a veteran named Ron Kovic takes over. Kovic is driving as he explains calmly how three 30 caliber bullets had wounded him and left him paralyzed from the waist down for the rest of his life. He is young, angry, and articulate. He remembers seeing babies dying as civilians were napalmed, admitting "I still have nightmares."

The group traveled three thousand miles over five days across the South in a caravan of VW beetles and buses and battered four-door sedans. Kovic's interviews were interspersed with panning shots of freeways and traffic.

At one stop Kovic picked up a megaphone to lament that "what this trip does, I suppose, is work out our guilt for the crimes we've done. . . . Nixon will win [the election] but we're the biggest losers. The damage has already been done. It's corrupted America."

At night, the veterans and women traveling with them set up tents and ate communally. They bathed communally in rivers, their bodies silhouetted against pale evening skies, their dogs waiting on the riverbanks.

Driving through Texas, they were stopped and searched by state police. Driving through Louisiana, they were escorted by state police. Along the way, other veterans shared their anger and confusion over the war. One said he had such bad nerves he broke the fingers of a friend waking him up. Another said he conquered his heroin addiction with cough syrup and candy bars. By the time they reached Miami, they were keyed up for action, convinced they were the true patriots. "We've been there. We all got honorable discharges. We aren't subversives, communists, or draft dodgers. We think the war is wrong."

The veterans marched down the streets of Miami whistling "When Johnny Comes Marching Home Again" and raising their fists to shouts of "right on!" They chanted: "Babies keep on dying—Nobody seems to care."

Kovic moved in his wheelchair past barbed-wire barricades, police, and tear gas, into the conventional hall. "An ex-Marine who won the silver star and is paralyzed from the waist down begged for attention from his wheelchair and was answered by the cold, empty stares of delegates as Nixon made his acceptance speech," Leroy wrote in a film precis.

The film shows Kovic in the hall shouting: "Do you hear me when I say I'm in pain from this war?"

Operation Last Patrol became a niche favorite, portraying as it did the agony of antiwar veterans in the age of Nixon. Kovic was so inspired by the documentary that he immediately wrote his autobiography *Born on the Fourth of July*. It became a best seller and was made into a hit movie in 1989, directed by Oliver Stone and starring Tom Cruise as Kovic. The movie won two Oscars. Kovic got Cavestani a position as paid adviser for the film and as an actor playing several unnamed veterans. The two gave speeches describing how *Operation Last Patrol* inspired *Born on the Fourth of July*.[5]

Missing from all of this was Leroy. Kovic never acknowledged her in his book or in the Hollywood feature film.[6] Leroy was angry and disappointed that only Cavestani received public acclaim and credit for what was also very much her movie. She told friends that she fought to receive some financial compensation. She remained proud of *Operation Last Patrol*, though, and included it in the catalogue of her most important coverage of the Vietnam War.

By the time she finished making the documentary, Leroy made herself a promise: she would not return to Vietnam until she was certain she would photograph the war's end.

~ ~ ~

NORTH VIETNAM MADE another attempt to win the war militarily with a massive Spring Offensive beginning at the end of March 1972. President Nixon had made public the secret talks between Henry Kissinger and Le Duc Tho, and all sides seemed to be maneuvering for battlefield advantage in advance of a cease-fire. But North Vietnamese leader Le Duan was more ambitious: he wanted to overthrow the South Vietnamese government.

Hanoi sent 120,000 troops across the DMZ in its biggest offensive since Tet in 1968. With Soviet tanks and heavy artillery, the North Vietnamese captured territory deep in the South. But the ARVN counterattacked with massive American bombing support and pushed the communists out of An Loc and Quang Tri City. Under Vietnamization, American strength had been reduced to 140,000 troops remaining in the country.

The US also launched its first air attack on North Vietnam since 1968, signaling that Washington would escalate as necessary to halt the North Vietnamese. Kissinger said the bombing was "saving American honor." ARVN held off the North Vietnamese, and the offensive ended in May with a North Vietnamese defeat. But the communists held on to some of the newly captured territory in the South, which would prove critical in the months ahead.

The South Vietnamese army had been stronger than expected. Historians would later debate whether ARVN could have reversed the course of the war eventually and kept Vietnam divided. Nixon felt the renewed bombing of North Vietnam demonstrated how "we will demolish them" if they didn't accept his peace proposals.

That failed Spring Offensive helped convince the North Vietnamese of the wisdom of Ho Chi Minh. He had opposed the earlier Tet Offensive in the belief that the road to victory required the departure of the Americans first before defeating Saigon.

The North Vietnamese returned to the negotiating table over the summer, and both sides made concessions and rewrote proposals. In early October, Le Duc Tho wrote a nine-point peace agreement that included the essential new compromises needed from both sides and handed it to Kissinger. Under the plan, the United States would allow North Vietnamese troops to remain in place in the South. And Hanoi would drop its requirement that the South Vietnamese government and military be disbanded at the same time. That was the breakthrough Kissinger had been waiting for.

"We've done it," said Kissinger.[7]

After their three years of secret negotiations, both sides were pleased. American objectives were fulfilled with the agreement that the communists would release all American prisoners of war as the United States withdrew all of its troops and ended direct military involvement. The final terms were not unlike the McGovern plan proposed in 1972.

President Nixon and North Vietnamese prime minister Pham Van Dong agreed on the text and scheduled an official signing on October 30, 1972, days before the November presidential election.

But South Vietnamese president Nguyen Van Thieu was furious. He had been left out of the talks where, to his mind, the United States had accepted too many of North Vietnam's conditions in the peace accords, including recognizing Vietnam as a single nation and not two sovereign states. Under the agreement, there would be no withdrawal of North Vietnamese troops from the South, and no effective body to police a cease-fire. The political future of South Vietnam was not settled.[8]

Thieu refused to accept the agreement.

Back in Washington, Kissinger downplayed Thieu's intransigence as a misunderstanding. "Peace is at hand," he said at a press conference packed with one hundred reporters hoping to report that the Vietnam War was ending.

Nixon won reelection in November in a landslide, carrying all the states except Massachusetts and the District of Columbia.

Buoyed, Kissinger gave the North Vietnamese sixty-nine new amendments proposed by South Vietnam, expecting Hanoi to accept a few as a face-saving compromise for Thieu. But the North Vietnamese resisted Kissinger's pleas. The talks were officially declared at an impasse on December 16, 1972.

Two days later, the United States launched the largest aerial blitz of the war, attacking Hanoi and Haiphong for twelve days in what became known as the Christmas bombing. B-52 bombers and fighter jets dropped bombs around the clock on what was left of military targets, effectively destroying the city's air defense cover. The bombs hit city blocks and nearby villages. Bach Mai Hospital was hit twice. Schools, pagodas, markets, and apartment houses were flattened. At least 1,600 civilians were killed. Photographs of this destruction were published around the world and provoked mass demonstrations. Pope Paul VI said the bombing was the "object of daily grief," while Sweden's prime minister compared it to Nazi atrocities.[9]

After the bombing ended, Kissinger and Le Duc Tho returned to Paris, and the Paris Peace Accords were signed on January 27, 1973. They were essentially the same as those negotiated in October, before the Christmas bombing, with a few minor changes.

President Nixon announced the agreement from the White House: "We today have concluded an agreement to end the war and bring peace with honor in Vietnam and in Southeast Asia."

President Thieu told his public: "The signing of the agreement means the beginning of peace, but it does not mean peace."

~ ~ ~

WHEN I ARRIVED in Cambodia in January 1973, other reporters warned me that I was too late. The peace accords were about to be signed, and the war was effectively over. For a few weeks, I believed them and worried I had made the biggest mistake of my life.

My first sight of battle suggested otherwise. Neil Davis, a much-admired Australian cameraman who had covered Vietnam and Cambodia since 1964, took me down Highway 4 to the headquarters of Gen. Dien Del, one of Cambodia's best officers. We left as the city was waking up. Men in sarongs were pulling up metal grills to open their shops or drinking coffee on sidewalk stools. Monks in saffron robes were walking single file down the street, begging bowls in hand. We rolled down the windows to catch the still-cool morning breezes.

The city's boulevards merged into the highway, which led to the countryside. Sugar palms defined the horizon with silhouettes of farmers' thatched homes on stilts. We passed newly harvested rice fields that looked like an old man's stubble and thick knots of neem trees. On a small road, as we climbed out of the car, I heard the whipping sound of bullets. We ran away from the noise until Neil motioned me to fall on my stomach immediately. The danger had caught up with us. We waited "safely" behind teenage Cambodian soldiers firing M16 automatic rifles at the Khmer Rouge forward line. During a lull, we backed out and headed in the car closer to the general's base camp, where his aide waited for us.

We all walked single file down a path lined with dusty bamboo trees toward the headquarters. The bamboo disappeared, replaced by a row of wooden poles. The aide stood still. My brain stopped, refusing to register what was in front of me.

At the top of each pole was the severed head of a young man. Each seemed to have had his dark hair combed. Some had their eyes slightly open. I muffled a silent scream. Neil thought they were the heads of Khmer Rouge soldiers killed the day before.

When we met Gen. Dien Del, he assured us his men were not savages and that beheading was practiced by both sides, as if that was any consolation. As far as peace was concerned, he saw only more war. Vietnam and Laos may have signed the Paris Accords, but Cambodia had not.

Soon after, I began having irregular nightmares of beheadings. Judy, my oldest sister, had been beheaded in a car accident when she was twenty years old. Her death had plunged our family into years of despair. Now her face appeared in my dark dreams with those of the young Khmer Rouge soldiers.

I told myself that if the rumors of peace came true, I could leave Cambodia in a few months with enough experience to find a job back home in Seattle. I just had to survive until then.

～ ～ ～

IN FEBRUARY, THE news out of Vietnam was joyful: 591 American prisoners of war were released over sixty days. In parallel, American troops withdrew from Vietnam.

Reporters jockeyed for the assignment to fly to Hanoi and cover the return of the soldiers and airmen who had survived sometimes years of imprisonment, torture, poor nutrition, and insufferable conditions in North Vietnam. Back home, President Nixon invited them all to the White House for a dinner with Bob Hope as master of ceremony.

Before long, all of America's soldiers in Vietnam would be coming home. The killing of Americans there was over, and for the American public, the Vietnam War was done, just as President Nixon had promised.

Henry Kissinger and Le Duc Tho were awarded the 1973 Nobel Peace Prize, although Le Duc Tho became the only person in history to refuse it: the North Vietnamese negotiator declined the honor, saying there was no peace in Vietnam and accusing the US of breaking the truce.[10]

～ ～ ～

DURING MY FIRST three months in Cambodia, I lost fifteen pounds living on soup, coffee, and cigarettes.

The men in the resident and visiting foreign press corps were a mixed bag. At first, everyone wanted to take me to dinner—but too many felt the need to make a pass at me, and I was frightened by the attention. I looked and acted like a Seattle provincial far from home. Besides, I was stumped trying to read a French menu. It took me some time to figure out which colleagues I could trust, especially after Sylvana Foa was expelled.

Dith Pran, the top Cambodian journalist and fixer, noticed I relied on slow pedicabs to get around the city and had to beg for rides to the front. One day he saw me in the hotel's parking lot and handed me the keys to his green Volkswagen bug. "Bek Kar," he said. "Take my car. You're not a hippie. You're serious." Even better, Pran regularly checked to make sure I didn't blunder down the wrong highway for my sake and the car's.[11]

With the car I was golden, and within a month I could afford to rent Pran's car in time to chase the biggest story of the war that year.

At the open-air daily briefings, Am Rong, the military spokesman, certified that the North Vietnamese troops had withdrawn from Cambodia as required under the peace accords. That changed the whole character of the war. Cambodians were no longer fighting their traditional enemy. They were fighting each other: the Lon Nol government's FANK against the Khmer Rouge insurgents. To everyone's surprise, the Khmer Rouge were strong even without the Vietnamese.

Since the warring parties of Cambodia were not part of the Paris Peace Accords, the United State could focus all of its air power on the Cambodian front to aid the Lon Nol government. The US launched a massive new air campaign without publicly announcing this dramatic change in policy. The US command had been restrained in its official response to our questions about its military plans in Cambodia. The evidence, though, was everywhere. US bombs were saving the government of Lon Nol.

In the March 19, 1973, edition of *Far Eastern Economic Review*, I wrote that the extent and expanse of American bombing had increased at "unprecedented proportions" throughout the country and was no longer restricted to border regions.

"Villages barely scarred in three years of conflict were leveled. The fighting continues to plague densely populated regions and the tactical air support has become more lethal. Refugees are pouring into Phnom Penh, leaving their homes in the lush Mekong River region to escape the raids."[12]

Part of me worried that I was overstating the extent of the bombing. But you could hear the bombing from the capital. Kate Webb congratulated me, saying the article was strong.

Decades later, the secret government data on the bombing was made public, and the analysis showed the uptick began in March 1973. "During [July] an incredible 51,900 tons of bombs were dropped or eleven percent of the total of all bombs dropped on Cambodia during the ten years recorded."[13]

Those cold figures don't begin to describe the horror that enveloped Cambodia, once the focus of the war moved from the ground to the air. Bombing was a danger most Cambodians could not comprehend. Deadly fire bolts from the sky, with no discernible earthly origins, could only be explained by texts from their Buddhist faith, the clash of demons and gods. Fighter jets high in the air piloted by foreign men dropping bombs were as fantastic in their world as Garuda, the magical eagle-like bird that carries Vishnu, the Hindu-Buddhist god, across the heavens. Their fear was contagious. Their lives were ruined.

Phnom Penh became crowded with foreign journalists. Cambodia was the new front line. By April 1973, I was writing stories of the city under siege, with all highways and the Mekong River blocked by the Khmer Rouge and supplies of food and gasoline dwindling. Black-market prices of rice doubled in a week. The dry season heat was intolerable—it was like living under a sunlamp. I interviewed captains of the few tankers and cargo ships that successfully ran the blockade on the Mekong. Foreign families who were able to were leaving Cambodia.

Some days I was filled with resolve and excitement that I was reporting the story and giving voice to Cambodians. Other days I was near suicidal with the enormity of the destruction and feelings of loss that I couldn't describe. I stopped believing reporters who said they could push their emotions aside.

What saved me was the relentless pace of the news. Overwhelmed and understaffed, the *Washington Post* hired me in May as their Cambodia stringer. Lee Lescaze, the foreign editor, made it official in a letter, where he suggested I not overestimate my good fortune. "Our rates are $7.00 per hundred words and, I am afraid, no Post stringer grows rich writing for us. However, you will find, I hope, that we edit and display your stories intelligently."[14]

That was all true. In order to make a living and squirrel away savings, I also was the stringer for *Newsweek* magazine and NBC radio.

Many evenings I went to the military briefings, had a gin and tonic with the other journalists, and returned to work in my room at the Hotel Royale, now renamed Hotel le Phnom. I did not need to dine out with colleagues and was happy to hide in my room. One night in July, a knock on my door was followed by a soft, smoky voice saying: "Beth—open the door—it's Kate."

~ ~ ~

AFTER THE PUBLICATION of her book *On the Other Side*, Kate Webb's byline had almost disappeared. She wrote one major article predicting that Cambodia would be left out of any peace accord: "perhaps because the big powers are willing to let the usually-forgotten Cambodia fall whichever way it falls."[15]

She had been falling apart, personally, laid low by the accumulation of all she had endured. By her own account, she had become "a paralytic drunk" who had to be scraped off the ladies' room floor. "I suppose the medics would call it battle fatigue, whatever it was I was pretty worn out." In later years it would be called a severe case of post-traumatic stress disorder.[16]

She took time off, traveling to western United States for "a couple of good weeks gentling, or idling my motors around Big Sur."[17]

UPI relocated her to Hong Kong with the hope that her crippling obsession with Cambodia and Vietnam would fade. It didn't work. Her life and her thoughts were "still very much entangled with Indochina."

Until the knock at my door, I hadn't seen her since she met me at the airport as I was on my way to my new life as a war reporter.

"Kate!" I gave her a hug and asked her to wait while I finished a letter to my mother. She said, bleakly: "At least you have a mother to write to." I stopped typing, turned off the weak 1960s desk lamp, and pulled out a precious bottle of Scotch whiskey. Kate then told me in her cautious mumble the story of the car crash that killed her parents while she was at university. She was off her stride—she hadn't been around bombing for months and was skittish.

I pulled my two chairs onto the room's balcony, next to the large ceramic pots planted with vines. Mine was the smallest room in the hotel, but the twenty-foot ceiling gave an illusion of grandeur, and from the balcony I had a view of sunsets and the stars. It was my bastion. Kate put her feet on the railing and smiled. She loved the crumbling hotel and the city, even or maybe especially at wartime.

After finishing the Scotch, we slipped away to Café le Paradis for Chinese noodles. The Chinese quarter was quiet, the red- and yellow-tiled sidewalks slippery from evening showers. We were greeted with a smile and a request to order immediately. The owner wanted to close early. Kate asked whether the war would end after the bombing, and I said I thought it would go on and be more miserable. Since the Vietnamese communists had withdrawn to their own country, the atrocities on both sides had become even more extreme. The government soldiers displayed the heads of Khmer Rouge soldiers on pikes, while the Khmer Rouge disemboweled the corpses of government soldiers. The Khmer Rouge had told the French archaeologist Bernard-Philippe Groslier he could no longer maintain the temples of Angkor. Now that they were winning, neither Sihanouk nor the Khmer Rouge were willing to even talk to Lon Nol.

I knew better than to discuss my personal matters with Kate. I'd learned which subjects would set off her temper or her melancholy. One was women's liberation. I had come directly from university where I was a feminist who volunteered at a phone bank to help women find birth control, and I had joined a divorce cooperative when my brief marriage had fallen apart. She considered women with my views part of the problem, not the solution. And I considered her willfully blind to the obstacles women faced. So we stuck to the easy subject of whether Cambodia would be destroyed by the war.

"*Doucement en peu ici la*," the owner said, suggesting not only that we quiet down but also leave so he could close up.

The next day, Webb and I drove south, deep into Takeo Province. The American bombing was the biggest story of the war, and Webb had to survey the bomb craters. From a distance, craters looked like polka dots. Webb jumped into one and used the toe-to-heel measuring system to determine whether a B-52 had dropped the ordnance. Every detail was news that summer as Congress passed legislation to force President Nixon to end the air war in Cambodia. Nixon vetoed the bill, saying continued pressure was necessary since Kissinger was at a delicate stage of negotiating for peace in Cambodia, which was a lie. There were no negotiations.

Our articles from the front line would be scrutinized carefully, so we found witnesses to the bombing and fighting in the tired cavalcade of refugees on the road back to Phnom Penh. Cheng Hem, a middle-aged farmer, told me her home was bombed when government soldiers camped nearby and the Khmer Rouge came up behind them. "I saw a flame—a big flame—and my whole body shook. Houses were burning, and so was mine. My 12-year old daughter was inside."[18]

Hem pulled her dusty krama scarf across her face and turned away.

Kate and I knew the displaced would be at a loss when they arrived in the capital. Phnom Penh was overwhelmed by the 346,000 new refugees who had arrived since the bombing began. There was no room for them in the city, which in peacetime was home to just half a million people. The new camps were already full. These country people would be robbed by soldiers manning checkpoints on the highway and once in the city would be pushed to fetid holding areas near the river where they would live in squalor, cutting down trees along the city's boulevards to use for firewood and drawing their drinking water from the Mekong where they also bathed. They were also in danger of going hungry. US food aid meant for them was sold under the table to private merchants who hoarded the grain and then resold it for profit. The situation was a catastrophe.

Kate took me to a warehouse in Phnom Penh where she bought a 20-kilogram sack of rice, which Mr. Khauv from the UPI office then delivered anonymously to the people we had interviewed. It was an honest way to get around the rule forbidding journalists to pay for interviews.

On her last night before returning to Hong Kong, we had a couscous dinner at La Taverne opposite the PTT in the post office square with half a dozen other journalists who wanted to hear Kate's war stories. She obliged and for two hours enthralled the table. The next day she was waiting for her flight out of Pochentong Airport when Kishore Mahbubani, the young head of the Singapore mission, saw she was carrying a book he had lent her—*The ABC of Relativity* by Bertrand Russell. He gave her a friendly wave and asked for his book. She smiled, waved back, and boarded her plane. She kept the Bertrand Russell.

Kishore did not let me forget that my friend Kate had walked off with his favorite philosophy book.[19]

Kate also took with her what little sense of female camraderie I had. I felt very dreary after she left. Although I had become accustomed to being without a close friend, her visit had reminded me how lonely I was.

I couldn't know then that I would never see Kate again.

~ ~ ~

BY THE SUMMER of 1973, Nixon had become preoccupied with the congressional Watergate hearings and his fear that they were heading toward his possible impeachment. Wanting to avoid a separate fight over the bombing of Cambodia, he reached a compromise with Congress and agreed to end the American bombing on August 15, 1973.

The *Washington Post* showcased the end of the bombing with three articles. David Greenway came from Hong Kong to write the main story from Phnom Penh about the strategic shift, which could determine the fate of Cambodia.[20] Tom Lippman flew from Saigon to the Korat Air Base in Thailand to report the last American plane to bomb Cambodia, which put an end to active American military involvement in the wider Vietnam War. The pilot of that plane played "Turkey in the Straw" on his harmonica.[21] I wrote from Battambang, the elegant Cambodian river city near Thailand that, like border towns in other wars, offered a quick exit for wealthier Cambodians, dissidents, and artists when the time came.[22]

Despite everyone's fears, Phnom Penh was still standing after August 15. The Khmer Rouge retreated, and I took my sole vacation from the war. I flew to Kashmir to be with Peter Gill, a British journalist who lived in India and whom I had met when he covered the bombing. The nights on Dal Lake in Srinagar were so quiet my ears vibrated. I read English-language novels and feasted on pulao and lamb curries. It was a relief to have a romantic escape with a kind and intelligent boyfriend, but after ten days I felt the same compulsive pull that had called Cathy Leroy and Kate Webb: I couldn't stand to be away from the war.

Nothing in my short life had ever mattered as much as witnessing Cambodia's war as a reporter. Every part of every day had meaning. I had never felt more involved, more alive, or more vulnerable. I had crossed a line and made a commitment to Cambodia that would be costly.

~ ~ ~

MEY KOMPHOT, A wise banker and good friend, was reading a Khmer-language paperback with a striking cover: a drawing of Cambodia shaped like a heart broken by the coursing Mekong River. The hotel's desk clerk was reading it, too, and so were Cambodian bureaucrats, teachers, politicians, and one of the fruit sellers at the Central Market. It was so popular I thought it had to be an escapist novel. Instead, it was a fiercely dark exposé of the Khmer Rouge.

Regrets for the Khmer Soul (in Khmer, *Sranaoh Pralung Khmer*) was the only firsthand account of the Khmer Rouge written during the war. The author was Ith Sarin, a school inspector who had grown alarmed by the corruption and incompetence of the Lon Nol government and had defected to the Khmer Rouge.[23] When he got to know the mysterious Cambodian communists, how they operated and what they hoped to accomplish, Sarin realized they were an existential danger to his country. He escaped and wrote the book to urge his fellow citizens to change their ways and fight back, to "bring light to some of the secrecy of the Khmer problems and to expose the great danger from the communists inside the country."

His testimony was lifesaving. The Khmer Rouge were highly secretive and refused to allow foreign reporters into their zones. Any reporter who had tried had been killed, one of the reasons the death rate among journalists in Cambodia was so high. Prince Sihanouk frequently warned journalists he could not assure their security should they attempt to visit the Khmer Rouge zones.

This book helped answer the question: Who were the Khmer Rouge? They were winning the war, yet we foreign reporters had yet to even publish the name of their leader or describe their organization or their vision for a communist Cambodia.

I was working on this story with Ishiyama Koki, the Kyodo news correspondent and one of my closest colleagues. Koki was my shield, a colleague who was happily married and treated me like a friend and nothing more. He had translated several of George Orwell's books into Japanese and considered Orwell's *Homage to Catalonia* a blueprint for analyzing Cambodia's war. We paid his assistant to translate *Regrets of the Khmer Soul* into English.

Sarin's account was thorough. On the positive side, farmers saw the Khmer Rouge as "very tough and strong in nature," providing basic services like building dams, dikes, ponds, and houses with a "modest and simple" demeanor. Their rule was highly organized and required communal living, which was often resented.

But the Khmer Rouge also exhibited an "iron discipline." They hid their communist party, calling it the organization; they demanded strict adherence and ruled by fear. The Khmer Rouge cultivated that fear by saying their organization was omnipotent and "has as many eyes as a pineapple and cannot make mistakes."

Sarin also demolished the belief that the Khmer Rouge were loyal allies of the North Vietnamese or anyone else. At meetings he attended, the Khmer Rouge "encouraged hatred" of North Vietnam and Prince Sihanouk. The farmers were heartbroken at the insults against the prince. All of this led to Sarin's change of heart and his escape back to Phnom Penh.

The Lon Nol government eventually banned the book and jailed Sarin. But *Regrets* remained in circulation, passed from hand to hand.

I spent weeks that turned into months chasing down confirmations and additional information about the Khmer Rouge. The most difficult aspect of the task was confirming that Saloth Sar was the secret leader of the Khmer Rouge. He would be known later as Pol Pot.

As this research was underway, Ishiyama Koki was ordered back to Tokyo in late October. Our Khmer language class, which included the Japanese photographers Ichinose Taizo and Mabuchi Naoki and me, held a going-away party for him. We drank tea and gave Koki a piece of antique silk. He surprised us with gifts. Mine was a new automatic Japanese camera that he called Beth's *baka-chong*, or idiot camera.

A few weeks after Koki left, Taizo disappeared while trying to photograph the Khmer Rouge at the temples of Angkor. We were stunned and sickened. His death was confirmed several months later.

Finally, in March 1974, "Who Are the Khmer Rouge?" was published in the *Washington Post* Sunday Outlook section. Quoting liberally from Sarin's book, I described the Khmer Rouge organization and its leaders, why they refused to negotiate for peace, and why they were in a position to win the war.[24]

The reaction was awful. The CIA at the embassy in Phnom Penh called it black propaganda because I described a split between the Vietnamese and Cambodian communists. Officials in other embassies called it CIA propaganda because I was so critical of the Khmer Rouge. My journalist colleagues ignored it as too hypothetical since I hadn't interviewed the Khmer Rouge myself.

Three days later, I followed up with a front-page article in the *Washington Post* that described in detail how an American military attaché was illegally advising the Cambodian army. US Army Maj.

Lawrence W. Ondecker had taken command of the Cambodian troops in the besieged riverport of Kampot, eighty miles south of Phnom Penh during a Khmer Rouge offensive. He ordered a counterattack that saved the garrison and many lives, including mine.[25] I was standing near Ondecker and taking notes through the whole ordeal, the only journalist foolish enough to have traveled by helicopter to report on this critical battle. Members of Congress, including two dozen senators, demanded an investigation since "Congress had passed a law banning direct American U.S. military involvement in Indochina."[26] Ondecker was removed, and the US embassy prohibited the staff from speaking to me unless accompanied by the press officer. When the newly arrived US ambassador John Gunther Dean gave his first press conference in Phnom Penh, he went out of his way to humiliate me.

Then, two days after those articles appeared, my father died in Seattle. I had made an emergency trip to see him in January, using up my savings to buy the airplane ticket to spend two weeks with him while he was alive. When we said good-bye, he promised he would make it through his third open-heart surgery. When I received the cable confirming that he hadn't made it, I couldn't go home so I went to the rocky beaches off Vung Tau, Vietnam, for the weekend. It was one of the few peaceful places left in Indochina.

~ ~ ~

The foreign editor of Kyodo News Service was waiting for me one night before dinner. It was April, and he had flown from Tokyo to Phnom Penh with bad news. Koki had lied about his transfer back to Japan. He had not gone home. Instead, he had crossed over to the Khmer Rouge zone months ago, about the same time as Taizo, and then disappeared. The editor knew I was a close colleague and asked if I could help find him. I felt walls closing in. I was angry with Koki for trusting the Khmer Rouge and angry at Tokyo for waiting so long before making his disappearance public so that we could all look for him.

Methodically, I talked to the intelligence officers at various embassies, French planters, and priests, as well as Cambodian officials and businessmen; all were discouraging.

That Sunday I attended mass at the cathedral, as I often did, and sat in the back pew. It was the only sanctuary where I was able to grieve for my father, Koki, and the country that was being destroyed by war.

My community of journalist friends was disappearing. James Fenton, the precocious British poet who had become my buddy after Koki left, was going back to London for the summer. The most literate foreigner in the city, Fenton wrote news articles for the *New Statesman* that read like polished essays. His poems—the few he showed me—were crystalline. He saw everything and was very funny. He had a tailor sew matching jeans for us out of the USAID flour sacks. Around Phnom Penh, he fit in easily, befriending simple shopkeepers and top diplomats alike. Renji Sathiah, the Malaysian charge d'affairs, threw him a farewell party in May, where we were required to wear white in honor of James's love for his swinging-London white suit.

Françoise Demulder, the French photographer who had moved to Phnom Penh right after the bombing ended, was one of my only journalist friends still living in Cambodia. She had arrived with Yves Billy, a photographer and her boyfriend since her teens. A model in Paris, she had little to do in Cambodia, so she followed Yves to the battlefield and eventually started taking photographs herself. When she turned professional, her photographs outsold Yves's and their relationship fell apart.

Françoise shied away from the press crowd and the daily briefings. We routinely met at the home of the French diplomat Louis Bardollet, who fed us good meals, played the piano, and took us waterskiing on the Mekong when the war permitted. She felt protected in the French community and had no intention of leaving.

The situation with the resident male press corps was getting rough, and some of their arguments were physical. Reporters openly brought prostitutes to the hotel and press parties; the young Cambodian women resembled others I had interviewed in brothels after being sold by their destitute families. Steve Heder, the American freelancer who became an academic, had recently married a Cambodian woman and was staying in Phnom Penh. He saw the atmosphere among journalists become one of "anything goes. The more you went off the rails, the better. It was cool—whoring, drinking, drugs. I didn't understand it then as a right or wrong thing—just crazy."[27]

The behavior of the press corps was a reflection of the disintegration of Cambodia. Clinics treated children wrapped in dirty bandages with nothing more than aspirin in sugar water. Sadism abounded. A five-year-old boy who sold wine bottles full of a gasoline and oil mixture for motorcyclists was burned alive outside the Central Market when a passerby threw a flaming towel at his merchandise.

After the 1974 dry season offensive, Phnom Penh was no longer safe. The Khmer Rouge regularly shelled the city. A group of us covering an attack heard cries from a burning building and carried out the wounded one night—an improvised, desperate rescue that was caught on film. The next day I received a cable from my top boss at the *Washington Post* saying: "No More Florence Nightingales. Will not repeat not pay hospital."

Even the French ordered all of their nonessentials out: men and any wives still in the country.

The smell of death was not restricted to battlefields. In refugee camps, the overcrowded hospitals, and the city streets, I grew accustomed to the stench of blood, urine, and decay. The rational part of me knew there was no good end. I believed my own reporting. It was clear that soon I had to leave, and I wrote my family that if I waited until the end I would be carried out in a straitjacket or a body bag.

It still took months before I could bring myself to leave this country of horrors that seemed so beautiful to me. One of my last articles was a tribute to the Cambodian journalists who were at the core of the reporting of the war. From my first weeks they had supported me and become my friends. Most had never seen their name in print until they appeared in my article called "Cambodia's Hero-Journalists."

After nearly two years, I left in August 1974, feeling I was abandoning the country. I'm sure Kate Webb felt the same when UPI told her to move to Hong Kong in 1972. What I could barely comprehend was how Kate had survived nearly six years of the war and still lobbied to return to cover the end.

~ ~ ~

FRANCES FITZGERALD PUBLISHED a three-part series on the Viet Cong about the same time my article on the Khmer Rouge appeared. Rather than move on to another subject, FitzGerald had continued watching Vietnam and had returned to report on the other side. In theory, reporters were permitted to cross into Viet Cong territory after the signing of the Paris Peace Accords in 1973, but the Saigon government considered such visits illegal. FitzGerald walked across the invisible border without any invitation and with no idea what she would find. She entered near Can Tho in the Delta, an area she knew well.

She and David Greenway of the *Washington Post* walked across a flat plain of unkempt wild grasses and bamboo toward a hamlet of small clay homes that led to bunkers deep underground: the "liberated zone" of the Provisional Revolutionary Government (PRG), formerly known as the Viet Cong. Young girls guided the journalists to the edge of a tree line where PRG soldiers appeared. By accident, the two Americans had walked into a zone at the edge of a military base.

"Strangely," FitzGerald said, "I never felt in danger."

It was still an active war zone: the promised cease-fire had never held. Once US troops withdrew in exchange for the release of American prisoners, all bets were off. "The accords did not settle the central question over which the war had been fought: the question of who controlled South Vietnam," FitzGerald wrote in the *Atlantic Monthly*.[28]

Once inside the VC zone, the top political officer shook their hands. "We welcome you and it does not matter if you are journalists or CIA because we have won the war."

Over meals of rice, fish, and tea, the political officers spent hours explaining why they believed they were winning the war, that the American withdrawal was an admission of defeat and a victory for them. Their lectures concluded with a description of peace under the communists, "where everyone had a house and enough clothes and no one took bribes." At times these officials reminded FitzGerald of the American colonels who had given military briefings back in Saigon.[29]

She made one more trip to the other side and pretended to have been captured by the PRG to avoid any trouble with the Saigon authorities.

There, she assessed the varying strengths of the two sides. North Vietnam and the PRG controlled two-thirds of the territory of South Vietnam, while the Saigon government controlled the vast majority of the population. The ARVN had grown to one million soldiers, and the United States had resupplied Saigon with massive military shipments before the peace accord was signed.[30]

She summed up the state of what she called the "cease-fire war" in the New York Times in early 1974. Since peace had been declared, fifty thousand troops had been killed, the same annual rate of casualties since 1965, except none were American. For the first time in twelve years, there was no bombing of North Vietnam. The United States still paid $3 billion or 80 percent of South Vietnam's budget. China and the Soviet Union still supplied North Vietnam. President Nixon had held historic summits in Peking and Moscow to begin a thaw in the Cold War, negating much of the earlier ideological motivation for fighting the war.

"Mr. Nixon's measures have not insured a stable situation," Frankie concluded. The cease-fire "stalemate" was artificial and would require American intervention to continue. She hoped the American public wouldn't allow the US to resume fighting. The price was already too high, she wrote, even higher than the cost of President Johnson's war.[31]

But it would not be Nixon's war for long. President Richard M. Nixon resigned on August 9, 1974, rather than face impeachment over the Watergate scandal.

~ ~ ~

FRANKIE FITZGERALD SPENT Christmas 1974 in Hanoi and stayed on through the New Year of 1975, becoming one of the very few journalists who reported from all three sides of the war.

North Vietnam surprised her, for its unexpected similarities to the South and its contrasts. In the countryside, the poverty and lack of development was a shock. It seemed nearly feudal. She wrote that the landscape hadn't change since the "the nineteen-twenties or the seventeen-twenties."

In Hanoi, the surprise was the similarities. The city looked like a French provincial town, although ill kempt, just as Saigon had been before the American buildup. On Christmas Eve, she walked to the old French cathedral, the night air scented with orchids, passed throngs of young Vietnamese walking around the square in an old-fashioned paseo, and entered the church that, like in Saigon, was "filled to over-flowing even at ten o'clock for the midnight mass." Children slept in the aisles.

Her hotel, the once grand Metropole, was the dilapidated cousin of the Continental in Saigon, down to the off-yellow paint and the bath-tubs that had lost much of their enamel. Renamed the Thong Nhat, or Reunification, the Hanoi hotel's public spaces were gloomy. Guests invited one another to their rooms for drinks. Outside, the sidewalks were filled with pedestrians and bicyclists, as lively a street scene as in Saigon, but the people of the North were wearing "green military jackets and pith helmets . . . a monochrome procession."[32]

FitzGerald's twenty-three-page *New Yorker* article on her journey to North Vietnam described the real-life conditions and aspirations, the humor and the subterfuge. The often-rote propaganda, she wrote, proceeded "like some ideological freight train over all the old tracks, from the independence of North Vietnamese policy to American im-perialism in the South."

The most important propaganda message, "indeed the only one," was the familiar statement of Ho Chi Minh that "there is nothing more precious than freedom and independence."

Missing during the three-week visit was any meeting with the mili-tary. The North Vietnamese denied FitzGerald any military briefings. "They steered us away from military affairs (we met no high military officers, and, doubtless because of all the convoys on the roads, we did not travel south)."

FitzGerald left Hanoi as the North Vietnamese launched their final offensive, although she only learned the details after she returned to New York on January 11.

Phuoc Binh, the capital of Phuoc Long Province in South Vietnam, fell to a North Vietnamese tank assault on January 7, 1975. It was the first provincial capital to fall to the North since 1972, but the North Vietnamese said nothing to the group that this might become the final offensive of the war.

The new American president, Gerald Ford, responded to the new offensive by saying the US would not supply air support to South Vietnam during the fighting.

～ ～ ～

KATE WEBB WAS stuck in Hong Kong on the UPI desk, reading the wire stories as the North Vietnamese tanks pushed east and then south. The Thieu government in Saigon had expected a dry season offensive but not one aimed at the cities.

Hanoi was following a strategy of "escalation and improvisation." The army would proceed south as long as they could defeat the ARVN and pull back when they met stiff resistance. Just before leaving Hanoi to lead his troops in the South, North Vietnamese general Van Tien Dung met with Le Duan and told him he was optimistic that "if we win great victories we might be able to liberate the south this year."

The victories added up. By the end of March 1975, the NVA had captured Ban Me Thout and the Central Highlands, Pleiku City and its airport, and Quang Tri and Da Nang, allowing the North Vietnamese to revise their goal: they would be in Saigon by mid-May.

President Ford announced that the US Navy would evacuate South Vietnamese from the cities threatened by the North.[33]

In Cambodia, the Phnom Penh government was also near collapse. Lon Nol had been sent on a goodwill tour manufactured by the Americans to replace him with better military leaders. It was years too late. The Khmer Rouge had encircled the capital and cut off all supply routes.

Webb felt a need to report the war's end. Her editors agreed but did not send her to the war zones; they instead assigned her to Clark Air Base in the Philippines, where she covered the American evacuation from South Vietnam. Webb was at the base when the Marines began the final evacuation of Cambodia on April 12, 1975. Helicopters landed on a playground near the embassy, and heavily armed Marines escorted the waiting diplomats, journalists, and Cambodian officials and families onto the helicopters that flew them to US aircraft carriers in the Gulf of Thailand.

Alarmed, Webb used the military system to patch through to UPI in Hong Kong to reach the UPI's remaining Cambodian journalists who had declined the offer to evacuate. Early on April 17, she cabled one of the reporters as he sent a story from the PTT Office on the square. In her imagination, Kate could see him typing the keys as they exchanged jokes over the wires. He said he deserved a pay raise. She was about to answer when he interrupted with what became his last message. The Khmer Rouge were entering the post office. He had to go.

Webb went straight to the bar on the air base and drank martinis until four in the morning when members of the Filipino band ended their set and carried her to her hotel room.[34]

~ ~ ~

THE NEWS FROM Cambodia was shocking. On the first day of victory, the Khmer Rouge ordered everyone out of Phnom Penh. Immediately. The entire population was herded like cattle out of the capital to the countryside. Soldiers in black pajama uniforms shot any protestors. Men, women, children, students, and patients in hospitals: they were all sent marching down the highways. Government officials, soldiers, and professionals were identified and murdered.

Ly Eng, the journalist who was Webb's close friend and sometime lover, was last seen fleeing the Khmer Rouge in his sports car.

Horror over Cambodia was eclipsed by the coming collapse of South Vietnam. The North Vietnamese were closing in on Saigon. They had taken Xuan Loc, the last line of defense of Saigon. President Thieu resigned on April 21, blaming the United States for signing the Paris Peace Accords and turning its back on his country. Two days later, President Ford rejected any suggestion that the US would launch a last-minute bombing campaign to save Saigon. He announced that the Vietnam War was "finished as far as America was concerned."

All that was left was the evacuation of Americans and their Vietnamese allies. Ambassador Graham Martin had resisted repeated assertions from within the embassy, beginning in early March, that the end was near. The initial evacuation plans were drawn up to use the runways at Tan Son Nhut Air Base. That option was destroyed by the communists' heavy bombardment on the night of April 29.[35]

Kate Webb was reassigned from Clark Air Base to the USS *Blue Ridge*, the navy command ship in charge of the forty-vessel American armada waiting off the coast of Vietnam to receive evacuees and transport them to the Philippines. The ships had been waiting there since the fall of Da Nang one month earlier. She was one of a select few pool reporters on the ship and was responsible for writing stories to be used by all news organizations.

Ron Moreau, a *Newsweek* magazine reporter fluent in Vietnamese, was another pool reporter on the USS *Blue Ridge*. Although he was only two years younger than Webb, Moreau considered her an icon. It was an "honor to be reporting with her. I hoped I could get her to talk about her exploits, but she was all business, interviewing everyone, not seeming to pay attention to me and to the fact that she was the only woman on the ship."[36]

The pace was nonstop. The largest helicopter operation of its kind was thrown together later than anyone wanted. On April 29, President Ford and Secretary of State Kissinger gave the order to evacuate, and the American armed forces radio played the song "I'm Dreaming of a White Christmas," the signal in Saigon to depart. Panic and chaos ensued. Desperate crowds tried to board buses to pickup zones from which helicopters would ferry them to the American ships thirty miles off the coast. Families and friends were divided. Bribes as large as $200,000 were offered to get past Marines guarding the buildings, whose roofs were being used as helicopter landing pads for the evacuation.

Moreau never saw Webb sleep as helicopter after helicopter landed on the small ship, discharged the Americans and Vietnamese from Saigon and then turned around to pick up more. She interviewed the arrivals and then filed nonstop stories through the ship's communications room.

One of the last to arrive on board was Tom Polgar, the CIA station chief, who had burned embassy files and sent the last message to Washington. "It has been a long fight and we have lost. . . . Those who fail to learn from history are forced to repeat it. Let us hope that we will not have another Vietnam experience and that we have learned our lesson. Saigon signing off."[37]

On April 30, 1975, after the US embassy had shut down and all the Americans evacuated, Webb filed this report:

> The 40 American ships involved in the Vietnam evacuation operation moved out to a new holding area today about 50 miles off the coast. Navy spokesmen said that the operation was officially over. More than 6,000 people, including about 900 Americans, were flown out of Saigon in the last phase of the American airlift and landed on the decks of vessels that were waiting 30 miles offshore. Among the last to leave was the American Ambassador, 61-year-old Graham A. Martin. He appeared drawn and weary as he stepped out of a Marine helicopter before dawn onto the deck of the Blue Ridge.[38]

And with that, Kate Webb wrote the end of the decades-long American involvement in the Vietnam War.

⌒ ⌒ ⌒

ONCE SHE REALIZED the end was near, Catherine Leroy put aside her assignments and projects and flew to Saigon from Paris. She arrived in the middle of April and booked a room at the Continental Hotel with most of the remaining press corps. But she wasn't chasing the story as she normally did. Adding historic photos to her portfolio was not uppermost in her mind. She had come as a witness.

When she walked the streets, she dutifully had her camera, but she was in a thoughtful mood, remembering the city nine years earlier when she first arrived and how life had exploded all around her. Since 1969, she had covered Middle East conflicts. Beirut was becoming a second home. But Vietnam always remained very close to her. She felt she owed it to herself, to her profession, and to those who had touched her life deeply, like Vernon Wike, the medic she photographed on Hill 881, to be in Saigon at this moment.

Seated on the familiar Continental terrace, she watched the growing panic as hundreds, then thousands, fled by the day. They carried bulging suitcases and briefcases of gold bars. Parents searched for children lost in the scrum. Parts of the city were burning. Ambulances raced toward Grall Hospital where she had recovered from her foot injury. That Saigon, her old Saigon, had disappeared. Now it was in the chaos of something new.

The biggest surprise was on April 29, as the signal to evacuate went out. To her amazement, nearly all the American journalists left the city on helicopters, landing on the USS *Blue Ridge*.

Leroy understood their editors had told them to leave, but still, they could have ignored those orders. "That was very interesting that the American media left because this was the end of their story of war . . . it would have been worthwhile if they had stayed."[39]

European journalists and photographers found themselves filling in for the absent Americans.

Françoise Demulder had flown into Vietnam from Cambodia and was working with Leroy, her role model. The two teamed up on April 30 as the North Vietnamese moved into the city. They photographed the looting of US installations. The American embassy was pillaged. Furniture, office equipment, and supplies were scattered on all floors and into the street. To avoid a battle, the South Vietnamese government had broadcast its surrender over the radio. The sound of cannons ended. Policemen and ARVN soldiers were shedding their uniforms all over the city.

When North Vietnamese troops entered Saigon, there was no fighting or bloodshed as the soldiers, called *bo doi*, marched as if in a victory parade. They shouted *giai phong*, or liberation. The two French women ran ahead of the column of troops and arrived at the Presidential Palace, the seat of power of the South Vietnamese government, in time to record the first NVA tank—Tank 843—crashing through its gate.

James Fenton was there as well, riding on the back of that tank. He had flagged it down on its way to the palace. "The tank speeded up and rammed the left side of the palace gate. Wrought iron flew into the air, but the whole structure refused to give. I nearly fell off. The tank backed again, and I observed a man with a nervous smile opening the center portion of the gate. We drove into the grounds of the palace and fired a salute."[40]

Fenton had been named acting bureau chief of the *Washington Post* one day earlier, after the departure of the American staff. His was the only front-page article from Saigon in that paper the day the war ended.

Demulder photographed the exact moment of the tank crashing into the Presidential Palace. Her image was reproduced around the world and became one of the memorable shots of the war's end.

Leroy followed the troops as they marched through the palace gardens to accept the surrender of the South Vietnamese government. She photographed them at an impromptu press conference on the palace balcony and as they raised their flag, officially taking power in the South.

"I wanted to be there, to see it happen."[41]

⌐ ⌐ ⌐

EACH OF THE three women who had redefined the role of women in war reporting, and who, individually, had won extraordinary accolades and suffered for their work, was there as the war in Vietnam finally ended. Frankie FitzGerald witnessed the final assault from the North from bomb-scarred Hanoi; Kate Webb watched each shattered US evacuee arrive aboard the USS *Blue Ridge*; and Cathy Leroy was there, an almost silent observer, as the gates of the old regime were torn from their posts and years of death and ruin for the idea of a US-sponsored state of South Vietnam were finally brought to an end. It was over.

Epilogue

Aᴛᴇʀ 1975, ᴛʜᴇ Uɴɪᴛᴇᴅ Sᴛᴀᴛᴇs ᴡᴀɴᴛᴇᴅ ᴛᴏ ᴇʀᴀsᴇ ᴛʜᴇ memory of Vietnam and the first war America had lost. Once it had helped Vietnamese, Lao, and Cambodian refugees settle in America, the US largely turned its back on the countries of Indochina. At the State Department, the diplomats overseeing Vietnam, Laos, and Cambodia gave their group the nickname Very Lost Causes.

The American veterans of the war felt they were left adrift. When Jan Scruggs, a veteran, established the fund that built the memorial to their fallen comrades in Washington, DC—the striking black granite wall of names designed by Maya Lin[1]—the opening in November 1982 began with a parade of often-weeping veterans, grateful for the welcome home parade they had never previously received. Gen. John W. Vessey Jr., the chairman of the Joint Chiefs of Staff, attended. President Ronald Reagan did not.[2]

Bobby Mueller, another veteran, helped establish Vietnam Veterans of America in 1978 because traditional veteran groups did next to nothing to lobby for the specific care and support Vietnam veterans needed. The group initiated informal relations with Vietnamese veterans in Vietnam and, as a nonprofit fund, shared the 1997 Nobel Prize for Peace for the campaign to ban land mines.[3]

The US finally established normal diplomatic relations with Vietnam in 1995 and ended its severe sanctions against the country.

~ ~ ~

CATHERINE LEROY, KATE Webb, and Frances FitzGerald did not forget Vietnam. During the first years after the Vietnam War, Catherine Leroy was on fire. She won the 1976 Robert Capa Gold Medal Award honoring courage as well as artistry for her coverage of street fighting in Beirut during the Lebanese civil war—the first woman to win that award. She also fell in love in Beirut with Bernard Estrade, a French reporter for Agence France-Presse. Estrade was the physical and emotional opposite of Leroy—large, solid, and a stabilizer in the relationship. They were partners for most of the war.[4]

Estrade was posted to Hanoi, and Leroy spent two months in Vietnam in 1980. She traveled around the country, photographing the changes to mark the fifth anniversary of the end of the war. She moved about in relative freedom compared to her last days in the South in 1975.

From 1977 to 1986, she was under contract with *Time* magazine and covered conflicts in Northern Ireland, Cyprus, Afghanistan, Iran, Iraq, Angola, China, Pakistan, and Libya.[5] In 1983, she coauthored *God Cried* with Tony Clifton, a *Newsweek* correspondent.[6] In the midst of this hectic transient working life, her relationship with Estrade unsurprisingly fell apart. He was the only partner she ever had.

Leroy's assignments dried up not long after she left war coverage in the early 1990s. She was never good at business and found herself with little money. She lived in Los Angeles where she drove around in a 1968 black Mustang and eventually ran a website called Piece Unique, where she sold used haute couture apparel as well as her war photographs.

Fred Ritchin, dean of the school at the International Center of Photography and a close friend of Leroy's, spoke to her every Friday during those years. "She never really recovered from what she suffered in Vietnam. She felt left out—others had gone on to a certain amount of prestige and financial success. She felt marginalized, cast aside, not appreciated. She was broke.[7]

For the thirtieth anniversary of the war's end in 2005, she published the book *Under Fire: Great Photographers and Writers in Vietnam*, giving credit to her colleagues for what she considered model war coverage.[8] She managed to mount a few exhibits of her Vietnam work, but by then she had largely disappeared from public view, unknown to the photographers—female and male—making their names in newer wars in Asia, the Middle East, and Africa.

Her last assignment was that same year. *Paris Match* sent Leroy to Arizona for a reunion and report on Vernon Wike, the medic she had photographed on Hill 881. Wike was a wreck. He had married four times and no longer spoke to his daughters. In her photographs, he looks lost, his arms tattooed with the names of his dead comrades. "Vernon is haunted," Leroy wrote.[9]

So was Leroy. She died in 2006, one week after she was diagnosed with cancer. Shortly before she died, she told Fred Ritchin that she was proud of what she had done in Vietnam—that she had climbed the summit.

Her friends, led by Robert Pledge, founder and head of Contact Press Images, did not allow her accomplishment to disappear. Pledge, along with Ritchin, the editor Dominique Deschavanne, and other photographers, collected all of her photographs and papers for the first time and created the nonprofit French foundation, or dotation, to preserve her work. From Paris and New York, they painstakingly translated all of her letters, carefully stored her photographs, and created a sophisticated website called Dotation Catherine Leroy that features her work and her story.

More broadly, the number of women war photographers and photo editors today are her legacy, of the woman who broke through at great cost, winning unprecedented honors and creating a new way of seeing war.

~ ~ ~

KATE WEBB QUIT journalism not long after the war's end. UPI had her sent to Singapore, but her boss in Hong Kong visited regularly and insisted she have an affair with him. She refused. She told her sister Rachel, "That's not part of my job description."[10] But the boss complained to New York headquarters that Webb was not performing well. She demanded that New York remove his complaints from her file. When UPI refused, she quit and moved to Indonesia. She became a public relations director for a hotel in Jakarta.

She was sufficiently angry that she stayed out of daily journalism for ten years. Webb did try to keep her hand in as a freelancer, but without the structure of a staff job she flailed, missing deadlines and disappointing editors. Her drinking did not help. In Jakarta, she began a lifelong, off-and-on relationship with John Stearman, a down-home American engineer working for oil companies in the region. She moved in with him and his two young daughters until they returned to the United States and he accepted jobs around the world.

After that lost decade, Webb returned to full-time journalism, joining Agence France-Presse in 1985. In her second career, Webb covered much of Asia, living in Seoul, Delhi, Kabul, and finally in Jakarta again. She covered major stories: the ongoing Soviet occupation of Afghanistan, the 1991 Gulf War, the assassination of Indian prime minister Rajiv Gandhi, Hong Kong's handover in 1997, and the United Nations intervention in East Timor. She endured a kidnap attempt in Kabul when an assassin dragged her out of her hotel room by the hair (she was rescued by colleagues) and a motorcycle accident in Delhi that badly injured her right shoulder. She never changed. She always championed her local staff—once threatening to quit if they weren't treated better by the wire service—and generosity was second nature to her. She invited an Afghan family to live with her in Delhi after they escaped the war and sent money for life-saving medicine to the daughter of a friend of a friend whom she had never met.

Through it all she remained a stellar wire service reporter. She was the pool reporter in August 1997 when the isolated communist country of North Korea briefly opened its doors. Peter Mackler, her Agence France-Presse boss in Washington, sent out a company-wide note praising her reporting: "Her pool copy really sparkled. It was abundant, timely, well-written and full of good color detail and quotes that pool members eat up." Among those pool members who Mackler said appreciated her work were future Pulitzer Prize winners Nicholas Kristof of the *New York Times* and Kevin Sullivan and Mary Jordan of the *Washington Post*.[11]

She repeatedly returned to Indochina, always reporting on the dissidents and those left behind by history. Her last visit to Cambodia was in 1993, long after the genocide and just as the country had found peace. Her final return to Vietnam was in 2000. She found those trips "very depressing." "Time marches on but humankind does not progress," she wrote to her aunt, Alison Sims.[12]

One year later she retired. She told Agence France-Presse she was "too old to keep up with front-line reporting and that was the only kind I liked." She also complained about the insane demand for constant updates. "It's like we're all mosquitoes dancing on the surface of a pond. We have to move so fast that reporting has suffered. It's nowhere as meticulous as it was."[13]

Webb bought herself a small farm outside Sydney in Hunter Valley from her beloved aunt. Her plans included inviting John Stearman to join her. They had seen each other irregularly over the decades and had talked of retiring together. But Stearman died working in South America. Webb wrote an essay for *War Torn*, a collection of nine personal stories by women who reported from Vietnam. Then, except for one year teaching journalism at Ohio University, Webb spent her retirement catching up with her family and growing vegetables in Australia. She died of cancer in 2007; at her side were her sister, Rachel, and brother Jeremy, as they had been so many times before.

Agence France-Presse created the Kate Webb Prize in 2008, an annual award given to a locally employed Asian journalist for exceptional work in difficult or dangerous conditions in the region, a fair description of the circumstances the young Kate Webb found herself in in 1970. In 2019, her image appeared on an Australian postage stamp honoring women in war.

∽ ∽ ∽

FRANCES FITZGERALD'S ARTICLES on the war and Vietnam appeared in the *New Republic*, the *New York Times*, *More Magazine*, the *New York Review of Books*, and other publications for years after the war ended. If a woman reporter was invited on a panel to discuss the war, it was inevitably Frances FitzGerald.

She attained the stature of a public intellectual, writing books that challenged worn truths and winning praise from the New York editors who mattered most. William Shawn of the *New Yorker*, who had published the excerpts from her book, singled her out as "one of the best non-fiction writers of her generation," while Robert Silvers of the *New York Review of Books* called her a "master of complicated ideas and difficult issues."

Within the world of letters and foreign affairs, she played major roles as president of the PEN American Center promoting freedom of speech, as president of the Society of American Historians, and as an active member of the Council on Foreign Relations.

She never lost her place in the rarified circles of New York society, either, and dated a series of accomplished and often glamorous men.

Her later books were eclectic. Her investigation of the dull and aimless history books used in American secondary schools showed how they deprived Americans of any real sense of their own history. She profiled four prophetic communities for signs of where the United States was headed in 1986: a gay activist community in San Francisco, an ashram in Oregon, the fundamentalist church of Jerry Fallwell, and the Florida sun city retirement community. She next turned to military matters in a deep investigation of the multibillion-dollar Star Wars defense program of Ronald Reagan, which, like all of her books, was a critical success.[14]

After returning to Vietnam with the photographer Mary Cross to cowrite a photojournalist book, *Vietnam: Spirits of the Earth*, her most recent book to date is *The Evangelicals: The Struggle to Shape America*, which was published in 2017 when she was seventy-seven years old. It was uniformly praised, particularly by academics. The American Scholar said it succinctly: "FitzGerald's brilliant book could not have been more timely, more well-researched, more well-written, or more necessary." She won the 2017 National Book Critics Circle Award for that book—forty-five years after she had swept the awards for *Fire in the Lake*.

In 2020 the Society of American Historians awarded her the inaugural Tony Horwitz Prize for lifetime work of "wide appeal and enduring significance."

At fifty, FitzGerald married Jim Sterba, a well-respected foreign correspondent for the *Wall Street Journal* who had covered the Vietnam War. They met late in their lives. He wrote of their courtship and marriage in *Frankie's Place: A Love Story*, portraying himself as the Spencer Tracy to her Katherine Hepburn, a Midwestern journeyman to her Brahmin diva.

Some later critics raised doubts about *Fire in the Lake*. When the 2017 multipart PBS documentary on the Vietnam War by Ken Burns and Lynn Novick offered what it called a full reading list to accompany the series, the fifty-eight history books did not include *Fire in the Lake*, the most honored book on the war.[15]

Fredrik Logevall, the respected historian of Vietnam, warned that while parts of the book did prove problematic with later research, he feared that some of the criticism was tinged with envy. He said: "Whatever we want to call it—a first-cut history—this book stands up very well even though she didn't have access to archives. I would put it on a short shelf of really important books on the war. It's of enduring importance."[16]

But then Kate Webb's *On the Other Side: 23 Days with the Viet Cong* was not on the Ken Burns list of recommended Vietnam books; nor was Catherine Leroy's *Under Fire: Great Photographers and Writers in Vietnam*. In fact, the Burns list did not include a single published work by any of the female journalists who covered the war.

~ ~ ~

THE WAR DID not end for me as I thought it would. Back in Washington, DC, now a staff reporter at the *Washington Post*, I was upended by the sparse news coming out of Cambodia. After throwing everyone out of the cities and towns, the victorious Khmer Rouge isolated the country completely. No telephone, no mail, no cables, no air traffic save from Vietnam and China. All borders shut. The few refugees who escaped spoke of executions and hunger, of a regime that treated people like work animals. I was desperate to go there and see for myself. After four years petitioning the government of the Khmer Rouge, I received a visa and set out in December 1978 with one other American reporter, Richard Dudman, and Malcolm Caldwell, a British professor, to report from Cambodia. We were the first and last journalists allowed in Pol Pot's country.

For two weeks we were taken around the country on prearranged schedules with no time to explore on our own. We were kept under guard at all times, essentially under house arrest. We were shown only staged happy villagers and happy workers. Yet the Khmer Rouge could not hide what was missing. All normal life was gone: empty towns, empty schools, empty markets, empty pagodas and churches and mosques. No one lingered on the streets. On our last day, we interviewed Pol Pot himself. For nearly two hours, he lectured us on Vietnam's plan to invade Cambodia and the need for NATO to come to his aid. That night at our guesthouse, Cambodian assassins attacked us, threatening me and Dudman and killing Caldwell. We waited hours before we were rescued. The next day we left for home, and the Vietnamese did invade and overthrew the genocidal regime of the Khmer Rouge.

Shaken by the experience and my horror at what the country went through, I spent the next five years researching and writing a history of the nearly four years of Khmer Rouge rule, entitled *When the War Was Over*. They devastated the country, killing off nearly a quarter of the population through starvation, neglect, and murder, attempting to erase the culture and civilization, and leaving a nation utterly traumatized. I have continued to report from Cambodia.

My journalism career was traditional. After the *Washington Post*, I became the senior foreign editor of National Public Radio and then I joined the *New York Times* as an editor and then reporter in the Washington bureau. I am the mother of two grown children and a grandmother. My husband is Bill Nash, a retired army major general, who led the peacekeeping mission for the US Army in Bosnia in 1995 and who, as a young lieutenant in Vietnam, was part of the 1970 invasion of Cambodia.

This book was triggered by my appearance in 2015 as an expert witness at the genocide trial of senior Khmer Rouge leaders. The Extraordinary Chambers in the Courts of Cambodia was established to try the senior surviving Khmer Rouge leaders on charges of crimes against humanity and genocide from 1975 to 1979. It was the only international criminal tribunal ever convened to address the long Vietnam War or its consequences. It was constructed so that foreign officials and foreign nations were excluded from scrutiny, allowing China and the United States to escape judgment.

The courtroom in Phnom Penh was solemn during the three full days of my testimony. Robed Cambodian and international jurists sat on all sides of me. The two surviving defendants, Nuon Chea, number two to Pol Pot, and Khieu Samphan, the head of state, were seated to my right. I felt bolted to my chair by the profound realization that my work could help convict these monsters. The first day's transcript filled 107 pages.[17]

Although there were thousands of witnesses, there were no more than a handful of expert witnesses like me. The prosecution went over minute details from my book, my interviews with senior Khmer Rouge figures, and from that rare firsthand trip through the country under Pol Pot and my subsequent research—all damning. On the last day, the defense predictably attempted to destroy my credibility. Anta Guisse, a French lawyer, represented the defendant Khieu Samphan.

"I'm going to finish with this question," she said and then quoted from a 1986 review of my book by David Chandler, a respected professor of modern Cambodia. He criticized me for writing my book because I was only a journalist and not an academic. He claimed I hadn't done sufficient original research even though I was the only author who had reported from Cambodia during the war and the revolution and who had done countless and often exclusive interviews.

"Do you have anything to say?" Guisse asked.

Yes, I said. Then I read the positive reviews printed on my book jacket from the *Los Angeles Times*, the *Financial Times*, the *New York Times*, and the *Washington Post*. Guisse said I hadn't answered the question. She pushed me. I was hoping not to get into a petty dispute over one bad review during a genocide trial, but at the same time I was not going to allow that review to undermine my testimony. So I explained how David Chandler had been selective in his dismissal of journalists writing history. Every other journalist who had written a book on modern Cambodia, even novels, had received a nice review from Chandler. I was the exception. How was I different?

"I am the only woman journalist who wrote such a book."[18]

Guisse, a French woman of color who had spoken about sexism in the international legal field, thanked me for the "clarification" and sat down.

The two defendants were convicted of genocide.

And something became clear to me. No one knew what it had meant to be a woman covering the Vietnam War. I had never tried to tell the story. Now, through the extraordinary pioneering lives of Catherine Leroy, Frances FitzGerald, and Kate Webb, I have.

Acknowledgments

THIS JOINT BIOGRAPHY would have been close to impossible without the unconditional and generous cooperation of Frances FitzGerald, the Catherine Leroy Foundation, and the family of Kate Webb. They held nothing back from their archives, agreed to lengthy interviews, and asked nothing in return. Every page of this book reflects their open minds and respect for history, even and especially when my inquiries exposed flaws in those they love. They were always gracious, and I am deeply grateful.

The Frances FitzGerald Collection at the Howard Gotlieb Archives of Boston University holds extensive materials donated by Frankie from her earliest life through her extensive career, including notebooks, articles, and manuscripts from Vietnam. Frankie patiently answered my questions over three years, most often in person, welcoming me at her home and supplying leads when asked. No issue was off-limits.

The members of the board of the Dotation Catherine Leroy approved my request to delve into their foundation's archives of Catherine's photographs, papers, and records, as well as videotaped interviews of those who knew her. Robert Pledge in New York and Dominique

Deschavanne in Paris sat for extensive interviews and gave me access to material unavailable to the public. They never pushed back when I asked for more access and went to great lengths to help me locate French journalists who knew Catherine in Vietnam.

Rachel Webb Miller and her husband, Geoff Miller, welcomed me to their home in Sydney, Australia, where I searched on my own through large plastic bins that hold the papers and records of Kate Webb. When I discovered items that had been overlooked, we untangled cryptic notes and papers together and then made photocopies at the local library. They answered countless questions, and in Brisbane, Rachel and her brother Jeremy Webb sat through a final daylong interview about Kate's life. I appreciated their quiet hospitality, especially after some wrenching discussions about their sister's life. The family plans to house Kate Webb's papers in an Australian library.

I also want to thank Professor Joyce Hoffmann, who opened her files at Old Dominion University in Norfolk, Virginia. She is the author of *On Their Own: Women Journalists and the American Experience in Vietnam*, an almost encyclopedic survey of women who covered the war. Hoffmann's extensive records were very helpful and gave me leads for my own research.

In the same vein, I would like to thank the women who contributed essays and testimonials to the collection *War Torn: Stories of War from the Women Reporters Who Covered Vietnam*. Several aided my research, especially Denby Fawcett, Jurate Kazickas, and Laura Palmer. Their essays filled many holes in the narrative of women's struggles, especially those by Anne Morrissy Merick and Ann Bryan Mariano, who was a former colleague of mine at the *Washington Post*.

Librarians at Boston University and the Library of Congress were more than helpful, ensuring I found all the materials I needed. The librarians at the National Archives in suburban Maryland answered all of my questions and organized the timely release of the classified Vietnam personnel records of Catherine Leroy.

I want to thank Edward Friedman, professor emeritus at the University of Wisconsin and a scholar of Asia-US relations, for carefully reviewing much of the book.

I have wanted to write this book for years, but every time I tried, it was too difficult emotionally. So I started small, going back to the University of Washington to verify my memories and notes in what, at times, veered between an investigation and a twelve-step program. Thank you to my former professors Frank F. Conlon, historian of South Asia; Michael Shapiro, author of a now classic modern Hindi language primer; and the late Daniel Lev, a scholar of Southeast Asian politics. Judith Henchy, Southeast Asian Studies librarian, helped transform me into a very active alumni. My Cambodia archives are under her excellent care.

After digging up my papers from the war, I had long informal conversations, not interviews, with literally countless old colleagues and friends and made multiple trips to Vietnam and Cambodia. Sylvana Foa was a touchstone. My close friend Karen DeYoung patiently read through several of my false starts. Thanks to the editor, Clay Risen, I finally found my footing in an opinion piece for the *New York Times*.

Critically, it was my immense good fortune that Clive Priddle, publisher of PublicAffairs, then took on this project. He saw the importance of the book and how to shape it. He was thoroughly engaged throughout. His thoughtful hands-on editing was exquisite. This book owes much to his editing, and I cannot thank him enough. Plus, he is a joy to work with.

His assistant, Anupama Roy-Chaudhury, and the team at PublicAffairs were always helpful. And I owe a special thanks to Peter Osnos, the founder and publisher emeritus of PublicAffairs. In 1978, Osnos was the *Washington Post* foreign editor who ensured I had the newspaper's full support for my eventful trip to Cambodia. Twenty years later, he published an expanded version of my Cambodia book in the first list of PublicAffairs. He and Susan Osnos have always been in my corner.

My agent David Halpern of the Robbins Office is practically family. For over thirty years, Kathy Robbins and David have been taking care of me, steering me away from publishing pitfalls and securing my writing career so carefully I can't imagine life without them.

Thank you, Christy Macy, Anne Garrels, and Karen DeYoung, again, for reading the early pages of *You Don't Belong Here* and giving me honest feedback.

Along the way, many friends encouraged me to stick with this project, however vague it seemed. Thanks, especially, to Diane and Dennis Kenny, Lynne Bundesen, Ann and Walter Pincus, Ann Cooper, and Larry Heintzerling; to my friends from Indochina days: Steve Heder, Victoria Butler, and Timothy Carney; to Murray Hiebert, John and Karen Burgess, Robert Kaneda, and Mark Storella; and to the Capitol Hill women's group of Megan Rosenfeld, Bonny Wolf, Lis Wackman, and Gayle Krughoff. Thanks, as well, to the congregation of St. Mark's Episcopal Church led by Rev. Michele Morgan.

And I have been inspired, as always, by the examples of Rithy Panh, Mu Sochua, and Pung Chhiv Kek (Galabru), Cambodians who have enriched their country and never given up.

This book is dedicated to my family, the blending of the Becker-Nash clan. On my Becker side that includes my sisters, Sue, Janice, and Mary, my son, Lee Hoagland, my daughter, Lily Hoagland, son-in-law, Thomas Minc, and grandson Raphael Minc. On the Nash side is Bill's sister, Jean Firmin, his daughter, Rebecca, son-in-law, Matthew Engelke, grandchildren, Harriet and Louis Engelke; his son, Bill, daughter-in-law, Susan Kaufmann Nash, and granddaughters Charlotte and Julia Nash. You don't know how good it is to have a family of such love and care.

Bill is my trusted first and last reader, my love who keeps life interesting. Mackey, our dog, gets us up in the morning.

Notes

EPIGRAPH

1. Richard Eder, "Shallow Graves—Two Women and Vietnam," Los Angeles Times Book Review, *Los Angeles Times*, April 20, 1986.

2. Peter Arnett, *Live from the Battlefield: From Vietnam to Baghdad, 35 Years in the World's War Zones* (New York: Touchstone, 1995), 220

PREFACE

1. Sylvana Foa to Elizabeth Becker, August 7, 1972, in the author's possession.

2. Emory Swank, "Expulsion of Sylvana Foa," confidential cable to US embassy, Phnom Penh, Cambodia (ID:1973PHNOM3809_b), April 22, 1973, declassified 2005.

3. Sydney H. Schanberg, "Credit Due on Deep Throat," *Village Voice*, June 29, 2005.

CHAPTER 1: PETITE LADY

1. Description of jump based on Catherine Leroy, "Vietnam Narrative," unpublished manuscript, Dotation Catherine Leroy (DCL); Jacques Menasche, dir., *Cathy at War: Volume 1: Vietnam* (DCL, 2016), 72 mins.; and Leroy letter to father, DCL, February 1967.

2. Stanley Karnow, *Vietnam: A History* (New York: Viking Press, 1983), 512.

3. G. C. Lorentz, J. H. Willbanks, D. H. Petraeus, P. A. Stuart, and B. L. Crittenden, *Operation Junction City, Vietnam 1967: Battle Book* (Ft. Leavenworth, KS:

Combat Studies Institute, 1983), prepared for Advanced Battle Analysis, US Army Command and General Staff College.

4. Robert Pledge interview with Don McCullin, March 17, 2012, in Menasche, *Cathy at War*.

5. George P. Hunt, "A Tiny Girl with Paratroopers' Wings," *Life*, February 16, 1968, 3.

6. John Garofolo, *Dickey Chapelle Under Fire: Photographs by the First American Female War Correspondent Killed in Action* (Madison: Wisconsin Historical Society Press, 2015).

7. Author interview with Hal Buell, January 7, 2019.

8. Author interview with Dominique Deschavanne, September 14, 2018.

9. Catherine Leroy, "Synopsis," unpublished, DCL.

10. Gary R. Hess, "Franklin Roosevelt and Indochina," *Journal of American History* 59, no. 2 (September 1972): 353–368.

11. Fredrik Logevall, *Embers of War: The Fall of an Empire and the Making of America's Vietnam* (New York: Random House, 2012), 224–231.

12. Logevall, *Embers of War*, 458.

13. Fredrik Logevall, *Choosing War: The Lost Chance for Peace and the Escalation of War in Vietnam* (Berkeley: University of California Press, 2001), 55.

14. Author interview with Christian Simonpietri, December 20, 2018.

15. Author interview with Simonpietri.

16. Pledge interview with Horst Faas, March 1, 2011, in Menasche, *Cathy at War*.

17. Jack Baird, "Ann-Margret and Her Band Perform in Vietnam," *Stars and Stripes*, March 17, 1966.

18. Description of photographing Buddhist crisis from Leroy letter to mother, DCL, April 8, 1966.

19. Description with gravestones from Leroy, "Vietnam Narrative."

20. Description of sleeping eighteen hours from Helene Cantin interview with Leroy, Radio Canada, Quebec, May 29, 1989.

CHAPTER 2: AS DIRTY AND TIRED AS THEY ARE

1. Daniel C. Hallin, *The "Uncensored War": The Media and Vietnam* (New York: Oxford University Press, 1986), 9–10.

2. Department of Defense, "Public Affairs Guidance (PAG) on Embedding Media During Possible Future Operations/Deployments in the (CENTCOM) Area of Responsibility (AOR)," declassified January 3, 2003, Federation of American Scientists, https://fas.org/sgp/othergov/dod/embed.html.

3. Jonathan Schell speaking at "Journalists Under Fire: Vietnam and Iraq," University of California television, April 16, 2005.

4. Catherine Leroy, "Vietnam Narrative," unpublished manuscript, Dotation Catherine Leroy (DCL).

5. Leroy, "Vietnam Narrative."

6. Leroy letter to father, DCL, September 20, 1966.

7. Nina Strochlic, "Daring Life of a Female War Photographer," *National Geographic*, August 17, 2018.

8. Leroy letter to mother, DCL, April 8, 1966.

9. Brothel incident based on Leroy, "Vietnam Narrative."

10. Leroy letter to father, September 20, 1966.

11. Author interview with Christian Simonpietri, December 20, 2018.

12. Interrogation in Co Luu based on Leroy, "Vietnam Narrative."

13. William M. Hammond, "Who Were the Saigon Correspondents and Does It Matter?," Joan Barone Shorenstein Center for the Press and Public Policy, Harvard University, John F. Kennedy School of Government, May 17, 1999.

14. Leroy letter to mother, April 8, 1966.

15. Author interview with Alain Taieb, July 16, 2019.

16. File of Catherine Leroy, in "Discreditation or Suspended Accreditation Correspondents Files," US Forces in Southeast Asia, Saigon, National Archives and Records Administration, released July 16, 2019, under the Freedom of Information Act.

17. "The unwashed one," in note by Clif Thompson, Da Nang, "Discreditation or Suspended Accreditation," October 26, 1966.

18. "Ugly Caucasian," "Discreditation or Suspended Accreditation," October 30, 1966.

19. Peter Arnett, *Live from the Battlefield: From Vietnam to Baghdad, 35 Years in the World's War Zones* (New York: Touchstone, 1995), 220.

20. Col. Rodger R. Bankson letter, "Discreditation or Suspended Accreditation," October 24, 1966.

21. Lt. Paul E. Pedisich letter, "Discreditation or Suspended Accreditation," October 27, 1966.

22. Author interview with Paul Pedisich, April 25, 2019.

23. Horst Faas letter to MACV, Saigon, "Discreditation or Suspended Accreditation," December 1, 1966.

24. Author interview with Tim Page, January 30, 2019.

25. Author interview with Page.

26. G. C. Lorentz, J. H. Willbanks, D. H. Petraeus, P. A. Stuart, and B. L. Crittenden, *Operation Junction City, Vietnam 1967: Battle Book* (Ft. Leavenworth, KS: Combat Studies Institute, 1983), prepared for Advanced Battle Analysis, US Army Command and General Staff College.

27. Denby Fawcett, "Walking Point," in Tad Bartimus, Denby Fawcett, Jurate Kazickas, Edith Lederer, Ann Bryan Mariano, Anne Morrissy Merick, Laura Palmer, Kate Webb, and Tracy Wood, *War Torn: Stories of War from the Women Reporters Who Covered Vietnam* (New York: Random House, 2002), 12–13.

28. Fawcett, in Bartimus et al., *War Torn*, 11–13.

29. Anne Morrissy Merick, "My Love Affair with Viet Nam," in Bartimus et al., *War Torn*, 105–106.

30. Denby Fawcett, "Nine Others Win Their Case," *Honolulu Advertiser*, August 3, 1967.

31. Author interview with Denby Fawcett, November 12, 2019.

32. Jurate Kazickas, "I Became a Feminist in Vietnam When the Officers Invited Me to Dinner—But Not to the Front Line," Veteran Feminists of America, Inc., VFA Pioneer Histories Project, September 2018.

CHAPTER 3: FORTUNATE FEMALE

1. Joshua Kurlantzick, *A Great Place to Have a War: America in Laos and the Birth of a Military CIA* (New York: Simon and Schuster, 2017), 125.

2. Author interview with Frances FitzGerald, April 6, 2018.

3. Frances FitzGerald, "Comparative Calm in the Hurricane's Eye," *Village Voice*, March 24, 1966.

4. Desmond FitzGerald letter to Frances FitzGerald, March 15, 1966, Frances FitzGerald Collection (FFC), Howard Gotlieb Archival Research Center, Boston University.

5. Bank account according to author interview with Frances FitzGerald, January 15, 2019.

6. Frank Wisner letter to FitzGerald, FFC, December 21, 1965.

7. "Telegram from the Office of the Secretary of Defense to the Embassy in Vietnam," DEF 6181, March 2, 1965, in *Foreign Relations of the United States, 1964–1968: Volume II, Vietnam, January–June 1965*, ed. David C. Humphrey, Ronald D. Landa, and Louis J. Smith (Washington, DC: US Government Printing Office, 1996), 395.

8. William Fulbright to Lyndon Johnson, in Stanley Karnow, *Vietnam: A History* (New York: Viking Press, 1983), 418.

9. Author interview with FitzGerald, January 15, 2019.

10. "Debutantes: The Smart Set," *New York Journal-American*, October 5, 1958.

11. Author interview with Ward Just, July 7, 2018.

12. Ward Just, *To What End: Report from Vietnam* (Boston: Houghton Miflin, 1968), 20.

13. Frances FitzGerald, "My Autobiography," black watch plaid notebook, FFC, 1952.

14. Author interview with FitzGerald, January 15, 2019.

15. Author interview with Meg Douglas-Hamilton, February 18, 2019.

16. Frances FitzGerald, "The Caliphate and the Kingdom," History 187, Radcliffe College, FFC, November 15, 1961.

17. Author interview with FitzGerald, January 15, 2019.

18. Marietta Tree letter to FitzGerald, Geneva, FFC, July 6, 1963.

19. Author interview with FitzGerald, January 15, 2019.

20. Martin Luther King Jr., "Opposes Vietnam War," *New York Times*, November 11, 1965, cited in "Vietnam War," Martin Luther King Jr. Research and Education Institute, Stanford University.

21. "Flamingo-pink ghetto" from Gail Sheehy, "Gail Sheehy Remembers Clay Felker," *New York Magazine*, July 2, 2008.

22. Adlai Stevenson encounter in FitzGerald, red EasyRite notebook, FFC, July 15, 1965.

23. Evan Thomas, *The Very Best Men: Four Who Dared; The Early Years of the CIA* (New York: Simon and Schuster, 1996), 322.

24. Clay Felker making a pass in FitzGerald, maple leaf notebook, FFC, circa December 1965.

25. Richard Paddock, "Thich Tri Quang, 95, Galvanizing Monk in South Vietnam, Dies," *New York Times*, November 20, 2019.

26. Don Moser and Sam Angeloff, "Irony of Riots on the Heels of Hard Fought Victories," *Life*, April 22, 1966.

27. Karnow, *Vietnam*, 444.

28. Author interview with Just, July 7, 2018.

29. Author interview with FitzGerald, June 19, 2019.

30. FitzGerald, Vietnam notebook, FFC, April 21, 1966.

31. Author interview with FitzGerald, June 19, 2019.

32. Author interview with Daniel Ellsberg, June 11, 2019.

33. Moser and Angeloff, "Irony of Riots on the Heels of Hard-Fought Victories."

34. FitzGerald, Vietnam notebook.

CHAPTER 4: A WHOLE NEW MEANING TO
THE PHRASE FOREIGN CORRESPONDENT

1. Frances FitzGerald, visiting Qui Nhon Hospital, typescript, Frances FitzGerald Collection (FFC), Howard Gotlieb Archival Research Center, Boston University, undated.

2. Neil Sheehan, *Bright Shining Lie: John Paul Vann and America in Vietnam* (New York: Random House, 1988), 580–585.

3. Stanley Karnow, *Vietnam: A History* (New York: Viking Press, 1983), 444–451.

4. Desmond FitzGerald to Frances FitzGerald, FFC, April 6, 1966.

5. Frances FitzGerald, "Background of Crisis: The Trivia in Truth," *Village Voice*, April 28, 1966.

6. John Phillips, "Language of Madness," *Village Voice*, May 5, 1966.

7. William Prochnau, *Once upon a Distant War: Young Correspondents and the Early Vietnam Battles* (New York: Times Books, 1995), 273.

8. Michael Herr, *Dispatches* (New York: Alfred A. Knopf, 1977), 233.

9. Author interview with Ward Just, July 7, 2018.

10. FitzGerald, loose paper addition to Vietnam notebook, FFC, August 1966.

11. Description of Alsop visit from Ward Just letter to FitzGerald, FFC, undated.

12. Author interview with Daniel Ellsberg, June 11, 2019.

13. Author interview with Frances FitzGerald, June 19, 2019.

14. Description of Frankie's house from author interview with FitzGerald, June 19, 2019.

15. Frances FitzGerald, "A Quiet Afternoon in a Rustic Setting," *Village Voice*, May 19, 1966.

16. Author interview with Just, July 7, 2018.

17. Author interview with FitzGerald, June 19, 2019.

18. Marietta Tree letter to FitzGerald, FFC, June 4, 1966.

19. Ward Just, *To What End: Report from Vietnam* (Boston: Houghton Miflin, 1968), 167–191.

20. Author interview with FitzGerald, June 19, 2019.

21. Author interview with Just, e-mail, July 26, 2019.

22. William Fulbright quoted in Karnow, *Vietnam*, 486.

23. George Kennan, "Vietnam Hearings," closed hearings before Senate Foreign Relations Committee, US Senate, February 1966, www.senate.gov /artandhistory/history/minute/vietnam.

24. Niall Ferguson, *Kissinger: 1923–1968; The Idealist* (New York: Penguin Books, 2015), 681.

25. Author interview with Ellsberg, June 11, 2019.

26. Henry Kissinger to FitzGerald, FFC, August 12, 1966.

27. Author interview with FitzGerald, June 19, 2019.

28. Fredrik Logevall, *Embers of War: The Fall of an Empire and the Making of America's Vietnam* (New York: Random House, 2012), 190–193.

29. "Frances FitzGerald: Author of *Fire in the Lake* Talks About Covering the War," interview for Vietnam Reconsidered: Lessons from a War conference, University of Southern California, February 1983.

30. Sheehan, *Bright Shining Lie*, 526.

31. Frances FitzGerald, "Life and Death of a Vietnamese Village," *New York Times Magazine*, September 4, 1966.

32. Robert Shaplen, "Letter from Saigon," *New Yorker*, October 1, 1966.

33. Jonathan Schell, "The Village of Ben Suc," *New Yorker*, July 8, 1967.

34. FitzGerald, Vietnam notebook, September 2, 1966.

35. Desmond FitzGerald to Frances FitzGerald, FFC, September 10, 1966.

36. Author interview with FitzGerald, April 6, 2018.

37. Just to FitzGerald, FFC, December 1966.

CHAPTER 5: VIOLENCE, MADNESS AND FEAR AND AGONY

1. Thomas C. Thayer, *The War Without Fronts: The American Experience in Vietnam* (Annapolis, MD: Naval Institute Press, 1985), 4.

2. Lewis Sorley, *Westmoreland: The General Who Lost Vietnam* (New York: Mariner Books, 2012).

3. Neil Sheehan, *Bright Shining Lie: John Paul Vann and America in Vietnam* (New York: Random House, 1988), 643–645.

4. Catherine Leroy letter to mother, Dotation Catherine Leroy (DCL), January 5, 1967.

5. Leroy, "Vietnam Narrative," unpublished manuscript, DCL.

6. Robert Pledge interview with Horst Faas, March 1, 2011, in Jacques Menasche, dir., *Cathy at War: Volume 1; Vietnam* (DCL, 2016), 72 mins.

7. Catherine Leroy, "Up Hill 881 with the Marines," *Life*, May 19, 1967.

8. Peter Howe, "The Death of a Fighter: Catherine Leroy, 1944–2006," Digital Journalist, August 2006.

9. CBS request according to Hugh Lunn, *Vietnam: A Reporter's War* (Lanham, MD: Cooper Square Press, 2001), 75.

10. Howe, "The Death of a Fighter."

11. Helene Cantin interview with Catherine Leroy, Radio Canada, Quebec, May 29, 1989.

12. Operation Hickory from Maj. Gary L. Telfer, USMC, Lt. Col. Lane Rogers, USMC, and V. Keith Fleming Jr., *U.S. Marines in Vietnam: Fighting the North Vietnamese, 1967* (Washington, DC: History and Museums Division, US Marine Corps), 26–30.

13. Menasche, *Cathy at War*.

14. "Cathy Le Roi Hit by Mortar," UPI, May 21, 1967.

15. S.Sgt. Russ Havonrd, "Lensgirl Faces Peril to Make It," *Stars and Stripes*, June 16, 1967.

16. Leroy, "Vietnam Narrative," 16–17.

17. Horst Faas letter to Forest Edwards, Hong Kong, DCL, May 25, 1967.

18. Faas letter to Sam Jones, Tokyo, DCL, May 25, 1967.

19. Faas letter to Monsieur and Madame Leroy, DCL, June 4, 1967.

20. Faas letter to Leroy, DCL, May 28, 1967.

21. AP approves payment for Leroy in John Koehler letter to Robert Tuckman, Saigon, DCL, July 12, 1967.

22. Leroy, "Vietnam Narrative."

23. Saigon cable to Paris AP office, June 17, 1967.

24. Neil Sheehan, E. W. Kenworthy, Fox Butterfield, and Hedrick Smith, *The Pentagon Papers: The Secret History of the Vietnam War* (New York: Racehorse Publishing, 2017), 589–590.

25. Nguyen Khac Vien, *The Long Resistance (1858–1975)* (Hanoi, Vietnam: Foreign Languages Publishing House, 1975), 202.

26. Author interview with Frances FitzGerald, June 19, 2019.

27. Ward Just letter to Frances FitzGerald, Frances FitzGerald Collection (FFC), Howard Gotlieb Archival Research Center, Boston University, December 1966.

28. Just poem to FitzGerald, Goodwood Hotel, Singapore, FFC, undated.

29. Just cable to FitzGerald, FFC, June 29, 1967.

30. FitzGerald, blue notebook marked "Kalb book Writer's Union," FFC.

31. Author interview with FitzGerald, June 19, 2019.

32. Letter from Gaga (Grandmother Peabody) to FitzGerald, FFC, July 1967.

33. Just letter to FitzGerald, FFC, October 1967.

34. Author interview with Ann and Walter Pincus, December 2, 2019.

35. Frances FitzGerald, "The Long Fear—Fresh Eyes on Vietnam," *Vogue*, January 1967.

36. Frances FitzGerald, "The Power Set: The Fragile but Dominating Women of Vietnam," *Vogue*, February 1967.

37. Henry Kissinger to FitzGerald, FFC, August 31, 1967.

38. Author interview with FitzGerald, January 15, 2019.

39. Paul Mus letter to FitzGerald, FFC, October 20, 1967.

40. William Conrad Gibbons, *The U.S. Government and the Vietnam War: Executive and Legislative Roles and Relationships* (Princeton, NJ: Princeton University Press, 1995), 894, footnote.

41. Author interview with Daniel Ellsberg, June 11, 2019.

42. Author interview with Ellsberg.

43. Author interview with FitzGerald, June 19, 2019.

44. Peter Davison letter to FitzGerald, FFC, November 29, 1968.

45. David Chandler, "Paul Mus (1902–1969): A Biographical Sketch," *Journal of Vietnamese Studies* 4, no. 1 (Winter 2009).

CHAPTER 6: HOW SHE CAME OUT OF THAT ALIVE IS A MIRACLE

1. Catherine Leroy letter to mother, Dotation Catherine Leroy (DCL), June 29, 1967.

2. Author interview with John Laurence, August 30, 2019.

3. Don North, "A Little Piece of Hell," *New York Times*, July 4, 2017.

4. Leroy, "Vietnam Narrative," unpublished manuscript, DCL.

5. Leroy letter to mother, DCL, December 6, 1967.

6. Terry Gross interview with Horst Faas, *Fresh Air*, WHYY, National Public Radio, November 5, 1997.

7. Details about General Westmoreland appraisal in Stanley Karnow, *Vietnam: A History* (New York: Viking Press, 1983), 514.

8. Author interview with Sam Bingham, January 29, 2019.

9. Don Oberdorfer, *TET: The Story of a Battle and Its Historic Aftermath* (New York: Doubleday, 1971), 2–40.

10. George C. Herring, "The Road to Tet," *New York Times*, January 27, 2017.

11. Karnow, *Vietnam*, 523–545.

12. Author interview with Bingham, January 29, 2019.

13. Catherine Leroy, "Soldiers of North Vietnam Strike Pose for Her Camera," *Life*, February 16, 1968.

14. Robert Pledge interview with Horst Faas, March 1, 2011, in Jacques Menasche, dir., *Cathy at War: Volume 1; Vietnam* (DCL, 2016), 72 mins.

15. John Laurence, *The Cat from Hue: A Vietnam War Story* (New York: PublicAffairs, 2002), 16.

16. Menasche, *Cathy at War*.

17. Pledge interview with Faas, in Menasche, *Cathy at War*.

18. Pledge interview with Don McCullin, March 17, 2012, in Menasche, *Cathy at War*.

19. Leroy, "Vietnam Narrative."

20. Leroy, "Vietnam Narrative."

21. Mark Bowden, *Hue 1968: A Turning Point of the American War in Vietnam* (New York: Atlantic Monthly Press, 2017), 391–441.

22. Brooke Gladstone interview with Leslie Gelb, *On the Media*, WNYC, National Public Radio, January 12, 2018.

23. Marcel Gugliaris interview with Leroy, Saigon, DCL, March 7, 1968.

24. Leroy letter to mother, DCL, April 8, 1968.

25. Author interview with Hal Buell, January 7, 2019.

26. Leroy letter to mother, DCL, March 19, 1968.

27. The editors, "An Editorial," *Look*, May 14, 1968.

28. Author interview with Susan Moeller, October 14, 2019.

29. Susan D. Moeller, *Shooting War: Photography and the American Experience of Combat* (New York: Basic Books, 1989), 410.

30. Leroy letter to mother, DCL, September 9, 1968.

31. Author interview with Dominique Deschavanne, September 14, 2018.

32. Leroy letter to mother, DCL, October 3, 1968.

33. Dirck Halstead quote from Donald R. Winslow, "Catherine Leroy: Vietnam War Photographer, 60," National Press Photographers Association, July 21, 2006, NPPA.org.

34. Leroy, "Synopsis," unpublished, DCL.

35. Leroy, "Only the Photographer," proposal for unpublished autobiography, DCL.

CHAPTER 7: THREE DEATHS

1. Kate Webb, "Highpockets," in Tad Bartimus, Denby Fawcett, Jurate Kazickas, Edith Lederer, Ann Bryan Mariano, Anne Morrissy Merick, Laura Palmer, Kate Webb, and Tracy Wood, *War Torn: Stories of War from the Women Reporters Who Covered Vietnam* (New York: Random House, 2002), 63.

2. John Woodrow Cox, "I Read My Own Obit: A Female Vietnam War Reporter's Harrowing Weeks as a POW," *Washington Post*, January 31, 2018.

3. Cox, "I Read My Own Obit."

4. Don Oberdorfer, *TET: The Story of a Battle and Its Historic Aftermath* (New York: Doubleday, 1971), 16.

5. Webb, in Bartimus et al., *War Torn*, 63.

6. Author interview with Dan Southerland, February 17, 2019.

7. Kate Webb, "War Torn: Women Reporters Who Covered Vietnam," panel discussion, National Press Club, September 24, 2002.

8. Webb, in Bartimus et al., *War Torn*, 64.

9. Joyce Hoffmann, *On Their Own: Women Journalists and the American Experience in Vietnam* (New York: Da Capo Press, 2008), 217.

10. Kenton Clymer, *The United States and Cambodia, 1870–1969: From Curiosity to Confrontation* (Abingdon, UK: Routledge, 2004), 41.

11. Kate Webb, interview, *Singapore Radio*, transcript, Kate Webb papers (KWP), private family collection, Sydney, Australia, April 5, 1988.

12. Author interview with Rachel Webb Miller and Jeremy Webb, November 7, 2018.

13. Religious News Service, "New Zealand Primate, 76, Dr. Campbell West-Watson Dies, Was Senior Anglican Bishop," *New York Times*, May 20, 1953.

14. C. M. West-Watson, "Geneva During September," *Christchurch Times* (New Zealand), KWP, 1931.

15. John Warhurst, "Webb, Leicester Chisholm (1905–1962)," in *Australian Dictionary of Biography*, vol. 16 (Melbourne: Melbourne University Press, 2002).

16. Author interview with Miller and Jeremy Webb, November 7, 2018.

17. Webb, illustrated journal or epistolary of her European travels, KWP, undated.

18. Author interview with Miller and Jeremy Webb, November 7, 2018.

19. "Court Told Girl, 15, Lent Friend Rifle to Suicide," *Canberra Times*, April 1, 1958.

20. "Court Told Girl, 15, Urged Friend Not to Suicide," *Canberra Times*, April 15, 1958.

21. "No Bill of Indictment in Webb Case," *Canberra Times*, May 1, 1958.

22. Frank Fenner, *Nature, Nurture and Chance: The Lives of Frank and Charles Fenner* (Canberra, Australia: ANU Press, 2011), 63.

23. Author interview with Miller and Jeremy Webb, November 7, 2018.

24. Tony Clifton, "Biography: Kate Webb," Australia Media Hall of Fame, April 30, 2019, halloffame.melbournepressclub.com.

CHAPTER 8: WE WERE LAUGHING

1. Kate Webb, "Highpockets," in Tad Bartimus, Denby Fawcett, Jurate Kazickas, Edith Lederer, Ann Bryan Mariano, Anne Morrissy Merick, Laura Palmer,

Kate Webb, and Tracy Wood, *War Torn: Stories of War from the Women Reporters Who Covered Vietnam* (New York: Random House, 2002), 66.

2. Kate Webb, interview, *Singapore Radio*, transcript, Kate Webb papers (KWP), private family collection, Sydney, Australia, April 5, 1988, p. 13.

3. Webb, fictionalized memoir, unpublished, KWP.

4. Author interview with Gene Roberts, January 28, 2019.

5. Webb, poem in notebook, KWP, undated.

6. Richard V. Oliver, "6 Top Viets Slain; US Rocket Blamed," UPI, in *Boston Globe*, June 3, 1968.

7. Webb, interview, *Singapore Radio*, 14.

8. Kate Webb, "Life and Death of a Copter Crew," UPI, in *Boston Globe*, October 8, 1968.

9. J. W. Cohn, "Women Cover the News, Too," *Women's Wear Daily*, in *Washington Post*, October 17, 1968.

10. Joyce Hoffmann interview with David Halberstam, Joyce Hoffmann papers, Old Dominion University, Norfolk, Virginia, January 7, 1998.

11. Webb, fictionalized memoir.

12. Author interview with Rachel Webb Miller, November 7, 2018.

13. "H.R. Haldeman's Notes from Oct. 22, 1968," Sunday Review, *New York Times*, December 31, 2016.

14. Author interview with Jeremy Webb, November 7, 2018.

15. Webb, fictionalized memoir.

16. Webb, fictionalized memoir.

CHAPTER 9: WHERE DOES THE STORY END?

1. Frances FitzGerald, "Death of a Chronicler," *Commentary*, March 1968.

2. MacDowell Colony, "Artists: Frances FitzGerald," Fall 1969, www .macdowellcolony.org/artists/frances-fitz-gerald.

3. Author interview with Alan Lelchuk, December 10, 2019.

4. Joyce Carol Oates, "A Conversation with Philip Roth," *Ontario Review* 1 (Fall 1974).

5. Frank Rich, Jean Bennett, Michael Kazin, James E. Thomas, Lucy Fisher, Chris Wallace, Lance C. Buhl, Robert L. Hall, Mark Helprin, Ernest J. Wilson, and Richard Hyland, "Echoes of 1969," *Harvard Magazine*, March–April 2019.

6. Linda Greenhouse, "How Smart Women Got the Chance," *New York Review of Books*, April 6, 2017.

7. Alessandra Stanley, "The Way It Was at Radcliffe," *New York Times*, June 7, 1992.

8. Author interview with Frances FitzGerald, June 19, 2019.

9. Author interview with Lelchuk, December 10, 2019.

10. Peter Davison letter to Frances FitzGerald, Frances FitzGerald Collection (FFC), Howard Gotlieb Archival Research Center, Boston University, August 1969.

11. John McAlister letter to Frances FitzGerald, FFC, September 16, 1969.

12. McAlister letter to FitzGerald, October 10, 1969.

13. Richard Soloman letter to FitzGerald, FFC, December 18, 1968.

14. Author interview with FitzGerald, June 19, 2019.

15. Henry Kissinger letter to FitzGerald, FFC, May 13, 1970.

16. Author interview with Lelchuk, December 10, 2019.

17. Author interview with FitzGerald, August 1, 2019.

18. Daniel Ellsberg, *Papers on the War* (New York: Simon and Schuster, 1972), 41.

19. Fern Marja Eckman, "Hooked on Vietnam," *New York Post*, July 21, 1972.

20. Kevin Buckley, "The Saigon Yale Club," Yale Class of 1962 website, July 15, 2004, www.Yale62.org.

21. Kevin Buckley investigation in Nick Turse, *Kill Anything That Moves: The Real American War in Vietnam* (New York: Picador, 2013), 249–250.

22. Kevin Buckley note to FitzGerald, Saigon, FFC, 1971.

23. FitzGerald letter to Buckley, FFC, February 22, 1972.

24. Kate Webb, "Highpockets," in Tad Bartimus, Denby Fawcett, Jurate Kazickas, Edith Lederer, Ann Bryan Mariano, Anne Morrissy Merick, Laura Palmer, Kate Webb, and Tracy Wood, *War Torn: Stories of War from the Women Reporters Who Covered Vietnam* (New York: Random House, 2002), 70.

25. Author interview with Rachel Webb Miller, November 7, 2018.

26. Elizabeth Becker, *When the War Was Over: Cambodia and the Khmer Rouge Revolution* (New York: PublicAffairs, 1986, 1998).

27. William J. Rust, *Eisenhower & Cambodia: Diplomacy, Covert Action and the Origins of the Second Indochina War* (Lexington: University Press of Kentucky, 2016), 143.

28. Craig Etcheson, *The Rise and Demise of Democratic Kampuchea* (Boulder, CO: Westview Press, 1984), 98–99.

29. Becker, *When the War Was Over*.

30. For journalists killed in Cambodia see Richard Pyle, "Press People Killed During Cambodia's Civil War, 1970–1975," *Cambodia Daily*, April 17–18, 2019; Newseum, "Journalists Memorial"; and "List of Journalists Killed and Missing in the Vietnam War," Wikipedia.

31. Sydney H. Schanberg, "Syvertsen of CBS News Feared Dead in Cambodia," *New York Times*, June 4, 1970.

32. Robert M. Smith, "Ex-Officer Tells About Song My Data," *New York Times*, June 12, 1970.

33. Children chasing napalm from Kate Webb, "War Torn: Women Reporters Who Covered Vietnam," discussion panel, National Press Club, September 24, 2002.

34. Kate Webb, "Bombers Hit Tang Kauk; Major Battle Developing," UPI, in *Hartford Current*, September 13, 1970.

35. Henry Kamm, "2 More Newsmen Slain by Reds in Cambodia," *New York Times*, October 29, 1970.

36. Webb, in Bartimus et al., *War Torn*, 71–72.

37. Elizabeth Becker, "The Cambodian Nightmare of Prince Sihanouk," *Washington Post*, February 27, 1980.

38. Kate Webb, interview, *Singapore Radio*, transcript, Kate Webb papers (KWP), private family collection, Sydney, Australia, April 5, 1988.

39. Author interview with Sylvana Foa, February 10, 2019.

40. Webb, in Bartimus et al., *War Torn*, 85.

41. Webb, fictionalized memoir, unpublished, KWP.

42. Webb, fictionalized memoir.

43. Elizabeth Becker, "Cambodia's Hero Journalists," *Washington Post*, June 17, 1974.

44. Webb, black moleskin notebook, KWP, 2001.

45. Craig R. Whitney, "Gloria Emerson, Chronicler of War's Damage, Dies at 75," *New York Times*, August 5, 2004.

46. Kate Webb, *On the Other Side: 23 Days with the Viet Cong* (New York: Quadrangle Books, 1972), 5–7.

CHAPTER 10: AGAINST THE ODDS

1. Kate Webb, *On the Other Side: 23 Days with the Viet Cong* (New York: Quadrangle Books, 1972), 20–27.

2. Webb, *On the Other Side*, 62.

3. Webb, 75.

4. Webb, 90.

5. Webb, 108–109.

6. Webb, 121–122.

7. Author interview with Rachel Webb Miller, November 7, 2018.

8. *Sunday Mirror* article, family scrapbook, Kate Webb papers (KWP), private family collection, Sydney, Australia, undated.

9. "Missing UPI Correspondent Is Reported Dead in Cambodia," UPI, in *New York Times*, April 20, 1970.

10. Douglas Robinson, "A Masked Toughness," *New York Times*, April 20, 1970.

11. Pat Burgess, "Kate's Clean War Led to Her Death," *Daily Mirror* (Sydney), family scrapbook, KWP, undated.

12. Mungo MacCallun, "Most Unlikely War Correspondent," *Daily Mirror* (Sydney), family scrapbook, KWP, undated.

13. Bill Pinwill, *A.M. Radio in Singapore*, KWP, April 26, 1970.

14. Webb, *On the Other Side*, 129–130.

15. Webb, 149–152.

16. Frank Slusser e-mail to Webb, KWP, March 8, 2007.

17. Australian newspapers, family collection, KWP, May 2, 1971.

18. Author interview with Miller and Jeremy Webb, November 7, 2018.

19. Kate Webb, "High Pockets," in Tad Bartimus, Denby Fawcett, Jurate Kazickas, Edith Lederer, Ann Bryan Mariano, Anne Morrissy Merick, Laura Palmer, Kate Webb, and Tracy Wood, *War Torn: Stories of War from the Women Reporters Who Covered Vietnam* (New York: Random House, 2002), 79.

20. Author interview with Sylvana Foa, February 10, 2019.

21. Webb, *On the Other Side*.

22. Author interview with Jeremy Webb, November 7, 2018.

23. Nan Musgrove, "A Hairbreadth from Horror," *One Magazine*, June 7, 1971.

24. Geraldine Willesee, "What Makes Katie Run?," *Woman's Day*, June 7, 1971.

25. Author interview with Gene Roberts, January 28, 2019.

26. Author interview with Foa, February 10, 2019.

27. Frances FitzGerald, "Vietnam I," *New Yorker*, July 1, 1972; "Vietnam II," *New Yorker*, July 8, 1972; "Vietnam III," *New Yorker*, July 15, 1972; "Vietnam IV," *New Yorker*, July 22, 1972; "Vietnam V," *New Yorker*, July 29, 1972.

28. Stanley Hoffmann, "An Account of the Collision of Two Societies," *New York Times Book Review*, August 27, 1972.

29. David G. Marr, "Fire in the Lake: The Vietnamese and the Americans in Vietnam," *Journal of Asian Studies* 32, no. 3 (May 1973): 564–565.

30. Fairbanks observation in Fox Butterfield, "The New Vietnam Scholarship," *New York Times Magazine*, February 13, 1983.

31. Taylor Branch, "Halberstam, FitzGerald, Ellsberg, Reporter, Poetess, Analyst," *Washington Monthly*, March 1973.

32. Author interview with Frances FitzGerald, June 19, 2019.

33. Author interview with Dan Southerland, February 17, 2019.

34. Myra MacPherson, "Frances FitzGerald: In Hardcover," *Washington Post*, August 29, 1972.

35. Author interview with Myra MacPherson, December 31, 2019.

36. Author interview with H. D. S. Greenway, July 31, 2018.

37. "Discussion with Middle East Correspondent Anthony Shadid," Shorenstein Center, November 14, 2007.

38. Anthony Marc Lewis, "Re-examining Our Perceptions on Vietnam," *Studies in Intelligence* 17, no. 4 (Winter 1973), Central Intelligence Agency Library, declassified July 2, 1996.

39. Fredrik Logevall, "Vietnam Reconsidered," televised panel at the Los Angeles Times Festival of Books, April 30, 2000.

40. Author interview with Fredrik Logevall, January 31, 2020.

CHAPTER 11: SAIGON SIGNING OFF

1. "Transcript of Nixon's Acceptance Address and Excerpts from Agnew's Speech," *New York Times*, August 24, 1972.

2. Joshua Rothman, "Watching George McGovern Run," *New Yorker*, October 21, 2012.

3. Janis Joplin at Woodstock from Facebook page of Frank Cavestani, www .facebook.com/frank cavestani, retrieved January 1, 2020.

4. Frank Cavestani and Catherine Leroy, dir., *Operation Last Patrol* (1973), documentary, no theatrical release.

5. Ron Kovic and Frank Cavestani, "Operation Last Patrol," panel, Loyola Marymount University, September 24, 2012.

6. Author tried repeatedly to interview both Kovic and Cavestani.

7. "Transcript of President Nixon's Address to the Nation on His Policy in Vietnam," *New York Times*, May 9, 1972.

8. Arnold R. Isaacs, *Without Honor: Defeat in Vietnam and Cambodia* (Baltimore, MD: Johns Hopkins University Press, 1983), 36.

9. Stanley Karnow, *Vietnam: A History* (New York: Viking Press, 1983), 652–654.

10. Flora Lewis, "Tho Rejects Nobel Prize, Citing Vietnam Situation," *New York Times*, October 24, 1973.

11. Elizabeth Becker, "The Interpreter of Memories from the Killing Fields," *Washington Post*, April 1, 2008.

12. Elizabeth Becker, "Ah . . . over here, Dick," *Far Eastern Economic Review*, March 19, 1973.

13. Holly High, James R. Curran, and Gareth Robinson, "Electronic Record of the Air War over Southeast Asia," *Journal of Vietnamese Studies* 8, no. 4 (Fall 2013): 104–107.

14. Lee Lescaze letter to Elizabeth Becker, May 25, 1973.

15. Kate Webb, "No Peace Talks in Cambodia," UPI, in *Mainichi Shimbun* (Tokyo), October 21, 1972.

16. Kate Webb, interview, *Singapore Radio*, transcript, Kate Webb papers (KWP), private family collection, Sydney, Australia, April 5, 1988, p. 36.

17. Webb letter to Camilla, KWP, January 13, 1973.

18. Elizabeth Becker, "Phnom Penh Being Flooded by Thousands of Refugees," *Washington Post*, July 13, 1973.

19. Author interview with Kishore Mahbubani, March 8, 2020.

20. H. D. S. Greenway, "A Flower in the Sky Ends the Air War," *Washington Post*, August 16, 1973.

21. Thomas W. Lippman, "Business as Usual with U.S. Pilots," *Washington Post*, August 16, 1973.

22. Elizabeth Becker, "Cambodians Seek to Escape War in Northern City," *Washington Post*, August 16, 1973.

23. Ith Sarin, *Regrets for the Khmer Soul*, 1973.

24. Elizabeth Becker, "Who Are the Khmer Rouge?," *Washington Post*, March 10, 1974.

25. Elizabeth Becker, "American Advises in Combat," *Washington Post*, March 13, 1974.

26. Department of State, "Alleged U.S. Advisors in Cambodia," confidential cable to US embassy, Phnom Penh, Cambodia, March 13, 1974, declassified June 5, 2005, www.wikileaks.org/plusd/cables/1974STATE050795_b.html.

27. Author interview with Stephen Heder, January 17, 2020.

28. Frances FitzGerald, "Vietnam: Behind the Lines of the 'Cease-fire' War," *Atlantic Monthly*, April 1974.

29. Frances FitzGerald, "Vietnam: The Cadres and the Villagers," *Atlantic Monthly*, May 1974.

30. Frances FitzGerald, "Vietnam: Reconciliation," *Atlantic Monthly*, June 1974.

31. Frances FitzGerald, "One Year After the Paris Accords," *New York Times*, January 28, 1974.

32. Frances FitzGerald, "Reporter at Large—Journey to North Vietnam," *New Yorker*, April 28, 1975.

33. Isaacs, *Without Honor*, 351–385.

34. Webb, in Bartimus et al., *War Torn*, 81.

35. Frank Snepp, *Decent Interval: An Insider's Account of Saigon's Indecent End Told by the CIA's Chief Strategy Analyst in Vietnam* (New York: Vintage, 1978), 407–413.

36. Ron Moreau, "Tributes to Kate Webb," *Correspondent*, January 2002.

37. Snepp, *Decent Interval*, 557.

38. John W. Finney, "U.S. Rescue Fleets Picking up Vietnamese Who Fled in Boats," *New York Times*, May 1, 1975, includes UPI pool report by Kate Webb from the USS *Blue Ridge* without Webb byline.

39. Carrie Collins interview with Catherine Leroy, "Vietnam War Reflections," C-Span, April 29, 1985.

40. James Fenton, "The Fall of Saigon," *Granta*, May 2, 2019.

41. Collins interview with Leroy.

EPILOGUE

1. History of the Vietnam Veterans Memorial, www.vvmf.org.

2. Philip M. Boffey, "Vietnam Veterans' Parade a Belated Welcome Home," *New York Times*, November 14, 1982.

3. Nobel Prize 1997 to the six organizations, including the Vietnam Veterans of America Foundation, that comprised the International Campaign to Ban Landmines, www.nobelprize.org.

4. Author interview with Dominique Deschavanne, September 14, 2018.

5. Author interview with Robert Pledge, June 20, 2019.

6. Tony Clifton and Catherine Leroy, *God Cried* (London: Quartet, 1983).

7. Author interview with Fred Ritchin, February 8, 2019.

8. Catherine Leroy, *Under Fire: Great Photographers and Writers in Vietnam* (New York: Random House, 2005).

9. Régis Le Sommier and Catherine Leroy, "They Were Soldiers Once," *Paris Match*, reprinted in *American Photo* 16, no. 5 (September–October 2005): 28.

10. Author interview with Rachel Webb Miller, November 7, 2018.

11. Peter Mackler, Agence France-Presse internal memo, Kate Webb papers (KWP), private family collection, Sydney, Australia, August 20, 1997.

12. Webb letter to Alison Sims, KWP, May 8, 2000.

13. "No Regrets: Kate Webb 1943–2007," *Correspondent*, May–June 2007, 7–9.

14. For a list of FitzGerald's published books, see www.francesfitzgerald.net.

15. PBS, "Full Reading List," *The Vietnam War*, a film by Ken Burns and Lynn Novick, www.pbs.org/kenburns/the-vietnam-war/resources/reading-list/full-list/.

16. Author interview with Fredrik Logevall, January 31, 2020.

17. Transcript of Trial Proceedings: Public, Case File No. 002/19-09-2007-ECCC/TC, Extraordinary Chambers, Courts of Cambodia, Kingdom of Cambodia, Trial Day 240, February 9, 2015, www.eccc.gov.kh/sites/default/files/documents/courtdoc/2015-02-17%2015%3A22/E1_259.1_TR002_20150209_Final_EN_Pub.pdf; and Elizabeth Becker, "Reporting Massive Human Rights Abuses Behind a Façade," *Columbia Journalism Review*, October 3, 2016.

18. Transcript of Trial Proceedings, Trial Day 242, February 11, 2015, www.eccc.gov.kh/sites/default/files/documents/courtdoc/2015-02-24%2013%3A59/E1_261.1_TR002_20150211_Final_EN_Pub.pdf.

Index

WILLIAM NASH

ELIZABETH BECKER is an award-winning journalist and author who began her career as a war correspondent for the *Washington Post* in Cambodia. She later became the senior foreign editor of National Public Radio and a *New York Times* correspondent covering international economics, national security, and foreign policy. She has been the recipient of numerous awards, including the duPont-Columbia Award and accolades from the Overseas Press Club, and was a member of the *Times* team that won the 2002 Pulitzer Prize for Public Service in covering 9/11. She is the author of three previous books, including *When the War Was Over: Cambodia and the Khmer Rouge Revolution*, the definitive book on the event that has been in print for thirty years. Elizabeth Becker lives in Washington, DC.

PublicAffairs is a publishing house founded in 1997. It is a tribute to the standards, values, and flair of three persons who have served as mentors to countless reporters, writers, editors, and book people of all kinds, including me.

I. F. Stone, proprietor of *I. F. Stone's Weekly*, combined a commitment to the First Amendment with entrepreneurial zeal and reporting skill and became one of the great independent journalists in American history. At the age of eighty, Izzy published *The Trial of Socrates*, which was a national bestseller. He wrote the book after he taught himself ancient Greek.

Benjamin C. Bradlee was for nearly thirty years the charismatic editorial leader of *The Washington Post*. It was Ben who gave the *Post* the range and courage to pursue such historic issues as Watergate. He supported his reporters with a tenacity that made them fearless and it is no accident that so many became authors of influential, best-selling books.

Robert L. Bernstein, the chief executive of Random House for more than a quarter century, guided one of the nation's premier publishing houses. Bob was personally responsible for many books of political dissent and argument that challenged tyranny around the globe. He is also the founder and longtime chair of Human Rights Watch, one of the most respected human rights organizations in the world.

.　　.　　.

For fifty years, the banner of Public Affairs Press was carried by its owner Morris B. Schnapper, who published Gandhi, Nasser, Toynbee, Truman, and about 1,500 other authors. In 1983, Schnapper was described by *The Washington Post* as "a redoubtable gadfly." His legacy will endure in the books to come.

Peter Osnos, *Founder*